DAUGHTERS OF QUEEN VICTORIA

by
E. F. BENSON

With eight half-tone plates

Copyright © 2013 Read Books Ltd.
This book is copyright and may not be
reproduced or copied in any way without
the express permission of the publisher in writing

British Library Cataloguing-in-Publication Data
A catalogue record for this book is available from the
British Library

E. F. BENSON

Edward Frederic Benson was born at Wellington College (where his father was headmaster) in Berkshire, England in 1867. He was educated at Marlborough College, where he proved himself as an excellent athlete, representing England at figure skating, and published his first novel, *Dodo* (1893), when he was 26. The novel was quite popular, and Benson eventually expanded it into a trilogy (*Dodo the Second*, in 1914, and *Dodo Wonders*, in 1921). Nowadays, Benson is principally known for his 'Mapp and Lucia' series about Emmeline "Lucia" Lucas and Elizabeth Mapp. The series consists of six novels and two short stories, and remains popular to this day, being serialized for Radio 4 as recently as 2008. Benson was also a respected writer of ghost stories – indeed, H. P. Lovecraft spoke very highly of him, especially his story 'The Man Who Went Too Far'. Benson died of throat cancer in 1940, aged 72.

cious Permission of His Majesty The King

THE ROYAL FAMILY EARLY IN 1847

from the painting by Winterhalter

he Queen's right is the Prince of Wales, in front of them Prince Alfred; Princess Alice and the Princess Royal are nursing Princess Helena.

BY THE SAME AUTHOR
Across the Stream
As We Are
As We Were
Charlotte Brontë
Ferdinand Magellan
The Kaiser and English Relations
King Edward VII
Queen Victoria
Francis Drake

LIST OF ILLUSTRATIONS

The Royal Family early in 1847 - -		*Frontispiece*
Princess Beatrice - - - - -	*Facing page*	40
The Princess Royal and her son - -	,, ,,	40
Princess Alice - - - - -	,, ,,	88
The Queen, with her dog Sharp - -	,, ,,	120
Princess Louise - '- - - -	,, ,,	152
The Empress Frederick - - - -	,, ,,	184
Group at Balmoral, 1896 - - -	,, ,,	216
The Queen dressed for her Diamond Jubilee, 1897 - - - - -	,, ,,	248

ACKNOWLEDGMENTS

MY MOST grateful thanks are due to H.R.H. Princess Helena Victoria for her gracious permission to quote from and to use H.R.H. Princess Christian's memoir and letters of Princess Alice, Grand Duchess of Hesse, and to the publishers, Messrs. John Murray ; to Lady Sysonby for a similar permission with regard to the *Letters of the Empress Frederick* by Sir Frederick Ponsonby, and to the publishers, Messrs. Macmillan ; and to Messrs. John Murray for a similar permission with regard to the *Letters of Queen Victoria*.

E. F. BENSON

DAUGHTERS OF QUEEN VICTORIA

INTRODUCTION

WHEN the young husband and wife, Prince Albert and Queen Victoria began to consider the education and upbringing of their family, the memories of their own early years were much in their minds. These experiences were remarkably dissimilar : indeed the only point in common between them was that neither had known the care of more than one parent. When Albert was only four years old his father, Duke Ernest of Coburg, was separated from his wife, and two years later he divorced her for reasons approved by the Mosaic law. Albert therefore and his elder brother Ernest were brought up as motherless children by their father and their grandmother, the Dowager Duchess of Coburg, and Albert had only the dimmest recollection of his mother whom he never saw again. He was an extremely conscientious little boy, and recorded in his infant diary his various small naughtinesses and his tearful remorse for them. He was as studious as he was conscientious, and before he entered his teens he drew up for himself so strenuous a time-table of his lessons that no Board of Education of to-day would have permitted it to be used in schools. He was devoted to his relations, especially to his brother Ernest, and his boyhood, consecrated to the acquisition of learning, was extremely happy.

He had, among these relations, a very able uncle, his father's younger brother. Uncle Leopold, three years before Albert's birth, had married into the English Royal Family and his bride was Princess Charlotte of Wales, the only child of George, Prince of Wales, and heiress after her father to the throne of England. But she had died in giving birth to a stillborn child, and Uncle Leopold could therefore never become the husband of the Queen of England nor the father of a future King. His election, however, to be King of the Belgians gave him a consolatory Crown, and he set himself to procure for his nephew the destiny of which he himself had been so cruelly robbed. Albert's Aunt Victoria, Duchess of Kent, was the mother of Princess Victoria, a girl just three months older than himself, and by the time these two children were ten years old, it had become a practical certainty that Victoria, if she lived, would become Queen of England, for her eldest paternal Uncle, now King George IV, never had another child, and his successor Uncle William, Duke of Clarence, though he had a large family by Mrs. Jordan, was without a legitimate heir. Albert understood while he was quite a young boy that Uncle Leopold and Aunt Victoria and his grandmother were making plans which concerned him and Cousin Victoria very closely, but he took little interest in these or in the female sex generally. He was the sort of boy who, if he had been of less distinguished birth, might have become an eminent Professor, possibly unmarried, in some German Academy of learning. As a young student at the Universities of Bonn and Brussels he was a good rider and he fenced well, but he regarded all forms of sport and physical exercise as merely the needful refreshment for a mind weary of study, and he could not understand how people like his father would spend whole days hunting or shooting : a brisk walk with a like-minded friend, beguiled by a discussion on German modes of thought, was sufficient relaxation for so serious a youth. He looked on social functions, such as balls and evening parties with their senseless chatter, as a great waste of time, and when obliged to go to one, far preferred a conversation with a savant in a corner to dancing. In spite of these traits and tastes there was no touch of the prig about him, for his preferences were wholly sincere and devoid of all consciousness of superiority. He had been a very pretty boy, and was growing into an extremely handsome young man.

Very different were the conditions of life in the Royal Household at Kensington Palace in which Princess Victoria of Kent was being brought up. It consisted, as regards her earliest impressions, of five persons. First, there was her widowed mother, the Duchess of Kent, whose husband had died when the Princess was a baby of eight months old. By a previous marriage to Prince Charles of Leiningen she had another daughter, Feodore, nine years older than her half-sister Victoria, and Feodore was the second personage in this Kensington quintet. She was a very pretty girl, Victoria adored her and Victoria's uncle, King George IV, on the few occasions on which they met, obesely ogled her. The third was the governess of the two girls, Fräulein Lehzen, daughter of a Hanoverian pastor, whom the King created Baroness Lehzen. The fourth member of the party was an Irishman, Sir John Conroy. He had been an equerry of the Duke of Kent's, and was now Controller of the Duchess's Household. The fifth and the most potentially important of them all was the Princess Victoria herself, a plain child but of exuberant vitality. She gobbled her food, she laughed with wide open mouth, she was naughty and self-willed and hated her lessons, but loved all forms of activity and diversion, her pony, her dogs, her dolls' house, dancing, the play and the opera. When she was seven years old her beloved Feodore, now approaching marriageable age, was taken back to Germany by the Dowager Duchess of Coburg, her grandmother and Albert's, and Victoria was left companionless but never alone, with a troupe of tutors to give her the education suitable to a little girl who would one day be Queen of England.

Albert would have revelled in this life which afforded such opportunities for acquiring knowledge, but to Victoria, in spite of diversions, it was a sad and lonely childhood. Even before Feodore's departure, and far more so after it, there had been little brightness in the household, and Feodore writing to her half-sister confirmed this gloomy impression. The only happy hours, she said, that they had spent together in England were those when, staying at Uncle Leopold's house at Claremont, they went out driving or walking alone with Lehzen and escaped for an afternoon from the very uneasy domestic atmosphere. Certainly the Duchess was very strict with her two daughters, but there was something more than that, felt by the elder, Feodore, then, and felt by Victoria also when she grew a little older. This was their mother's dependence on Sir John Conroy. Charles Greville, the most scandalous of the world's best diarists, duly commented on this. He reports a conversation he had with the Duke of Wellington in which he asked him whether he believed that the Duchess was Conroy's mistress and the Duke said that he supposed that was so, adding, on another occasion, that he fancied that Princess Victoria must have seen " some act of familiarity " between the two that would account for the girl's frozen dislike of her mother, which subsequently was so manifest, and for her detestation of Conroy. That such was the mischievous tittle-tattle of scandalmongers was certainly the case, and our most injudicious Duchess gave ample cause for the wagging of unfriendly tongues. It must be remembered on the other hand, that until Victoria ascended the throne at the age of eighteen, she always slept in her mother's room, which seems an unlikely arrangement to be made by a woman who was carrying on a secret intrigue.

But whether this was so or not, there was sufficient cause for the Queen's unhappy recollections of her childhood. By day and night she was under the scrutinizing eye of her elders, she lived as on a desert island encompassed with guards. Lehzen was a friendly guard, but Lehzen loathed Conroy, and there were thus two camps in that small and isolated household. Her mother, with Conroy at her elbow, was far too strict with the girl; indeed, after her death in 1861, when the Queen read the Duchess's diaries of those early years, she was filled with amazement and remorse to find that they breathed the tenderest love and solicitude for her. She had never suspected that beneath that crust of hardness and severity there had glowed this deep affection. It is true that in the Princess's diary, which, under her mother's orders, she wrote regularly from the time she was thirteen, there are many records of treats and pleasures, concerts and operas and visits to country houses, but the diary had to pass her mother's reading and was written with the necessary discretion. These diversions did not make for happiness. It was a sad childhood, and when, as soon as possible after her accession she moved to Buckingham Palace, she said goodbye to the " poor old Palace " at Kensington as a home where she had passed through many " painful and disagreeable scenes." In later years she referred to the last six or seven years she had passed there as a time " of great misery and oppression."

It was not only in the domestic ordering of her house that the Duchess showed a great want of wisdom in her daughter's upbringing, but in her conduct towards Victoria's relations. Her position was a very difficult one, and she made the worst of it. She had come to England as the Duke of Kent's bride without a word of English to her tongue, and after eighteen months of marriage she had been left a widow with a daughter, who, as it soon became certain, would be Queen of England. Her brothers-in-law disliked the Duchess personally, they were jealous of her and of her fatherless child, and instead of attempting to conciliate them or behaving as was befitting the mother of a little girl between whom and the throne there still stood two of her uncles, she gave herself airs of ludicrous self-importance, as if she was the mother of the Queen already, and responded to their dislike with petty defiances. More especially was this the case when the irascible Duke of Clarence succeeded his brother as William IV. She neglected no opportunity of enraging him. She would not answer the Lord Chamberlain's enquiry as to whom she wished to have as her page at his Coronation, and when on the third application, the King countersigned this polite request, she discovered that his brothers were to take precedence of her and Victoria and declined to go at all : Victoria, she said, could not stand the fatigue, and she took her down to Sir John Conroy's cottage at Osborne in the Isle of Wight, where Victoria, who had set her heart on going to the Coronation, cried her eyes out. The King offered her the use of the Royal Yacht : she did not even thank him, but used the yacht freely, sailing about in the Solent and the Channel. Ships of the Royal Navy always fired a salute when a member of the Royal Family was on board, and these poppings of guns became so incessant that the Admiralty politely asked her to waive her right to them. Sir John Conroy replied that, as her confidential adviser, he could not recommend her to give way on this point, and an Order in Council had to be issued that the Royal Yacht should only be saluted when the King or Queen was on board.

Every year she took the Princess with Conroy in attendance on Royal progresses: they stayed at big houses like Chatsworth or Burghley or Belvoir, and visited neighbouring Boroughs where the Mayors and Corporations gave them a civic welcome. These progresses were admirable in themselves: they took the Princess into the county towns and rural districts of her future realm, but the Duchess's want of tact, in her exploitation of Conroy, was consummate. At Burghley Lord Exeter read an address of welcome and Conroy handed him the Duchess's reply exactly in the manner of a Prime Minister conveying the gracious message of the Sovereign: at Oxford he received the freedom of the city. Again, when the Duke of Wellington asked audience of her in order that he might personally explain the Regency Bill, one of the provisions of which was that in case King William died while Victoria was still a minor, she should be regent, the Duchess replied through Conroy that she was out of town and requested the Duke to address all future communications to the Controller of her Household.

When Princess Victoria was just seventeen, her uncles on both sides of the family simultaneously made the first definite moves with regard to her marriage. Her Uncle William wanted her to marry Prince Alexander, the younger son of the Prince of

Orange, and asked him and his two boys to stay with him at Windsor, while the Duchess of Kent, instigated by brother Leopold, asked Duke Ernest of Coburg to bring his two sons Ernest and Albert to stay with her at Kensington Palace for a visit of three weeks. King William in a fury said he would not allow the Coburg aspirants to set foot in England, but there was no statute in the law of the land which could enable him to prevent them, and the Coburgs braved the Royal displeasure and came. All four young men danced with the Princess at the ball her mother gave on Victoria's birthday, but in her eyes Albert excelled them all for charm and beauty and intellect and gaiety. She had never seen him before, but she knew what was intended and her heart thrilled with maidenly ecstasy. On the tearful morning of the cousins' departure she wrote to Uncle Leopold:

" I must thank you, my beloved uncle, for the prospect of *great* happiness you have contributed to give me in the person of dear Albert. Allow me then, my dearest Uncle, to tell you how delighted I am with him, and how much I like him in every way. He possesses every quality that could be desired to make me perfectly happy. He is so sensible, so kind, and so good, and so amiable too. He has, besides, the most pleasing and delightful exterior and appearance you can possibly see. I have only now to beg you, my dearest Uncle, to take care of the health of one now so *dear* to me, and to take him under *your special* protection. I hope and trust that all will go on prosperously and well on this subject of so much importance to me."[1]

[1] *Letters of Queen Victoria*, I, i, p. 62.

It may be taken for granted that her mother read this letter before it was despatched, and that it gave her and the recipient equal pleasure.

The conditions of the sad and lonely childhood were resumed. The Duchess of Kent, as a crow of triumph over the King's defeated Oranges, showed her scorn of his authority by an act of monstrous impertinence. She had asked him to let her add to the apartments which she occupied (by his grace and favour) at Kensington Palace seventeen new rooms : it was as if she was already planning an establishment for Victoria and Albert. The King refused, and she proceeded to annex them in direct disregard of his orders. The extensive alterations rendered Kensington uninhabitable, so she went to her brother Leopold's house at Claremont, with Victoria, Lehzen and Conroy. While she was there the King, still ignorant of what was going on at Kensington Palace, asked her and Victoria to come to Windsor for Queen Adelaide's birthday, and to remain there for his own birthday a week later. She answered that she would prefer to remain at Claremont over her own birthday, which was on the same day as the Queen's, but would come down to Windsor with Victoria for the birthday of the King, arriving the evening before. He had gone to London that morning to prorogue Parliament, and he must have received some private information about his sister-in-law's alterations at Kensington Palace, for on his way back to Windsor he looked in, and found that she had appropriated those seventeen rooms. He proceeded to Windsor, boiling with fury, and got there after dinner to find his wife entertaining his party of guests who included the Duchess of Kent and Victoria. He made some loud remarks about the infernal liberties she had taken, but said nothing to her directly.

Next day was his birthday, and there was a dinner of a hundred people. The Duchess of Kent sat next him, and opposite him was the Princess Victoria, greatly enjoying herself. After dinner his health was proposed, and in answer to it he made a gobbling, eloquent speech, in which he said that he hoped to God he would live long enough to see the Princess come of age on her eighteenth birthday, so that she would ascend the throne in her own right and not be subject (according to the Regency Bill) to " a person sitting near me who is surrounded by evil advisers and who is herself incompetent to act with propriety in the position in which she would be placed." . . . This person had repeatedly insulted him, and had kept his niece away from him, but he was determined to stand it no longer. . . . On and on went this tirade while the guests, among whom were his Ministers, sat aghast. Princess Victoria burst into tears, and it was with difficulty that the Duchess was persuaded not to go back to London that very night, taking the sobbing heiress to the throne with her. " Very awkward, by God," said the Duke of Wellington. Nothing, of course, can excuse the caddishness of the King in making this brutal public attack on a woman who was sitting beside him as his guest, but the Bluff Sailor had never learned the elements of manners. It must be admitted also that for years his sister-in-law had been deliberately rude to him, and this piratical seizure of those rooms at Kensington was almost as unpardonable as his reprisal.

Again the isolating rigour of her mother's control closed round Princess Victoria for one more winter of discontent. She continued to write in her diary those minute elaborate entries which were proper for her mother to see, and kept to herself all that she silently brooded over in the heart through which ran a vein of iron. Next May, being eighteen years old, she came of age, and the King wrote his niece an autograph letter assigning her an income of £10,000 a year independent of her mother. He sent Lord Conyngham to Kensington Palace, with instructions to deliver this personally to Princess Victoria. Sir John Conroy received him, and when he had explained his errand, the Controller of the Household admitted him into the room where the mother and daughter awaited him. The Duchess asked for the letter to be given to her, but Lord Conyngham said it was for the Princess. When the Duchess learned its contents she made her final *gaffe*. She would still be paying all the expenses of Victoria's board, lodging and education, and she claimed that £6,000 of this grant ought to go to her. But the days of her domination were over: a month later the King died and there was no longer any question whether Victoria should have an independent income of £10,000 a year or £4,000. The Queen of England had long thought over what she intended to do when this day came. At six that morning she went alone, without her mother, to see the Archbishop of Canterbury and Lord Conyngham who had come from Windsor to announce to her the King's death. She received Lord Melbourne alone three hours later, and subsequently four officers of State. At intervals throughout the day she had interviews with Baron Stockmar, whom Uncle Leopold had sent to England in anticipation of the King's death, and to whom he had enjoined her to give her complete confidence. She ordered that her bed should be taken out of her mother's room, and established herself in a suite of her own. She dined alone, for all day her mother had been popping in on her with advice and suggestions and queries, and the Queen of England had had enough of it. She bade her a dutiful good night, and for the first time in her life she slept alone in her own room.

CHAPTER I

NO one, least of all perhaps her mother, had suspected that this homely little girl with the projecting blue eyes and the mouth that she opened so very wide when she laughed, had such an indomitable will. Her complete self-reliance, her immense personal dignity amazed all who came in contact with her, and she took up the power and responsibility of Sovereignty as if she had been Queen all her life. The shell of the chrysalis cracked and the metamorphosis to a winged and jewelled being was accomplished without any stretching of folded membrane and fluttering expansion. To her mother she was ruthless in intention and in act. The Duchess had looked forward to the day when Victoria would be Queen of England and herself the honoured counsellor and friend, directing and guiding her and perhaps paying back with bitter interest the snubs which she had undergone from Victoria's relations, and which her own lack of wisdom had so largely brought upon her. Instead, she ceased to exist, her life was blighted at the precise moment when she imagined it would burst into flower. As for Conroy, the Queen conferred on him a baronetcy and a pension of £3,000 a year for his services to her parents and never spoke to him again. She was Queen: her mother knew that now, and in the years to come her children would know it also.

Two years passed, during which Victoria continued to show fresh facets of her unrivalled firmness : she routed Sir Robert Peel singlehanded over the affair of the Ladies of her Bedchamber and she took her own line (and an implacable line it was) over the deplorable affair of Lady Flora Hastings. But with all her native dominance, she always demanded throughout her life to have by her some man to whose judgment she could trust, or on whom she depended for her sense of comfort. Since her early girlhood she had exalted Uncle Leopold to the oracular seat : now she deposed him and established Lord Melbourne in his place as counsellor, and, in private life, as her personal friend, whose presence in such affairs as State functions gave her the feeling of being protected. No longer did she listen to Uncle's conversation, which she had once likened to reading a most improving book, with unquestioning faith. She shut the book up. Uncle felt hurt : he protested that he only desired the love of his dear niece, but she was quite aware that he very much desired to advise and control the Queen of England as well, and to that she did not intend to submit for a moment. She sought the oracles of her Prime Minister, for how should the Sovereign of a nice little foreign country, though he assured her that he was most ready to instruct her in the very difficult art of Constitutional Monarchy, understand the far vaster policies of England ? " Dear Uncle," as she subsequently wrote, " is given to believe that he must rule the roast everywhere.

However, that is not a necessity." And there was a subject on which Uncle's heart was set which she did not want to discuss.

It was the only subject affecting her intimately on which she could not make up her mind. She was twenty now, and three years had elapsed since the birthday party and ball her mother had given at Kensington Palace when Albert had made so engaging an impression, and when, writing to her uncle, she definitely implied that she accepted him as her future husband. She had not seen him since and neither of them had yet shown any desire to meet again. Her life had undergone an enormous change since then: she hugely enjoyed being Queen of England, and she was not sure she would like to be under a husband's control as a dutiful wife must be. She told Lord Melbourne that she did not wish to marry for two or three or even four years yet, and she called particular attention to her having made no actual promise. But in the meantime Albert was being kept dangling, and he had intimated that he did not intend to dangle for ever. He had been received with approval on their only meeting, but he had remained on approval ever since, and if the goods, so to speak, were not going to be ordered, they must be released. Endless were her vacillations. She thought the fact that Albert was younger than herself (the difference being three months) was an objection, and she reminded Melbourne that he himself did not like the match. Eventually she consented to see Albert again, on the understanding that she was absolutely free to refuse him. In October, 1839, he came to Windsor with his brother Ernest, equally determined that she must say the word now or for ever hold her peace. At the first sight of him all hesitation was over. He was perfection, she loved him more than she could say. It mattered not that Melbourne still disapproved, or that a very large body of public opinion shared Melbourne's view, or that Albert was younger than she. The Queen of England intended to marry him, and, with loverlike humility, she thought it a great sacrifice on his part to consent.

The marriage took place on February 10, 1840. The Queen had ordained that they should have only two days of uninterrupted solitude at Windsor for their honeymoon, and when Albert, fearful of being plunged so soon into the pomp of Court life, asked for a small extension, she was very much the Queen. "You have not at all understood the matter," she wrote to him. "You forget, my dearest love, that I am the Sovereign and that business can stop and wait for nothing. Parliament is sitting, and something occurs almost every day for which I may be required, and it is quite impossible for me to be away from London ; therefore two or three days is already a long time to be absent. I am never easy a moment, if I am not on the spot and see and hear what is going on." Perhaps also in the capacity of bride she thought that the first trial trip of the *Victoria and Albert* into the unknown seas should not be without escort for long, for she added, " I must be surrounded by my court ; I cannot keep alone. This is also my wish in every way."[1] So after two days the Court and the

[1] *Letters of Queen Victoria*, I, i, p. 269.

Queen's Ministers and her mother and Lehzen streamed down on them, and the honeymoon was over. It is strange to think how completely in later years the Queen ceased to regard the session of Parliament as a reason for her presence in London.

In the summer a new Regency Bill had to be passed before Parliament was prorogued, for the Queen expected to have a baby in the following November. Socially, Prince Albert's stiff and un-English manners had not rendered him very popular, but it is evident that the fine qualities of his character had already earned him high respect, for the Bill provided that, should the Queen die in childbirth, he should be sole Regent till her child came of age: he would thus for eighteen years be King of England in all but name. The Bill passed its third reading in both Houses without opposition.

On November 21 the Queen gave birth to her first child, a daughter. According to the barbaric usage of the day Ministers of the Crown, with Archbishop Howley of Canterbury and the Bishop of London, were assembled in the room adjoining that in which the Queen was in unanæsthetized labour, and of which the door was open. There was a little disappointment when Dr. Locock, who was within with the midwife and Prince Albert, was heard saying to the mother: " Oh, Madam, it is a Princess ! " but a confident voice from the bed answered him, " Well, next time it will be a Prince." Then the new-born girl was brought out in a blanket on a tray as Nature had just made her, so that the Lords temporal and spiritual might see with their eyes and hear with their ears (for the young lady seemed vexed) that there was now an heiress in the direct line to the throne of England. The distinguished company then dispersed amid a jubilation of saluting guns and pealing church bells, congratulating themselves that another life intervened before the detestable Hanoverian Ogre, Ernest, Duke of Cumberland, uncle of the Queen and now King of Hanover, could ascend the throne of England. Uncle Leopold was equally delighted : he rejoiced to think of the " *deep, deep* share " he had in this event, and, with that firm grasp of the obvious which was characteristic of him, told his niece that " children of our own, besides the affection which one feels for them, have also for their parents sentiments which one rarely obtains from strangers." But he did not say quite the right thing when he hoped that she would presently be the Mamma " *d'une nombreuse famille.*" She told him that such was not her wish. Childbearing involved " hardship and inconvenience " to herself (men seldom thought of that) and her country would not welcome a *nombreuse famille* any more than she. A quantity of Princes and Princesses would have to be properly provided for which would be a great expense. That was undeniably true : the country had not shown much gratitude for the privilege of supporting the numerous offspring of George III, or, for that matter, of granting an annuity of £50,000 to Uncle Leopold himself on his marriage with Princess Charlotte. Nor, in years to come, did the country appreciate similar substantial privileges which were periodically accorded it.

But the Queen's scruples were short-lived, and never again for her own sake or for that of her country did they trouble her. She revised her previous opinions also about never discussing political affairs with Albert. From the first she had surrendered to him as the perfect and adorable husband of Victoria, but as Queen of England she had shut the door of the Council chamber on him, and was resolved, as on the day of her accession, always to see her Ministers alone. But then it was her mother whom she intended to exclude, and now within a year of her marriage every door was open to Albert, and he took part in the Queen of England's affairs of State as a matter of course. From then until the day of his death his wisdom was her constant adviser and her guide.

The Princess Royal throve as a healthy baby should. Within a month she was too heavy for the Queen to carry, but Albert was a capital nurse and she liked being danced in his arms. Her mother's fond eye saw promise of her Pussie growing up to be very much like her father, and indeed that was a most shrewd and perceptive observation if the Queen referred to Pussie's dawning intelligence. Within a year of her birth there was another addition to the family. No Prince of Wales had been born to the Sovereign for eighty years, and the only discontent was Albert Edward's sister, who was not at all pleased with her brother. The Queen was sure that everybody, like herself, must fervently pray that he, too, should " resemble his angelic dearest father in *every, every* respect, both in body and mind."[1] She had felt " low " after her baby's birth ; she found London like a dungeon, and the family of four went down to Windsor. Pussie showed signs of great precocity : her mother recorded that she was quite like a grown-up person, quiet and observant, and casting coquettish glances at the Hussars who rode beside their carriage. Bertie, on the other hand, showed no signs of precocity, and when in the autumn his parents came back to Windsor from their first visit to Scotland it was a disappointment to find him so little grown either in mind or body, whereas Pussie had not only grown in stature, but was developing a remarkable degree of independent intelligence. Her mother was afraid that she had grown also in her capacity for being naughty, but that tendency seemed to spring from the curiosity of an inquiring mind. Bertie as yet was only ten months old, which was little early to write him down a dullard, but a dark saying of Baron Stockmar's, " Education begins at birth," troubled his father's mind. It was not at any rate too early to organize the coming schemes of education for the Royal children, and before Pussie was three years old the general lines of these were established. Sarah, Lady Lyttelton, was the President of the Board, and under her (for the present) were an English, a German and a French governess, who, as the children were weaned from the nursery, would teach them their lessons and look after them at their play. These governesses were very trustworthy women,

[1] *Ibid.*, p. 367.

and all of them were allowed to seek audience with the parents and lay before them any small problem that might arise about their charges. The Queen was delighted with the domestic freedom of these arrangements, and wrote to Uncle Leopold : " Indeed, dearest Uncle, I will venture to say that not only *no Royal Ménage* is to be found equal to *ours*, but *no other ménage* is to be compared to ours, nor is anyone to be compared, take him altogether, to my *dearest* Angel." What gave her peculiar pleasure was that everybody was struck with " Albert junior's " likeness to his dearest papa. But again these were early days yet.[1]

In such happy domestic circumstances the Queen became increasingly fond of a quiet life in the country. Before her marriage she adored London with its gaieties and entertainments : she could dance all night and be fresh and brisk for her early appointments with her Ministers next morning. But Prince Albert hated to sit up late, and though devoted to music would fall asleep in the middle of an evening concert, and the heavy atmosphere of London oppressed and fatigued him. At once the Queen was aware of similar symptoms of her own, and instead of longing to get back to town from Windsor, she vowed that she would be happy and content never to see her metropolis again. She would even, she thought, be glad to resign the estate and splendours of sovereignty altogether for this perfect family felicity, and after a quiet week at Claremont which Uncle Leopold had lent her she wrote to him : " God knows how

[1] *Ibid.*, p. 594.

willingly I would always live with my beloved Albert and his children in the quiet and retirement of private life." But in spite of the fervency of this exclamation how disconcerted she would have been if some malevolent fairy had taken her at her word and, with a wave of his wand, had granted her the boon ! For such a resignation would have rent her : she revelled in her great inheritance. Indeed, being Queen of England was already far more to her than any inherited office. It permeated her consciousness ; to be Queen was one of her qualities, as integral a part of her character as her indomitable will or her sense of motherhood. She would not have resigned her Sovereignty now, even when the presence of Albert rendered domesticity so blissful, any more than she dreamed of doing so when in the long desolation of her widowhood she recoiled from the duties which it entailed on her.

But she longed for some *angulus terræ* to which she could retire without ceasing to be Queen and which should be her own personal property, " free from all Woods and Forests and other charming Departments which are the plague of one's life." These perhaps were rather ungrateful expressions, for the Woods and Forests maintained her little garden at Buckingham Palace, and her little park at Windsor at the charges of the nation. Windsor was " beautiful and comfortable," but her instinct was just that of the young matron who wants to get out of handsomely furnished lodgings into a cottage of her own, however humble, somewhere in the country. The Queen had pleasant memories (now divorced from the sad circumstances of childhood) of the Isle of Wight, where she and her mother had stayed with Sir John Conroy : it was more remote than Windsor, which could now be reached from London in three-quarters of an hour by the new railway ; the Solent was an additional fence, and in 1843 she purchased Osborne House with eight hundred acres of ground, subsequently increased to two thousand. The house was far too small, and it was at once demolished, and then came an added, a consecrated joy, for Prince Albert, with the professional assistance of that rising architect, Mr. Cubitt, planned a residence better suited to the dignity of the Queen and to the accommodation of her growing family. It was furnished and decorated in accordance with his artistic tastes, and he laid out the grounds also, cutting openings in the ilexes to give *blicks* of the sea, and planting an avenue of those stark inhospitable trees called monkey-puzzlers.

Pussie was three this year, and she was truly a most gifted child. She, like her Papa in his boyhood, loved her lessons and already spoke French and English fluently : German (the language her parents habitually spoke together) scarcely needed tuition. These linguistic attainments rather overlapped each other in her small head, for she pronounced German with an English accent and English in the German mode. Her intelligence, too, already went far deeper than this glib lip-service, she could reflect on the meaning of what she learned. One day she had committed to memory a stanza of Lamartine's, and, going out presently on her pony in Windsor Park with her French governess, she waved her infant hand and exclaimed (with Lamartine) "*Voilà le tableau qui se déroule à mes pieds!*" Surely very remarkable in a child of three: her mother thought it was more like a person of twenty to have understood and applied "this difficult passage." This same year a second daughter was born to the Queen, Princess Alice, a very plump and sunny girl, on whom her father, who now made the most apposite English puns, bestowed the nickname of Fatima.

While Osborne was still in the throes of decoration and fresco, a second son was born, Prince Alfred. His destiny was fixed from birth, for Albert's father had died that year, and his brother, now Duke Ernest of Coburg, had succeeded him. In youth the two had been inseparable, but Ernest had ruined his health by scandalous courses, and, though he had reinstated himself in his brother's eyes by marrying, it was extremely unlikely that he would beget offspring. In this case a son of Albert's would succeed to the Dukedom of Coburg, and, since the Prince of Wales was earmarked for the throne of England, Alfred would inherit. Education (this was now a postulate) began at birth, and Prince Albert wrote to his brother: "The little one shall from his youth be taught to love the small dear country to which he belongs in every respect, as does his Papa." In the interval, more fortunate than his elder brother in being allowed to have a profession, he was to enter the English Navy as soon as he was old enough to become a naval cadet. He was a robust sky-larking boy, and his mother recorded how, romping on the staircase in the little old castle of Balmoral, he fell down the whole flight and might have been killed. But he escaped with a black eye, and appeared anxious to court death again. . . . Two more daughters, the Princesses Helena and Louise, two more sons, the Princes Arthur and Leopold, brought the offspring up to eight, and finally the birth of Princess Beatrice in 1857 completed the tale of a family which might now be considered *nombreuse*; the Queen had gladly suffered all the hardship and inconvenience of a loving wife, and it would soon be the nation's business, according to precedent, to provide for the dignified maintenance of her offspring.

During this long period of fertility she had positively gloated over her happiness in the family circle. Albert remained perfection; never once did he cast an admiring glance on any other woman, and throughout the years of her marriage the greatest domestic trial she ever experienced was when on his father's death he went to Coburg for a fortnight without her. She implored Uncle Leopold and his wife to hasten to England to enable her to bear her loneliness: " I have *never* been separated from him," she wrote, " even for *one night*, and the *thought of such* a separation is quite dreadful. . . . If I were to remain *quite* alone, I do not think I *could* bear it quietly. . . . I may be indiscreet, but you must think of *what* the separation from my *all* in *all*, even for a fortnight, will be to me. . . ."[1] Nor were the blessings

[1] *Ibid.*, I, ii, p. 8.

of this ideal marriage showered on herself and her children alone. "It has brought," she wrote later, "such universal blessings on this country and Europe. For what has not my beloved and perfect Albert done? Raised monarchy to the *highest* pinnacle of *respect* and rendered it *popular* beyond what it *ever* was in this country."[1] The Hanoverian dynasty, she once exclaimed, was finished. Henceforth the Royal Family of England were the House of Victoria and Albert. But this doting did not extend to her children; few women, indeed, if any, can fill the role of wife and mother with equal intensity. She was very fond of them, so said the admirable Lady Lyttelton, but she was very strict with them. And mixed with their dutiful love towards her, there was a very considerable awe. In earlier days, she had been not only Albert's wife but the Queen of England: now, in his regard, before the radiant sun of her personal devotion to him, the Queen of England was rapidly evaporating and soon there would be nothing of her left. But to her children, these two personalities of mother and Queen remained throughout their lives co-existent and effective. Mamma's wish must also be looked upon as the Queen's will.

The early years of the young family, particularly of the elder girls, was certainly extremely happy. The Queen must often have contrasted them with the memories of her own sad lonely childhood in Kensington Palace with its divided camps and its uneasy undercurrents. They adored their father and were

[1] *Ibid.*, I, iii, p. 325.

not the least afraid of him, and in Pussie, now promoted to the more dignified name of Vicky, he found a mind which in many respects exactly mirrored his own. She was quick to learn and retentive of memory, she had strong artistic tastes, even as he had, and while she was yet scarcely in her teens she was in these ways far more a companion to him than his wife. Victoria panted after him, glowing with admiration, but she did not care as Vicky cared for prolonged browsing on the subjects to which his mind instinctively turned in moments of leisure. Indeed, in the early days of their marriage, when Prince Albert had tried to enlarge the rather limited topics of conversation at dinner by the presence of artistic and literary folk, she had not at all approved, feeling that she would not be able to hold her own. There Uncle Leopold had backed her up on moral grounds : he considered artists dangerous people, people with whom it was not wise to be intimate. Possibly this alliance between the minds of the husband and the daughter gave rise to some subconscious jealousy. The Queen thought Vicky a plain child, whereas, without being beautiful, she had the most charming and attractive face. Alice, once Fatima, both parents were agreed, was the beauty of the family, and unfortunately they both agreed that Bertie was backward and stupid. He had become very shy and timid with his father, and whereas Lady Lyttelton's report of him, when he was still under the sway of governesses, was that he was singularly truthful, a rather later verdict was that he was much given to telling fibs. That is one of the unfortunate effects of any child's fear of a parent who, even from the highest motives, is too apt to mark what is done amiss.

On Prince Albert's birthday the children always produced for their father evidence of their progress in various forms of Art. He listened to their recitations, their performances on the piano and violin, and they made him presents of their needle-work, their sketches and their essays in composition, and jointly they gave their parents delightful surprises of a more elaborate sort. One year, on the anniversary of their wedding-day, they acted for them, with the help of governesses sworn to secrecy (though we suspect that the parents had an inkling of what was in store for them), a scene out of Racine's tragedy *Athalie*. Vicky, aged eleven, played Athalie, " a long and difficult part," and recited in admirable French the dream in which Rachel had risen to the topmost of her tragic splendour. Alice doubled two parts, " Joad " the high priest (with a white beard) and " Josabeth." Bertie and Alfred and Helena and Louise (aged three) had minor roles. Two years later on the recurring anniversary they produced some tableaux, representing the four Seasons with verses from Thompson's celebrated poem, which the Seasons duly recited. Then all were grouped together, and, throned in stage-clouds behind, Helena, who appeared as the Empress Helena, recited some more verses written for the occasion by the famous Mr. Martin Tupper, author of *Proverbial Philosophy*, who held a high place in Prince Albert's literary esteem. They could not have prepared a surprise more to his taste.[1]

[1] Princess Christian, *Alice*, pp. 4, 5.

The picture is certainly a very pleasant one; one can imagine the girls immensely enjoying their tableaux, confident that their poses and their well-spoken verses would delight their father. Perhaps Bertie, now aged twelve, in his icicled beard as Winter, was not enjoying himself so much; it was not unlikely that Prince Albert would tell him he had not spoken his lines as properly as his sisters, for where Bertie was concerned he was quicker to censure than to approve, and he took a very gloomy view of his character and his abilities. While his son was quite a child, he had told Lord Wriothesley Russell that Bertie's education was designed to make him as unlike as possible to the Queen's uncles: this was only really a paraphrase of her own ardent desire that he should grow up in every respect like his dearest beloved Papa. But Lord Melbourne was not very sanguine: there was nothing, he thought, less malleable than character.

Prince Albert was not a clubbable man: to sit talking for the mere sake of human intercourse was to him a waste of time, when he might have been reading a book. He concluded therefore that anybody who liked to sit talking with his fellows, unless some useful discussion occupied their tongues, was idling. The only book that Albert never cared to study was the book of human nature, nor did he consider that anything worth learning could be drawn from it. A huge destiny awaited Bertie, and it was his father's duty to fit him for it by cramming him with the nutriment which he himself would have so eagerly assimilated. Except under strict supervision, he was never allowed to consort with boys of his own age. Tutors prowled round him, like the hosts of Midian, and sent regular and unsatisfactory reports of his progress to a genuinely distressed Papa. Prince Albert's disappointment with a son, who, both he and Stockmar agreed, was a stupid and lazy boy degenerated, in spite of his paternal love, into something resembling dislike. So, in this domestic life which the Queen found quite idyllic, there was always this discordant note, and it is strange that she, remembering her own sad childhood did not remonstrate with her husband about this *régime* of snubs and strictness. And yet how could she? Albert to her was the incarnation of wisdom and all his judgments were true. She accepted his views on Bertie as being frivolously inclined and stupid and on the treatment that would fit him to become an enlightened and responsible King. It was not till many years after her husband's death that she began to see in her son the value of those genial qualities which Albert had rated too low.

But it was no wonder that the Queen adored her young and devoted husband, to whose guidance even in affairs of State she now so rapturously surrendered herself. She felt that he was more fit to rule than she, and her *métier* as Queen became almost subsidiary to her *métier* as wife. She wrote to her Uncle Leopold that she was ever more strongly convinced that " we women, if we are to be good women, *feminine* and *amiable* and *domestic*, are *not fitted to reign.*" The despatch-boxes from her Ministers still arrived before breakfast, but she pressed the keys into his hand, and often he got to work on their imperial contents before she joined him: she was content to abide by his judgment in the shaping of her own decisions.

But the desire for remote domesticity grew. Osborne was too easily accessible, the Isle of Wight was almost suburban, and she wanted some wilder and more untrammelled home. She rented a small Highland Castle at Balmoral on Deeside: the distance from London was an advantage rather than otherwise. Here she could live the simple life with him and the children among glens and lochs and mountains. There was deer-stalking for Albert, who made an exception in favour of that form of sport, which he found fatiguing but most interesting. For herself there were visits to the crofters with presents of tea and petticoats, and there were picnics on the hill, and they made great excursions into the wildest unpopulated districts, staying incognito in country inns with only a lady and gentleman in attendance, and dining off skinny chickens. Sometimes they were identified and that was great fun, too; in her diary which rivals that of Pepys for sheer sincerity and gusto, the Queen gleefully records an occasion when their hosts discovered who she was and were frightened out of their wits. That innocent pleasure never failed her, the fun of being incognito was not complete unless after a while there came disclosure; lacking that, it was like a play in which the high-born heroine takes a situation as housemaid, and remains permanently unidentified. But soon old Balmoral Castle became too small for the growing family. She and Albert had each a private sitting-room, but there were only two reception-rooms in the house, a dining-room and a billiard-room, and the Minister in attendance had to do his work in his bedroom. She purchased it with an estate of 25,000 acres, and Albert planned yet another Paradise for her. Down came the little Scotch Castle and in its place there rose from his architectural designs a more royal abode built of granite, and bristling with turrets and monograms. It was all Albert's creation, and in their picnics and great expeditions and their intercourse with the Highlanders the Queen passed the happiest months of the year. The new Castle was ready for habitation in 1855, and, like Osborne, was the Queen's personal possession, and its woods and forests were uncontrolled by any meddlesome Governmental Department.

Prince Albert had a great gift for organization. He had put a stop to the prodigiously wasteful housekeeping in the Royal Palaces, and during these years the Queen had kept up the due splendour of the Crown, purchased two large estates at Osborne and Balmoral, building and furnishing thereon family residences, and had magnificently entertained many Royal visitors from foreign countries without asking the country to contribute to that great expense : all had been paid out of the Civil List. In 1852 she had come into a substantial private windfall, when a certain Mr. John Camden Neild left her his entire fortune of £500,000. His father had been a silversmith in St. James's Street and had supplied plate to King George III and the Prince Regent, and he himself was a very philanthropic man. He had large landed estates in Buckinghamshire and elsewhere, and must have been among the first to start allotment gardens, for he made over plots of land to his labourers and gave prizes to those who raised the best crops. The Queen accepted this unusual legacy, no doubt with the Prince Consort's approval, for Mr. Neild appeared to have no relations, and out of it purchased annuities for his servants, and put up a stained-glass window in the church at North Marsham where her benefactor habitually worshipped. Uncle Leopold sent her his warm congratulations: it was only in England, he said, (certainly not in Belgium) that wealthy and loyal subjects manifested their affection for the Crown in so agreeable a manner. He advised her to let the money accumulate as a provision for her children.

In the spring of 1855 the Emperor Napoleon III and the Empress Eugénie paid a State visit to England. The Queen and Prince Albert returned the visit in August taking with them their two eldest children, the Princess Royal, now fourteen years old, and the Prince of Wales, a year younger. The Queen was in ecstasies at their magnificent reception in Paris and the brilliance of the fêtes in their honour, and she found the Emperor amazingly attractive. She felt she had made a real friend and that all misunderstandings and enmities between the two countries had been wiped out by this personal contact of which the symbolical climax was that interesting moment when she and the Emperor stood together, her arm in his, in the moonlight, beside the tomb of Napoleon I, while the Heir Apparent of the English throne knelt beside his mother. She always put a very high value on Royal cordialities, but she would have been astonished to know that the impression of Paris formed by her small and (she was afraid) stupid son, kneeling in a kilt beside her, would have a far greater effect on the future relations of the two countries than her own presence. The Empress Eugénie, she wrote to Uncle Leopold, took but a small part in their reception. " The dear Empress, whom we are all very fond of, we saw comparatively but little of, as for *really* and *certainly very* good reasons she must take great care of herself. . . ." The Empress expressed the same thing (and yet concealed it) by starting the fashion of the crinoline. Prince Albert did not share his wife's enthusiasm. His insight doubted whether the Emperor was a man with any high moral sense, and he thought the French a frivolous people. Vicky, as was subsequently apparent, shared her father's misgivings.

Straight from the dazzle and pomp of Paris, the four returned to the simple life at Balmoral, occupying the new Castle for the first time. The earliest guest they received there was Prince Frederick William of Prussia, eldest son of Prince William of Prussia, and nephew of the childless king. Prince Frederick had visited England once before, on the occasion of the Great Exhibition in 1851, and, though the Queen's eldest daughter was then only a girl of ten, she had roused in him remote matrimonial dreams. He had thought much about her since, and her parents had thought much about him, and now he was invited to Balmoral as a prospective son-in-law. The girl was not yet fifteen, but he had obtained the consent of his parents and of King Frederick William to his proposing marriage. He was enchanted with her, and asked her parents' leave to speak. She was a little young yet to make so momentous a decision, and the Queen suggested that he should wait until Vicky was older and had been confirmed. But he wanted it settled now, and, perhaps remorsefully remembering how long she had kept Albert dangling, the Queen allowed him to indicate his intentions by the delicate device of picking a sprig of white heather and presenting it to the girl with " an allusion to his hopes." Vicky responded most favourably to this allusion, but then, appalled at her own unmaidenly conduct, went in floods of tears to her parents and confessed. As she had done exactly as they desired, they found no difficulty in forgiving her. The two were evidently much attracted to each other, and, at parting (so Prince Albert wrote to Stockmar in calm detachment from these human weaknesses) " an abundance of tears were shed. While deep visible revolutions in the emotional natures of the two young people and of the mother were taking place, by which they were powerfully agitated, my feeling was rather one of cheerful satisfaction and gratitude to God for bringing across our path so much that was noble and good." They were all of one mind, and there was none of that ugly avuncular wrangling which had attended the Queen's choice of her suitor, when in 1836 her Uncle William's candidate was Prnce Alexander of Orange, and he threatened to forbid the landing in England of the Coburg candidate put forward by her Uncle Leopold and the Duchess of Kent.

No public announcement of the engagement was made for the present, but Prince Albert told Lord Clarendon, the Foreign Minister, saying that he might pass the news on to Lord Palmerston, and the Queen told Uncle Leopold. The secret, of course, at once ceased to be a secret, and the opinion of the English Press was far from favourable. Prussia at that time was only one of many German States, and the Hohenzollerns were considered " a paltry German dynasty " not worthy of being allied with the eldest daughter of the Queen of England. *The Times* gloomily prophesied that she would become very anti-English in feeling and, as a source of danger to international cordiality, would be soon sent back to England " an exile and a fugitive." Uncle Leopold also was critical. He must have written to the Queen a letter not very appreciative of Prince Frederick, for she replied to it.

" One word about Vicky. I must say she has a quick discernment of character, and I have never seen her take any predilection for a person which was *not motivé* by personal amiability, goodness, or distinction of some kind or other. You need be under no apprehension whatsoever on this subject."[1]

[1] *Letters of Queen Victoria*, I, iii, pp. 198, 199.

The Queen was justified a thousand times over about this. In all the troubles that befell her daughter in her married life, her one sanctuary and stand-by was the unfailing nobility and devotion of her husband.

Prince Albert shrugged his shoulders at these malicious and ignorant comments of the Press and at Uncle Leopold's doubts. His mind was made up, and it did not matter what people said. Both he and the Queen, in spite of her recent infatuation with Paris and the Emperor Napoleon, were strongly pro-German, as from their almost unmixed German blood was only natural, and they had long believed that a very great expansion was coming to the State of Prussia and its paltry dynasty. Prince Albert some years before had written one of his most thoughtful memoranda for the benefit of the King, recommending certain liberal reforms in the constitution of the State. If he adopted these suggestions Prussia " would become the leading and directing power in Germany, which other Governments and people would have to follow, and in this way would come to be regarded as one of the most important European powers, seeing that in the European scales she would weigh as Prussia *plus* Germany." This idea now formed the principal dogma in his creed of international politics, and he envisaged a Confederation of German States under the controlling hegemony of Prussia allied with England. Prussia would develop into a Continental Power of huge military strength, and with England's invincible command of the sea, the two would keep the peace of Europe inviolate.

Both would be inspired by enlightened and liberal aims, and an era of progress and prosperity, of free trade and commerce, as foreshadowed by the Great Exhibition, would dawn on a distracted world. The history of the ensuing eighty years has both proved the Prince's foresight and shattered his idealistic visions.

It was little wonder then that both the Queen and he welcomed this alliance between the Royal Families, especially since they were to be united in the persons of their exceptionally clever daughter and this young man of so admirable a character, who, in the next generation, would wield the sceptre of Prussia. He was not intellectually brilliant, but so much the better ; the girl who certainly possessed his heart would also rule his head. She would be to him what her father now was to Victoria. Her fifteenth birthday was approaching, after that two years must elapse before she was of marriageable age, and in that interval her father implanted in her brilliant intelligence, so eager to learn, so masculine in its grasp and comprehension, the ideas and ideals that should inspire her future husband to frame the noble destiny of their countries. For an hour every evening he conversed with her on these high themes, firing her with his own enthusiasms, building up in her, solid and firm, his own convictions, and fitting her to be his missioner in the beloved land to which he had never ceased to belong. But nothing was further from his intention than directly to attempt, through this union of Royal Families, any Anglicization of Prussia. England, in his view, was by no means a model State, and Germany, in matters of education, of thoroughness of organization, was far ahead of her. His aspirations were that his daughter, through her influence over her husband, should advance Liberal and democratic policies, the comprehension of which in Prussia would automatically draw the two countries together.

The betrothal was officially made public in May, 1857, and in the Queen's message to Parliament announcing it she asked that such provision be made for her daughter " as was suitable to the dignity of the Crown and the honour of the country." This was the first occasion on which the country had been asked to contribute to the support of the *nombreuse famille*, now consisting of nine members, and there was a little uneasiness as to what the response might be. Prince Albert would have liked the dowries and annuities for all his children as they came of age or married to be settled now in order to save any bother later, but as the youngest was as yet only two months old, the Government thought that this was looking too far ahead. Nor did they feel sure that the dowry of £40,000 with an annuity of £8,000 which they intended to ask for the Princess Royal would be granted very graciously ; it would be much wiser not to present to the country the total estimate of its future indebtedness. But all went well : only fourteen members of the House of Commons voted against the grant, and the Prince regarded this as practical unanimity, inspired by the respect of the Nation for the Crown.

The marriage was fixed for January 25, 1858.

PRINCESS BEATRICE

THE PRINCESS ROYAL, CROWN PRINCESS
OF PRUSSIA, AND HER SON

In England the alliance with the paltry dynasty was still regarded as a poor match for the Queen's eldest child, and official Berlin, very sensitive then—as now—to a superior attitude on the part of a foreign State, thought of a telling rejoinder. The Prussian Foreign Minister called on the British Ambassador in Berlin some months before the wedding, and told him that it was the custom for Princes of the House of Hohenzollern to be married in Berlin. Little did he realize with whom he had to deal. This impertinent suggestion was duly conveyed to the Queen who dealt with it in her most summary manner. She commanded her Foreign Minister, " to tell Lord Bloomfield not to *entertain* the *possibility* of such a question as the Princess Royal's marriage taking place at Berlin. The Queen *never* could consent to it, both for public and private reasons, and the assumption of its being *too much* for a Prince Royal of Prussia to *come* over to marry the *Princess Royal of Great Britain* in England is too absurd to say the least. . . . Whatever may be the custom of Prussian Princes, it is not *every* day that one marries the eldest daughter of the Queen of England. The question therefore must be considered settled and closed."[1]

So there was no more heard of that, and the Queen arranged that the wedding should take place at the Chapel Royal in St. James's Palace, where she herself had been married. A week before that date a galaxy of Royal personages and their suites arrived ; they were so numerous that the Prince Consort wrote to

[1] *Ibid.*, p. 321.

the Dowager Duchess of Coburg that it would be a most dexterous feat to find room for them all " in a very limited palace," and that if he succeeded in housing them there he was thinking of going on a professional tour as a conjurer. A unique festival of entertainment ensued. One night at Her Majesty's Theatre there was a gala performance of *Macbeth*, followed by a farce, *Twice Killed*. " We made," wrote the Queen with gusto in her diary, " a wonderful row of royalties." Next evening there was a State Ball, and the evening after a gala performance of Balfe's *Rose of Castile* with another farce. There was a State Dinner, with Mr. Henry Leslie's Choir to sing afterwards. Then on Saturday the bridegroom arrived. After lunch the whole Royal company attended a demonstration by Mr. Rarey of his method of taming vicious horses, and after dinner there was a gala performance of *La Sonnambula* ; to-night no farce followed, for at midnight the hours of Sunday would begin. That day was spent in worship and rest, and on Monday the wedding was celebrated in the Chapel Royal, St. James's Palace : " the second most eventful day in my life," wrote the Queen, " as regards feelings." She noticed how small the " old " Family had become, but the young Royal Family, the dynasty of Victoria and Albert more than made up for that dwindling. She walked with her two eldest sons, one on each side of her (" which they say had a most touching effect ") and three daughters followed. All was happiness and joy at this wedding of the first of her children, and she said that she could have embraced everybody. The newly-married couple went for their honeymoon to Windsor, and there was a State Concert at Buckingham Palace. Two days' solitude was allowed them, and then, as on the marriage of the Queen and Prince Albert, the Court followed them. " Everybody," the Queen recorded, " was full of the universal enthusiasm, of which the Duke of Buccleuch gave us most pleasing instances, he having been in the thick of the crowd, and amongst the lowest of the low." Next day they all returned to London, and a fourth gala performance took place at Her Majesty's Theatre consisting of *The Rivals*, and a roaring farce *The Spitalfields Weaver*. The two days preceding the departure of the bride and bridegroom to Germany were dreadful ; the Queen was constantly in tears, and even the sight of her baby daughter, now eight months old, saddened her " as dear Vicky loved her so much and only yesterday played with her." But the separation which Princess Frederick felt most was the parting from her father. " I think it will kill me," she said, " to take leave of dear Papa."[1] But the thought that he had entrusted her with this international mission, and the fact that she was truly in love with her partner, with whom she would carry it out, consoled her, and she set forth to take up the new life which promised so brilliantly.

Princess Frederick was received very cordially in Berlin ; she had youth and charm and intelligence, and her new relations and the high circles were most willing to give her a fair chance. At the same time

[1] Martin, *Life of Prince Consort*, IV, 157–169.

she was the centre of critical eyes, which watched her very closely. Bismarck was still at the German Embassy in Paris, and was not in office at Berlin for four years yet, but he saw her there soon after her marriage, and was at once aware from his own observation and from what he heard that she was prejudiced against him because of his " alleged anti-English feelings." His verdict, however, was conditionally favourable and agreed with the general impression. He did justice to her charm and intelligence, he noted with equal justice that she was not clever at concealing her real sentiments, and he wrote to General Gerlach : " If the Princess can leave the Englishwoman at home and become a Prussian, she may be a blessing to the country." But to leave the Englishwoman at home was just what the Princess could not bring herself to do, and what her parents would not permit. Her father continued his tutorial offices, writing to her every week long letters of advice, which could not have tended to Prussianize her : he told her that if her path of life was not always smooth, she must take such trials as designed to strengthen her mind and " not to be seduced by familiarity into approval of that which, while it was unfamiliar, the reason could not recognize as good or fitting." In fact she must not adapt herself to new ways. To her mother she wrote, as desired, every day of her life.

This policy of not leaving her alone was the worst possible : the Queen wished to exercise over her the old maternal authority, and the Prince backed that up by telling her : " Your place is that of your husband's wife and your mother's daughter. You will desire nothing else, but you will also forego nothing which you owe to your husband and your mother."[1] The Queen's will, in fact, was to be as binding as before and to be as paramount as the duties which her new position imposed on her. Then, when they had been married only a few months, the Prince Consort planned an injudicious sort of visit. They were to have met him at Coburg, but that had to be abandoned, and he wrote to Stockmar that, instead, he would go to their Castle at Babelsberg, " on which I must then make a sudden descent and take them by surprise. To do this with effect, however, no hint of my intention must reach them beforehand." But what he saw pleased him and he wrote to the Queen : " The relations between the young couple are all that can be desired. I have had long talks with them both, singly and together, which gave me the greatest satisfaction." A couple of months later both the Princess's parents paid a fortnight's visit to her. Though the Queen said that this visit was quite unofficial, she took two of her ministers with her, and her late Foreign Minister, Lord Clarendon.

Indeed, with these visits and this daily letter to her mother and the weekly letter to and from her father, it was the Princess's parents who hindered her from identifying herself with her new country, and encouraged her to be critical of it. Perhaps also it was not wise of her father to procure as her private secretary Ernest Stockmar, the son of his old tutor, who had lived so many years very intimately with him and the Queen in England. She was continually

[1] *Ibid.*, IV, p. 176.

comparing English and German ways of life to the great disadvantage of the latter: baths, sanitary arrangements, the method of eating boiled eggs, the decoration of the dinner-table, were all ordered better in England, to which she always referred as " home." With all her cleverness she was not sufficiently tactful to refrain from criticism of sheer trivialities. She found the etiquette of the German Court ponderous and boring, and tried to lighten it in her own house by the society of musicians and artists, a thing quite unheard of in Royal circles in Prussia. A further odd cause of offence against Prussian ideas of Royal dignity, about which her father-in-law subsequently complained to the Queen, was that she went out driving with only two horses to her carriage instead of four. The only chance of the Princess's drawing England and Germany together was that she must first win the confidence of her adopted country by conforming to its usages. To do that, she must understand it, and the way of understanding lies in appreciation rather than criticism. To be sure, she was very young and needed guidance, but she should have been told to seek that from her husband's parents rather than her own, not only because they knew better what Prussia expected (and did not expect) from her Princesses, but because the fact of her seeking it from them would have roused in them the kindly protectiveness of which she stood in need. To do otherwise could only result in her influence over her husband alienating him from them. This was exactly what happened, and herein lay one of the chief causes of her troubles and her tragedy.

A fortnight before the expected birth of the Princess's first baby in the following January, the Queen sent to Berlin her favourite physician, Sir James Clark, so that an English eye should watch over her : an English nurse followed, and the Prince Consort would have liked his old tutor, Baron Stockmar, to have gone to Berlin also for the event. The delivery was very difficult : it was doubtful whether either mother or son would survive, and it was not till two days afterwards that it was discovered that the baby's left shoulder was so seriously injured that, in spite of all subsequent treatment, Prince William's arm remained permanently powerless. Possibly this was not known for some time to the mother's parents, for the Prince Consort, writing to Stockmar a week after, spoke of the joy in Berlin over the birth of the " strong healthy boy," and the Queen writing to Uncle Leopold on the same day alluded to the " dear little boy, improving so much and thriving in every way." It much distressed her that a political crisis in England prevented her going to Berlin for the christening ; it was heart-breaking, she was never so disappointed, and she blamed the constitution of Prussia for her inability to attend it : " It is a *stupid* law in Prussia, I must say, to be so particular about having the child christened so soon." But Lord Raglan and Captain De Ros represented her, and the Prince Consort intended to question them more minutely on their return as to whether Vicky was getting out of doors, for in fresh air alone (whatever German doctors said) could she recover her health and strength : or was she " growing weak and watery, by being baked like a piece of pastry?" Other medical advice followed in the next Wednesday letter; it was as if there was no reliable practitioner in all Prussia. Sea air would be the right thing for her, and she ought soon to take shower-baths and wash in cold water.

Not content with these supervisions the Queen felt that Prussia was threatening to " monopolize " her daughter. The Princess's new relatives had been making difficulties about her going to England whenever her mother wished, and the Queen wrote very gloomily to Uncle Leopold about the chance of her being allowed to come over for her birthday : " It is a melancholy sad Easter, but what grieves me most—indeed, distracts me (for I have had nothing but disappointments in that quarter since November)—is that in all probability Vicky will be unable to come in May ! It quite *distracts me* ! "[1]

Happily this distraction was composed, for Princess Frederick was allowed to come to Osborne for a week and her mother found her flourishing and well and gay, and a most dear companion, and her father thought that she was " much matured physically and morally and has all the elements of a distinguished character." In spite of this reassurance the Queen would not relax the maternal hand nor allow her daughter the manumission reasonable for a married woman.

Later in the year Lord Clarendon was in Berlin and gave Charles Greville an account of an interview which he had had with Baron Stockmar, on the

[1] *Letters of Queen Victoria*, I, iii, p. 419.

subject of Princess Frederick, who had evidently spoken intimately to her old friend.

> "I want to talk to you [said the Baron] on a very important matter, and to invoke your aid. It relates to this 'poor child' here. Her mother is behaving abominably to her, and unless a stop can be put to her conduct I know not what may be the consequences, for she is not in good health, and she is worried and frightened to death. The Queen wishes to exercise the same control and authority over her that she did before her marriage, and she writes her constant letters full of anger and reproaches, desiring all sorts of things to be done that it is neither right nor desirable that she should do, and complaining of her remissness in writing to her sisters or to Miss Hildyard (her late governess) and her forgetting what is due to her own family and country till the poor child is made seriously ill, and put in a state dangerous to her in her actual condition."

Stockmar followed this up by writing to the Queen in the same sense in which he had spoken to Lord Clarendon. It was the kind of letter, he said, that would much astonish her. The effect of it was that when Lord Clarendon returned to England, the Prince Consort sent for him, knowing that Stockmar had already spoken to him on the subject, and they had a very frank talk about it.[1]

The episode is instructive. It exhibits the fearful difficulty of Princess Frederick's position. Already in Prussia she was growing unpopular for not leaving the Englishwoman at home, while her mother was

[1] *Greville Diary*, December 12, 1859.

upbraiding and reproaching her for doing so too thoroughly. For one so young, so devotedly attached to her home, so sincerely anxious to do her duty in her new sphere it was a cruel dilemma. She would have required the wisdom of Solomon and the patience of Job to avoid its horns.

CHAPTER II

AT home meantime the rest of the family were growing up. The Prince of Wales, in the pangs of unmitigated education, had been sent for a winter to Rome under the care of General Bruce, and, on his return to England he was placed at Edinburgh University to fill up in study the months of the deplorably long vacation, before he went to Oxford. " Never relax " was Stockmar's advice to his father and the Prince applied it to his son as rigorously as to himself, but it was disappointing to find that perpetual cramming and invigilation bred in him no love of books nor instinct of self-discipline. He was eighteen now and a bride must soon be sought for him. His father had already cast his eye over the Protestant Royal Families of Europe and with the assistance of Uncle Leopold drew up a list of seven eligible Princesses, to be further enquired into.

Next to him, eighteen months younger, was the second daughter Alice. She was sixteen years old in April, 1859, and was confirmed just before her birthday. According to the formidable Coburg ritual she had first to pass a *viva voce* examination, conducted by the Archbishop of Canterbury in the presence of her parents and her governess Miss Hildyard. Since Princess Frederick's marriage she had been the eldest daughter at home, and her mother in her diary always speaks of her with the warmest affection, as the greatest comfort to her and a treasure of a child. But mixed with her affection was that maternal possessiveness with which the Queen always regarded her daughters. " I shall not let her marry," she wrote to Uncle Leopold, " as long as I can reasonably delay her doing so."[1]

Next to Alice came Alfred : if his elder brother was a disappointment, he did much to compensate for it. As destined for the Navy, he had to start early on his career, and was already lost to the permanent home circle, for six months after his eldest sister's marriage he passed his midshipman's examination, and on his parent's return from their visit to Germany, he met them at Osborne, very smart and shy in his new uniform. The Queen and his father were extremely proud of him. The examination, said the Prince Consort, was particularly difficult (although the usual one) and he sent Lord Derby, the Prime Minister, all the papers, with an account of Alfred's brilliance. Lord Derby appears to have been very much impressed and replied with suitable gravity : " I could not but be very grateful that no such examination was necessary to qualify Her Majesty's Ministers for their office, as it would seriously increase the difficulty of forming an Administration." The small boy went out on his ship to Malta, and the tactful Governor wrote to say that he had been received with " reverence and loyalty." He came home

[1] Martin, *Life of Prince Consort*, IV, 427.

when he was sixteen to be confirmed, and the Prince Consort was rejoiced to find that he had a brain " in which no prejudice can maintain a footing against straightforward logic." That was a boy after his own heart, and perhaps he turned with a sigh to the latest report from General Bruce about Bertie, then an undergraduate at Oxford. He lived with his Governor and an Equerry in a private house, Frewen Hall, under the strictest supervision. He did not attend lectures, but Professors of the University came to instruct him in English literature, German literature, Chemistry and Modern Languages, Modern History and Ecclesiastical History. He was not allowed to mix with other young men, or to dine in Hall, except on special occasions, but in spite of this invigilation and these bountiful opportunities for acquiring useful knowledge, he remained, as his father lamented, " neither fish or flesh." But in other respects the elder members of the family were very satisfactory : Alice was blooming into a very good-looking and graceful young woman and Alfred in his jolly life at sea earned golden opinions.

The Queen's resolve to keep Princess Alice at home as long as she reasonably could was remotely threatened next year, but she had no intention of letting the threat develop into an act of aggression. She asked to her party at Windsor for Ascot Week in June, 1860, Uncle Leopold and his two sons, and the two sons of Prince Charles of Hesse, brother to the childless Grand Duke. The party from Windsor attended the races as usual on two days, following the precedent set by King William and

Queen Adelaide. The Prince Consort could never understand how it was that people of intelligence could enjoy spending solid hours in seeing a cluster of horses flash past the Royal box at long intervals, and Ascot this year, he wrote to Stockmar, was more tedious than usual owing to the incessant rain. He noticed that the elder Hesse son, Louis, and Alice were mutually attracted, though " fortunately " (a clear allusion to the Queen's determination to put off Alice's marriage as long as she reasonably could) Louis did not approach them about it. But there was no doubt about the attraction, and he expected " further advances from the young man's family." He thought the Hesses good, respectable people, and they were well-connected, for the Empress of Russia was Prince Charles's sister, and Louis was the heir-presumptive to the ancient Duchy and occupied in Hesse exactly the same position as did Prince Frederick in Prussia. Like him he was a very moral and manly young fellow, and he was full of gaiety and high spirits.[1] The expected advances from his family followed. Princess Charles, Louis's mother, conveyed to the Queen how deeply her son admired Alice, and for themselves they would heartily welcome the match. But if the young man's parents thought that Louis was to be allowed to offer himself without any further delay, they were much in error. He should be asked to Windsor again in six month's time : that was quite soon enough for the present. Simultaneously there came good news from Berlin. Princess Frederick had

[1] *Ibid.*, V, p. 112.

given birth to a daughter, and the baby's Aunt Beatrice, now aged three, was much fussed by her new responsibilities. If she was asked by her Papa or Mamma to do something for them, she said : " I have no time. I must write letters to my niece."

Neither the Queen nor the Prince Consort had yet seen their first grandson, Prince William of Prussia, who was now eighteen months old, and the Prince Consort, writing in reply to his daughter's birthday letter to him in August, and thanking her for her gift of some chandeliers made of the horns of stags, made an odd allusion to this. He playfully mentioned her " tableau vivant " meaning her and her two children, and continued : " I console myself, however, with the hope of seeing your first work before long, and although you have always something to object to in it, yet it is to me a source of great delight."[1] It seems reasonable to infer that the Princess hoped that treatment might still restore her son's powerless arm, and, till then, shrank from her parents seeing him. But William could not remain for ever shrouded from them, and the Queen and her husband arranged to pay a visit to Albert's beloved Coburg in September to see their grandson for the first time. Prince and Princess Frederick and their son with his English nurse, Mrs. Hobbs, went to meet them there.

There came bad news to them on the journey. The Dowager Duchess of Coburg, Prince Albert's step-mother, was very ill, and his brother telegraphed asking them to put off their arrival. But one of

[1] *Ibid.*, V, p. 177.

Albert's principles was to carry out a plan when once it had been made, and they proceeded. Before they arrived they got tidings that she was dead, and the party was received at Coburg by their relations in the deepest mourning. But nothing marred the great moment. William, holding Mrs. Hobbs's hand walked in to see his grandmamma. She was enraptured with him, he was such a fine fat child with a beautiful skin, and as for the stricken left arm, she absolutely refused to notice it, and wrote in her diary of his very fine shoulders and limbs. Again and again she referred to him in the warmest terms; the dear little boy, so intelligent and pretty, so good and affectionate, the darling child, the clever child, and from that first sight of him till the end of her life, though often furious with his indiscretions and conceit and mischief-making, she never ceased to regard him with peculiar affection.

Family marriages were becoming a matter of pressing concern. Bertie was nineteen this year, and his father again turned to the list of eligible Princesses. Among them, fifth in order of merit was Princess Alexandra, daughter of Prince Christian of Schleswig-Holstein-Sonderburg-Glucksburg, whose mother was heiress to the throne of Denmark. The Prince Consort sent this list to Princess Frederick for her views, and having heard a very favourable report of this candidate, she arranged to meet her. Never had she seen a more lovely and fascinating girl, and she gave her father so enthusiastic an account of her that she was instantly promoted to the top of the list. Bertie was not at present told anything about her,

nor was there any thought of his being allowed to
see her. He had spent his long vacation this summer
in a tour through Canada and the United States and
General Bruce was afraid that his huge popularity
there had made him sadly conceited. So immediately
on his return he was sent back to Oxford, where
among more studious and gifted youths he would
learn his level.

Six months had elapsed now since Ascot Week and
at the end of November, according to plan, Prince
Louis was bidden to Windsor again, with just such
an intention as that for which Prince Frederick of
Prussia had been bidden to Balmoral, and one
evening he asked Princess Alice to marry him. They
went together to the parents, and, with many embraces, the engagement was permitted. But the young
couple were told that the marriage could not take
place for over a year yet, for so long a postponement
seemed to the Queen a reasonable delay, though she
herself had married after a three months' engagement.
It was in vain that Louis begged for a remission of
part of this sentence. The Prince Consort only told
him that he was making a great mistake in wishing
" to curtail the fairest moments of his life."

The Queen's desire not to part with her daughter
was at the root of the prolongation of these fair
moments, but she was immensely pleased at the
thought of having Louis, eventually, as a son-inlaw. She found him good, amiable, honest, modest,
warm-hearted, high principled and " unassuming."
It was " as if he was one of our own children," and
it brought sunshine to her home to see the two young

lovers together. She began to wonder whether the marriage need entail a very substantial separation, and, following that up, she wrote to Uncle Leopold that she hoped that she and Albert, " have gained a son, and shall *not* lose a daughter, for we shall be able to have them a good deal with us, Louis not having any duties to detain him much at home at present. I can't say what happiness and comfort it is to me. I feel my dear child will first of all have a peaceful, quiet, happy home without difficulties— and secondly, that she will not be entirely cut off from us and monopolized as our poor Vicky is." Her plan prospered, and presently she wrote again to her uncle, with fresh *Lobgesang* for Louis, to say that this had been arranged : " *Now*—that *all* has been so *happily* settled, and that I find the young man so very charming—my joy and my *deep* gratitude to God are very great ! He is *so* lovable, so very *young*, and like one of our own children—not the *least in the way*—but a dear, pleasant, *bright* companion, full of fun and spirits, and I am *sure* will be a *great* comfort to us, besides being an excellent husband to our dear Alice, who though radiant with joy, and much in love (which well she may be) is as quiet and sensible as possible."[1]

Certainly this was a very happy settlement for the Queen. Alice and Louis, though deeply in love with each other must put off their marriage for more than a year yet, and after that, since he was so desirable an inmate and had no particular duties at home, they

[1] *Letters of Queen Victoria*, I, iii, pp. 532, 533.

would make their principal home in England, where he would have no duties at all. This was Mamma's wish and the Queen's will and Alice took it quietly and sensibly, like a dutiful daughter and a loyal subject. Louis remained at Windsor over Christmas, instead of going home to spend that great family festival with his parents. The Prince Consort no less than the Queen considered him an accession to the party, and in moods of abstraction used to call him Fritz. He wrote to Vicky to tell her this, hoping that " her Fritz " would not be annoyed. The fact was, he tactfully explained, that the name Fritz connoted to him " the personification of a beloved, newly-bestowed full grown son." Among the Christmas gifts from Germany, there was none that gave him so much joy as a long Memorandum Princess Frederick had written on the advantage of introducing into the Prussian Constitution a law concerning Ministerial responsibility to the Sovereign. He was delighted with it : he agreed with every word of it : it showed a statesmanlike grasp of the subject. Vicky was indeed tackling the mission with which he had entrusted her with profound sagacity.

Though the date for Princess Alice's wedding was still remote the Queen announced the engagement in her speech from the throne at the opening of Parliament in February, 1861, and asked that due provision should be made for her. Once again the Prince Consort would have preferred that all future provision of the sort should be settled now—for who could tell what poisonous anti-monarchical principles might prevail before all his daughters were provided for ?—but Gladstone, now Chancellor of the Exchequer, thought that the country would not care to pledge itself so plentifully in advance. However, the House unanimously voted a dowry of £30,000 and an annuity of £6,000. The Prince considered this rather shabby : Alice would not be able to cut much of a figure on so small an allowance, but small though the sum was, a precedent had been set for younger daughters, which the country would be bound to follow on future occasions.

Until this year the Queen had never lost anyone, friend or relation, to whom she was emotionally attached. But in March her mother, the Duchess of Kent, died after a short illness. Years ago, owing largely to the influence of Prince Albert, the early estrangement between them had passed and was forgotten, and almost since her marriage the Queen had been on the most affectionate terms with the Duchess. Her grief was sincere and profound, but from childhood the thought of death and all details connected with it had held a strange fascination for her. She wrote in her diary a minute account of the hours during which she watched by her mother's deathbed, and of the associations they suggested, of the striking of the clocks in the silent house, and especially of the chiming of the repeater watch in a tortoiseshell case, which had belonged to her father, the sound of which had been so familiar to her when as a girl she had slept in her mother's room, but which she had not heard since the day of her accession. Now, sleepless through the night she heard once more the tinkled quarters, and it was just striking half-past nine in the morning when the breathing from the bed ceased. She held her mother's hand and kissed it, and Albert took her into the room next door. He brought to her the daughter with whom she was so loath to part, and left them together, saying to Alice: " Comfort Mamma." To the girl that was a moment of self-dedication which she never forgot. Year after year, during her married life abroad, she wrote to her mother on that day renewing her vow, and telling her that neither time nor distance could ever loosen the dear obligation then laid on her by her father.[1]

The Duchess's death produced an effect on the Queen that was strange in one possessed of so vigorous a vitality. She clung to her grief as if to something intrinsically precious which must be cherished for its own sake, and she surrendered herself to the luxury of self-pity:

> " Except Albert," she wrote to her uncle, " (who I very often don't see but very little in the day), I have no human being except our children, and that is not the same *Verhaltniss* to *open* myself to: and besides a *woman* requires *women's* society and sympathy sometimes, as men do *men's*. All this, beloved Uncle, will show you that without *dwelling* constantly on it, or *moping* or becoming *morbid* though the *blank* and the *loss to me*, in my isolated position especially, is *such* a *dreadful* and such an *irreparable one*, the worst *trials* are yet to come. . . . But the general sympathy for *me*, and approval of the manner in which I have shown my grief, as well

[1] Princess Christian, *Alice*, p. 197.

as the affection and respect for dearest Mamma's memory in the country is *quite wonderful and most touching.* . . . Dear good Alice was full of intense tenderness, affection and distress for me."

It did her good, she wrote, to abandon herself to her grief, interruptions to her indulgence of it were bad for her. It was only right that she should be without the " power of real enjoyment in anything." Her doctors agreed that she must not attempt to make any effort. " Long conversation, loud talking, the talking of many people together I *can't* bear yet ; it must come *very* gradually." Even the birthday of her youngest daughter three weeks later was most upsetting, because her grandmamma idolized her, and the presence of Louis was equally agitating : it made her " long and pine " for her mother because she would have been so happy and proud.[1] This fond embrace of sorrow foreshadowed the effect which the approaching tragedy of the Queen's life would have on her.

The Prince of Wales was sent to the Curragh Camp in Kildare to occupy his long vacation, and in August the Queen with her husband and her three elder children made one of her rare visits to Ireland, so that the Prince Consort could see if he was performing his military duties with proper ardour. He was not pleased with the tone of the young officers : they were not keen enough on their profession, and sport rather than military tactics furnished the conversation

---

[1] *Letters of Queen Victoria*, I, iii, pp. 556, 557.

at mess. Altogether there was too much relaxation and he arranged that Bertie should go to Berlin to stay with his sister, and observe how much more earnest young German officers were. He was now also told about the young lady who had been put at the head of the eligible Princesses, and he would be allowed his first sight of her on his way home. At present he received this news with complete indifference : it was just one more of the duties laid on him.

The Crown Princess had come over to England on the Duchess of Kent's death, and she and her husband came again in June and remained for nearly two months, so the Prussian monopolization of Vicky did not quite warrant the Queen's complaints, and now, when she and the rest of the family went up to Balmoral, Prince Louis joined them and remained till the middle of October. There, with her husband and her family surrounding and ministering to her, she recovered the sense of the happiness her marriage had brought her, and that supreme content began to obliterate her loss. " Every year," she once wrote in her diary, " my heart becomes more fixed in this dear Paradise, and so much more now that *all* has become my dear Albert's *own* creation, own work, own building, own laying out as at Osborne, and his great taste and the impress of his dear hand has been stamped everywhere."[1] With him beside her the pleasures and interests of life resumed their savour. In the mellow autumn weather they had many picnics on the hill, and there were two great expeditions. In

[1] *Leaves from the Journal of a Life in the Highlands*, p. 111.

one of these, after riding and driving all day, the Royal party were to sleep at a small inn fifty miles from Balmoral. But after dinner there was a most agreeable alarm. The sound of a drum and fife band was heard, and from the door of their inn they saw the six musicians who composed it parading the village street. The Queen thought they must have been recognized, and that this serenade was in her honour. But this proved a disappointment; the Prince Consort made discreet inquiries from the maid at the hotel, and found that this local band played regularly in the street twice a week, which the Queen thought very odd. Later, during the night, a commercial traveller arrived, demanding refreshment and a bed. This invasion was averted by the faithful Grant, who told him that the hotel was full up with a wedding party from Aberdeen, and he had to seek shelter elsewhere.[1] The Queen wrote rapturously to Uncle Leopold of these expeditions and of her wonderful Highland servant, John Brown. He had once been Albert's gillie, but she had now made him her personal attendant, and he took the most watchful care of her. He combined the offices of groom, footman, page, and indeed of maid, so handy was he with cloaks and shawls: it would be sorrowful to leave him behind when they went south.

The Prince of Wales came for a few days of holiday before going to Cambridge for the October term, having studied German military life and having seen his Princess. They were pleased with each other;

[1] *Ibid.*, pp 148, 149.

they accepted the destiny their respective parents had framed for them, and the matter was regarded as settled. The Prince Consort explained to his son that his marriage would be unpopular in Germany, for, since the accession of the Hanoverian dynasty in 1714, all the Kings of England and indeed practically every member of the Royal Family had married Germans, and Germany felt she had a monopoly of supplying wives to the Royal House. Bertie must therefore be very tactful, and very dutiful towards his innumerable German cousins. The Prince Consort was disappointed with the unintelligent way he received these counsels, and he could only report to Stockmar that Bertie seemed to understand him " as well as a boy of his age and capacity could. . . ." But education was not done with yet, and since academic study was not producing much blossoming of the mind, his father planned a foreign tour for him to take place after the end of the Cambridge term and to last until the following June. Egypt, Turkey, and Palestine, under the supervision of General Bruce, might do more than the combined Universities. The Court left Balmoral for Windsor, and the Prince began putting in hand the arrangements for the wedding of Princess Alice. She had been engaged for nearly a year, Parliament, months ago, had granted her dowry and annuity, and there was no longer any reasonable cause for delay. He selected a household for her suitable to what he considered her narrow means and with that passion for perfection in detail which was so characteristic of him, he had already rejected the stock designs for the lace on her bridal veil, and Honiton was at work on patterns of more symbolic significance.

King Frederick William of Prussia who had been insane for two years had died in January. The Coronation of King William took place in October and the Crown Princess's daily letter to her mother gave a most picturesque account of it. She, like the Prince of Wales, had a marvellous eye for ceremonial detail and described the costumes of her ladies-in-waiting, one in blue velvet, the other in red velvet, and herself in gold and ermine and white; the loud singing of chorales, the draughts and the bitter cold; the huge number of guests at the State Banquet; the moment when at the end of the second course the King asked for wine, which was the signal for all ladies and gentlemen-in-waiting to leave the room; the four hundred servants in livery belonging to the assembled Royalties. The new King was very gracious to her, he gave her a locket containing a piece of his hair, and made her Chef of the 2nd Regiment of his Hussars. This appointment unfortunately was received with much laughter from the Princess, for she thought it was a joke, but she was told it was quite serious, and that Prussian Regiments particularly liked having a lady as their Chef. The Queen loved to hear the minutiæ of Royal Pageantries, and Vicky, in case she had forgotten anything, promised to send her the newspapers as well.[1]

Lord Clarendon was the British representative at these celebrations, and he wrote to the Queen loud

[1] Ponsonby, *Letters of Empress Frederick*, pp. 31, 32

THE QUEEN DRESSED FOR HER DIAMOND JUBILEE, 1897

in praise of the grace and dignity of her daughter : to him the most beautiful feature of the Coronation ceremony was the exquisite manner in which she had done homage to her father-in-law. What struck him even more was her intellectual grasp : " If His Majesty had the mind, the judgment and the foresight of the Princess Royal, there would be nothing to fear, and the example and influence of Prussia would soon be marvellously developed. Lord Clarendon has had the honour to hold a very long conversation with Her Royal Highness, and has been more than ever astonished at the *statesmanlike* and comprehensive views which she takes of the policy of Prussia, both internal and foreign, and of the duties of a Constitutional King."[1] But this appreciation, though gratifying in itself, surely contained the seeds of perilous stuff. In Prussia it was not proper for any woman to have statesmanlike and Liberal views, especially if she was Crown Princess, or, if she had, she must keep her guilty secret undivulged. The new King had clearly foreshadowed an autocratic policy when he addressed the Prussian Chamber : " The rulers of Prussia receive their Crown from God. This is the signification of the expression ' King by the Grace of God ' and therein lies the sanctity of the Crown which is inviolable." Such a monarch would not be likely to appreciate his English daughter-in-law's views on the duties of the Constitutional King of Prussia. Moreover *The Times*, under the editorship of Delane, had lately been publishing a series of violent articles attacking all Prussian forms of

[1] *Letters of Queen Victoria*, I, iii, p. 584.

Government and the less the Crown Princess said about such matters the better.

The treacheries of the English autumn always tried the Prince Consort's health ; this year, however, he seemed to feel them less than usual, and was full of engagements that constantly took him away from Windsor for tiring days. He began to suffer from great fatigue aggravated by sleeplessness, and towards the end of November he caught a chill, and made it worse by travelling down to Cambridge on a bitter day to see General Bruce : the Prince of Wales had not been behaving as the heir to the throne should. The doctors at first diagnosed his indisposition as rheumatism, then as influenza, and it was not till he had been ill nearly three weeks that they pronounced that he had typhoid fever. But there were no unfavourable symptoms : they encouraged the Queen to believe that the illness was running a normal course, and that there was no cause for anxiety. His strength was well maintained, but suddenly his illness took a turn for the worse, and he died on December 14, 1861.

Throughout his illness Princess Alice had been her mother's chief support, and now she took upon herself the whole burden of the tragedy. She slept in the Queen's room, she saw the Ministers of the Crown, she made herself responsible for all immediate arrangements, and, most difficult of all, she managed to reach, by the mere force of love and sympathy, that stricken heart. She put aside her own grief for the father whom she had adored, and devoted herself body and soul to her mother. So complete was her self-surrendering service that Prince Louis thought she might decide to break off her engagement to him and remain with her.[1] During those first days, had it not been for her, the Queen might have irretrievably collapsed.

Once more she turned to her Uncle Leopold. It was he who in her girlhood had been her most trusted counsellor, it was he who had brought about her marriage, and though through all her wedded life with Albert beside her she had had no need of him, she now appealed to him to support her in the resolve which for the future was to direct her life :

"I am also anxious," she wrote, " to repeat *one* thing, and *that one* is *my firm* resolve, my *irrevocable decision*, viz. that *his* wishes, *his* plans about everything, *his* views about *every* thing are to be *my law*. And *no human power* will make me swerve from what *he* decided and wished, and I look to *you* to *support* and *help* me in this. I apply this particularly as regards our children—Bertie, etc.— for whose future he has traced everything so carefully. I am *also determined* that *no one* person, may *he* be ever so good, ever so devoted among my servants—is to lead or guide or dictate to *me*. . . . Though miserably weak and utterly shattered, my spirit rises when I think that any wish or plan of his is to be changed, or that I am to be *made to do* anything."

She begged him to come to stay with her at Osborne, but was curiously anxious that before he saw anybody

[1] Princess Christian, *Alice*, p. 307.

else in England, he should talk to her own physician, Dr. Jenner :

> " Pray do this," she wrote, " for I *fear much* others trying to see you first and say things and wish for things which I *should not* consent to."[1]

The significance of this insistence was often clear enough in the years that followed, when her Ministers, year after year, urged her to resume the public functions of Sovereignty again. She sent them to see Dr. Jenner in order that he should tell them that her health rendered her incapable of anything of the sort.

The Queen remained at Osborne for more than two months after the Prince Consort's death, and this seclusion began to form itself into the habit which eventually became so disastrous. A Council was held there in January, but it was so arranged that she need not meet its members face to face. She gave an interview afterwards to Lord Granville, and later in the month to her Prime Minister. Otherwise she saw none of her Ministers, but she asked that some Secretary of State should come down once a week for a night or for a Saturday till Monday. She would not promise to see him, if she did not feel well enough, but it would be " a support to her Majesty to feel that he was at hand, and his presence at the Queen's residence would probably have a good effect."

But she gave all diligence to such work as could be done in complete privacy. She read with the utmost care the despatches that were sent her, and more than

[1] *Letters of Queen Victoria*, I, iii, p. 606.

once complained that they did not contain sufficient comment and guidance to enable her to make the decisions which she must now arrive at without her husband's counsel. She felt sure that she could not live long, and the future of her children occupied her : she wanted a provision made for the Prince of Wales, should his marriage take place, for her younger sons on their coming of age or marrying, and for her daughters if she died before they came of age. Mr. Gladstone, the Chancellor of the Exchequer, made certain proposals on these points which were satisfactory to her.

Though she shunned any personal contact beyond that of her children and her household she found alleviation in writing to others of her loss. Lord Derby was on the Committee for a Memorial to the Prince, and to him she poured out in terms most simple and most moving the sense of her infinite misery. She wrote :

" She feels as though *her life* had ended on that dreadful day when she lost that bright Angel who was the idol, the life of her life ; and time seems to have passed like *one long dark day*.

" She sees the trees budding, the days lengthening, the primroses coming out, but *she thinks* herself *still* in the month of December ! The Queen toils away from morning till night, goes out twice a day, does all she is desired to do by her physicians, but she wastes and pines, and there is that within her *inmost soul* which seems to be undermining her existence. And how can it be otherwise ? The happiness and comfort of twenty-two years crushed *for ever* ; and the Queen who did nothing, thought of nothing, without her beloved and gracious husband, who was her support, her constant companion, her guide, who helped her in *everything* great and small, stands *alone* in her trying and difficult position, struggling to do her duty as she will to her last hour, with a broken, bleeding heart, and with but *one* consolation—to rejoin him again—*never to part*."[1]

For the next six months Princess Alice remained in intimate charge of the Queen. Her elder sister had been no less passionately devoted to her father, but she did not come to England after his death, nor indeed during the year that followed, and it is easy to understand how the Queen shrank from rather than sought that brilliant but more disturbingly emotional companionship. She needed only this gentler, more intuitive daughter, intensely sensitive, but never assertive, the presence of whom rather than any manifestation of its protectiveness was all that could yet reach her. In those months the girl, not yet nineteen, blossomed into womanhood. She had many material businesses to take on her shoulders, and became, as her married life showed, a most capable organizer; she had the desolate anguish of her mother always before her eyes, and, *durch Mitleid wissend*, her heart learned from it an infinite tenderness and an unwearied patience.

The Queen's uncle remained in England for a month. He was anxious to be of any possible use, but a letter he wrote her after he got back to Brussels suggests that he meditated services which were the

[1] *Ibid.*, II, i, p. 20.

last in the world that the Queen would accept. " You will recollect [he said] that our beloved Angel gave me at all times his confidence, that we rarely differed. Whenever you have the slightest desire I am always at hand to aid you. I have been intimately connected with the country, when, with the exception of a few ancients, none of the present people were, as it were, in existence or known of. I have for near half a century been a steady and devoted friend of the country, never taking the slightest advantage of anything for myself, or for any vanity, however trifling."[1]

But it was not that that the Queen wanted. She knew her husband's mind better than anybody and needed no interpreter of it : and (as she had expressed herself before, when she ascended the throne) she and her Ministers could manage the affairs of the realm without the aid of Uncle Leopold's advice, even though it was based on such extensive experience.

The Queen at once took in hand what she regarded as a sacred and immediate duty, namely to follow out the plans which the Prince Consort had made for his children. The first of these was the foreign tour that he had arranged for the Prince of Wales. He had sketched out the programme for this with the Prince's Governor, General Bruce. Certain fêtes and entertainments must now be cancelled owing to the Prince's deep mourning, and, since this was to be a long absence, General Bruce was instructed to keep the thought of Princess Alexandra constantly before him. The party, with Dr. A. P. Stanley as

[1] *Ibid.*, II, i, p. 26.

Chaplain, left England in February, as had been already planned, and travelled for four months. As they were nearing England again on their return, the Queen wrote to General Bruce telling him to remind her son that he was returning to a house of mourning and a stricken mother, and that any "worldly, frivolous, gossiping kind of conversation" would be very unwelcome.

Princess Alice's long-delayed marriage with Prince Louis was the next duty. It was celebrated at Osborne on July 1, 1862, soon after the Prince of Wales's return from his tour. But every note of joy was muted. Though the girl was to be united to this admirable young man whom she devotedly loved, and who had been welcomed by her mother as an ideal son-in-law, the Queen turned the wedding into a memorial service for her own husband, and the account of it in her diary is simply heartbreaking. In these last twenty years she had surrendered to him all that she knew of herself, her self-reliance, her independence, her iron will; and the abysmal depth of her self-pity was the measure of her loss. She truly loved this daughter who for the last six months had been her chief stay and comfort, but no reflected gleam from Alice's happiness could pierce her darkness. It was in no way conscious selfishness or weakness that caused this, but the imperishable memories which asserted themselves with a force she was powerless to withstand. She was helpless in the grip of her self-centred misery, and that marriage day must have been an appalling experience for others as well as herself.

She slept very little on the previous night, and early in the morning heard the muffled knockings in preparation for the " sad marriage." Alice came to see her, and she gave her a Prayer-Book, like the one her mother had given her for her own " happy marriage." They breakfasted together and went to look at the dining-room which the knockings had converted into a chapel. Over the altar was hung a family picture by Winterhalter : Albert's hand was stretched out as if blessing them. The arrangement of the cushions and chairs in blue cloth and of the curved altar rails was as at her own wedding. Only a few relatives had been bidden ; Prince Louis's two brothers and his parents, Albert's brother Ernest, Prince and Princess Augustus of Saxe-Coburg, Princess Feodore Hohenlohe, her own half-sister, and the Crown Prince of Prussia, and they breakfasted in the Council Chamber, where hung a picture of the Queen's wedding which she had sent for specially from Windsor. Alice came to see her in her wedding-dress with its flounce of Honiton lace and the corresponding pattern on her veil, which Albert had ordered instead of the meaningless stock designs. Whatever the Queen looked on reminded her of her own sorrow.

Her four sons conducted her to the chapel before anybody but the clergy was there and took her to her arm-chair close to the altar : the two eldest stood between her and the seats for the congregation so that nobody could see her. But the waiting while she heard the small congregation assemble made her, though unseen, very nervous, and the pauses before the bridegroom and the bride entered were most painful. The Duke of Coburg gave his niece away, since the Prince of Wales, who would naturally have done so, was shielding his mother from the eyes of her relatives. Even the bridegroom found no place in this sad stricken soul, for the Queen recorded that " when all was over dearest Alice who was wonderfully calm embraced *me*, who was *all* she had." When everybody had left the chapel the Queen rose and accompanied by her sons went to the Horn Room, the walls of which were covered with the antlers of Albert's stags, and dreadful scenes of weeping took place. Alfred had been crying bitterly all through the service, and now the Queen clasped him in her arms and broke down herself, and the younger boys joined in. The bridegroom's parents were admitted and told the Queen how deeply they felt for her, and tears rolled down the Archbishop's cheeks. The rest of the guests then came in singly, and she embraced them, and went upstairs to lunch alone with the bride and bridegroom. Alice, she noted for the second time, still remained calm and composed.

The bridal couple went off for their honeymoon to a house lent them in the Isle of Wight, and, after leaving them to themselves for one day, the Queen drove over from Osborne to have tea, making a long detour to avoid being seen in Ryde. Bride and bridegroom came back to Osborne for three days before they left for Darmstadt, and at length, on her last night, Alice cried bitterly too. " I strove," wrote the Queen, " to cheer her up by the prospect of an early return."[1]

Princess Louis and her husband had promised to come back to England for a long stay in the autumn, and regularly through the intervening weeks she wrote copious and loving letters to her mother, full of those innumerable details of daily life which the Queen loved to hear. They were full, too, of the tenderest solicitude for her loneliness and unhappiness. At first, with an exquisite delicacy, she made no allusion to her own happiness except to say that she would with a full heart give up some of it, if by so doing she could transfer it to her mother. Then the Queen asked her to speak of it, and she wrote :

"You tell me to speak to you of my happiness, our happiness. You will understand the feeling which made me silent towards you, my own dear bereaved Mother, on that point, but you are unselfish and loving and can enter into my happiness, though I could never have been the first to tell you how intense it is, when it must draw the painful contrast between your past and the present existence. If I say I love my dear husband, that is scarcely enough—it is a love and esteem which increases daily, hourly ; which he also shows me by such consideration, such tender, loving ways. What was life before to what it has become now ? There is such blessed peace being at his side, being his wife ; there is such a feeling of security ; and we two have a world of our own when we are together, which *nothing* can touch or intrude upon. . . . How he loves you, you know, and he will be a good son to you."

[1] Princess Christian, *Alice*, pp. 13-18.

And then she turned to consolation again, founded on her absolute child-like belief in the personal reunion of those who had loved on Earth, with a perception, extraordinary in so young a woman, of the quality of her mother's misery:

> "Take courage, dear Mama, and feel strong in the thought that you require all your moral and physical strength to continue the journey which brings you nearer to *Home* and to *Him*. I know how weary you feel, how you long to rest your head on his dear shoulder, to have him to soothe your aching heart. You will find this rest again, and how blessed will it not be! Bear patiently and courageously your heavy burden, and it will lighten imperceptibly as you near him, and God's love and mercy will support you. Oh, could my feeble words bring you the least comfort! They come from a trusting, true and loving heart if from naught else."[1]

After Princess Alice's marriage the Queen, still in the strictest seclusion, went up to Balmoral, accompanied by her three younger daughters and sons, and took in hand the accomplishment of the third of the Prince Consort's arrangements for his children, writing to the father of Princess Alexandra, and obtaining his formal permission for the Prince of Wales to propose marriage to her. She had not yet seen her; and now she went to stay with Uncle Leopold at Laeken, where the Princess and her parents came for her inspection. It was a terrible ordeal to receive them without Albert's support, but

[1] *Ibid.*, pp. 59, 63.

the beauty, the charm, the simplicity and dignity of the girl instantly won her heart, and the Prince was sent for from England to speak for himself, while his mother went on to Coburg to revisit the scenes of Albert's youth. He was accepted, and the Queen herself worded the announcement in the English newspapers. " The revered Prince Consort whose sole object was the education and welfare of his children had long been convinced that this was a most desirable marriage." For her that was a sacred ordinance, but Germany in general and Prussia in particular were schismatic, and the fact that the Crown Princess was known to have taken a hand in the match, added to her growing unpopularity. Apart from Germany's prescriptive right to furnish English Queens, such a marriage was regarded as an indication that England sympathized with Denmark in the trouble now brewing over the Duchies of Schleswig and Holstein. But Albert had foreseen such objections when he selected the bride, he had cautioned his son on the subject and that was sufficient.

This feeling against the Crown Princess was aggravated by the arrival in Berlin of Bismarck and the inauguration of what might be called his reign of twenty-eight years. He at once showed that the principles on which he intended to govern were precisely the opposite of the Liberal policies which she and her husband stood for. In his first speech in the Reichstag he declared that Parliamentary Government was dead : autocracy, which meant his autocracy endorsed by the King, had superseded it, and its implements were blood and iron. For the Crown Prince and Princess he had nothing but a shrug of his vast shoulders : as long as the King lived, these Anglo-Coburgs were next to negligible. But he kept his eye on them. The *Engländerin* had not left the Englishwoman at home, and her influence over her husband was paramount. Nor could he forget that the *Engländerin's* mother was Queen of England, and at once he fixed on her as the source and inspiration of these Anglicizing tendencies. She was by no means negligible, though as yet she had not acquired either in England or on the Continent that immense personal prestige which was subsequently hers, and for which Bismarck, though he sometimes spoke of her with jocose contempt, learned to feel the most sincere respect. He did not like the Danish marriage of the *Engländerin's* brother, which had now been arranged, but there was no prospect of a direct collision between Prussian and English interests. He devoted his energies to the reorganization of Prussia as a military power, and observantly ignored the Anglo-Coburgs until the time came to take notice of them.

This establishment of the Bismarckian régime was a very disagreeable experience for the Crown Princess and her husband, and the Queen suggested a scheme which would give them a good pretext for leaving Berlin for a few months, and also served a purpose of her own. She wanted to see more of her future daughter-in-law, and have some quiet, serious conversation with her, and she also wanted to give the

Prince of Wales something to do to occupy his spare time, of which he had twenty-four hours every day. Moreover, she did not think it desirable that the two young people should see too much of each other before their marriage. They might, as Melbourne had once suggested to her, find traits in each other which they did not like. It was far better that, in the traditional Royal mode, they should be irrevocably united before there was a risk of their making such discoveries, and should adjust themselves afterwards. So she lent the Prince her yacht, asked Vicky and Fritz to cruise with him in the Mediterranean, and signified her wish that Alexandra should spend ten days with her at Osborne.

The Princess's father, Prince Christian, brought her over, and then was sent away again, for the Queen was not equal to entertaining an adult Royal guest, for whom she might have to alter her way of life; moreover these conversations with his daughter concerned him, and were better held in his absence. He would certainly become King of Denmark, through his wife's inheritance, before long, and it must be impressed on Alexandra that though in her heart she might love her father and his country as much as she pleased, she must keep these filial and patriotic affections to herself, and above all she must not attempt to foster pro-Danish sentiments in Bertie. Prussia in conjunction with Austria was determined to rape the Duchies of Schleswig and Holstein and it would give great offence in Germany if the heir to the English throne, not always very discreet, showed himself Danishly disposed : Alexandra must leave the Dane behind when she married into the

English Royal Family. We may presume that the Queen did not try to expound the intricacies of the question of the Duchies to the Princess, for, as Lord Palmerston once said, only three people had ever understood it : one was himself, but he had forgotten about it ; the second was a German professor, whose intellectual triumph had been dearly bought, for his brain had succumbed under the effort, and he was now in a lunatic asylum ; the third was the Prince Consort. He had been convinced that Denmark had no valid claim to the Duchies, and that must be sufficient for Alexandra, as it was for the Queen.

These ten days at Osborne must have been a melancholy experience for the girl, for she and her brothers and sisters were used to a gay and rather romping family life (she herself turned " cartwheels " across a room with modesty and ease and elegance), and here the unremitting gloom of the Queen's widowhood darkened the house, and anything like laughter or lightness, not to mention cartwheels, were out of the question in her hostess's presence. Every day the Queen took solitary drives with her or sent for her to her room, and explained to her, as Albert had previously explained to Bertie, the supreme dynastic importance of not offending Germany and her future husband's innumerable German relations. Tact was required, and it may safely be said that what Princess Alexandra did not instinctively know on that subject was not worth learning. The girl had, too, a rare power of sympathy and comprehension, and there sprang up between them a warm and abiding affection. Alice and Louis came back from Darmstadt while she was at Osborne, to spend some months in England with their mother ; and Princess Alexandra founded a close and life-long friendship with Princess Helena, now the eldest unmarried daughter. From Osborne the Court moved to Windsor, and the Queen's Ministers were formally presented to the Princess, though the Queen did not attend that ceremony, and then her father came back to fetch her away. Bertie was now on his way home, and they were allowed to spend a couple of days together with the King of Hanover. The two young people then parted, not to meet again till the evening before their wedding.

The Queen had a second personal interview with the Chancellor of the Exchequer about the settlements to be made on them. Thanks to the masterly management of the Prince Consort the estates of the Duchy of Cornwall, which at the Prince of Wales's birth had only been worth £13,000 a year, now yielded £62,000, and the Sandringham estate had been purchased for him out of accumulated capital. Gladstone proposed to bring the Prince's income up to £100,000, with a separate income for the Princess of £10,000, to be increased, in case of her widowhood, to £30,000. The Queen thought this a meagre provision ; supposing the Prince died, leaving a family of young children, how could their mother bring them up on £30,000 a year ? Gladstone agreed that in such a deplorable event a fresh provision would have to be made.

The wedding was celebrated on March 10, 1863,

at St. George's Chapel, Windsor, where no Royal wedding had been held since that of Henry I. Westminster Abbey or the Chapel Royal at St. James's would have been more suitable for the marriage of the heir to the throne; but that would have entailed a public appearance in London for the Queen, and was therefore impossible. To her it was just such another revival of heart-rending memories as the wedding of Princess Louis had been, and she would have liked the marriage to have taken place on February 10, the anniversary of her own wedding-day, in order to link up those memories with an intenser poignancy. She did not put off her widow's mourning for the day, nor did she go into the Chapel herself, but sat withdrawn in a gallery above the chancel, so that she need not face the wedding guests. Except for Prince Alfred, who had been desperately ill with typhoid out at Malta but was now making a good recovery, all her children were round her, five daughters and three sons, and two sons-in-law, for Prince and Princess Louis, who had been living with her for over three months, were here still, and the Crown Prince and Princess of Prussia had come, bringing Prince William with them. But the very fact that her children were Albert's children heightened her sense of loss. She bitterly contrasted in her diary for the day her sad and desolate life with that of her two elder daughters who had such loving and admirable husbands, and when Bertie with his lovely bride left for their honeymoon at Osborne, she tortured herself with the memory of her own departure for Windsor, twenty-three years ago, with her adored bridegroom.

After the wedding the Crown Prince and Princess of Prussia went home, but that devoted and unselfish couple, Prince and Princess Louis, still stayed on. Princess Louis was soon to have her first child, but the Queen did not see the slightest cause for their leaving her because of that : rather it was a reason for their remaining. If a boy, the baby would be in the direct succession to the Grand Duchy of Hesse, but Windsor was Alice's ancestral home just as much as Darmstadt was Louis's. So the baby was born at Windsor, and, as it was a girl, it was christened Victoria, and the parents stayed there till the middle of May. Alice, after parting with her mother, wrote the warmest and most affectionate letter of thanks to her for her kindness to herself and her husband and her baby. The answer she received to this evidently conveyed some sort of reproach for her going away, for tender-hearted Alice had to protest, though ever so gently : " In to-day's letter you mention again your wish that we should soon be with you again. Out of the months of our married life, five have been spent under your roof, so you see how ready we are to be with you. Before next year Louis does not think we shall be able to come ; at any rate when we can we shall."[1]

Whatever may have been the terms of residence implied in the " happy settlement " under which the Queen had permitted their marriage, this seemed to her a shabby interpretation of them. She felt that they had failed her, and she wrote to Uncle Leopold about their desertion :

[1] *Ibid.*, p. 70.

"The good children have no duties at present to perform at home, no house to live in, and ought to be as much with me as possible. A married daughter I must have living with me, and must not be left to look about for help, and to have to make shift for the day, which is too dreadful. I intend (and she wishes it herself) to look out in a year or two (for until nineteen or twenty I don't intend *she* should marry) for a young sensible Prince for Lenchen [Princess Helena] to marry, who can during *my lifetime* make my house his *principal* home. Lenchen is so useful, and her whole character so well adapted to live in the house that (unless Alice lived constantly with me, which she won't) I could not give her up without *sinking* under the *weight* of my desolation. A sufficient fortune to live independently if I died and plenty of good sense and high moral worth are the only necessary requisites."[1]

Three times a week or oftener, after this warning that she and Louis might not be able to come to England again this year, Alice wrote her mother letters brimming with affection and sympathy and the tenderest recognition of her desolate life, but she tried also to convey to her that there were calls on them at Darmstadt which, after all, was her husband's home and heritage and therefore hers. Louis's father and mother had claims on him; he had to take his seat in the Chamber, which he should have done before, but he was in England; they had to do their share in Royal entertainments, and they were both very busy over their new house, which she herself had planned: these plans, alas,

[1] *Letters of Queen Victoria*, II, i, p. 85.

proved to be beyond the scope of their finances and had to be cut down. She had taken into her service a little black Malay boy, who had been in Darmstadt two years, but had received no sort of education. She was having him taught to read and write, and when he had been instructed in religion she would have him christened. Twice a week Louis had to drill with his regiment, there was an industrial exhibition to open, there was a conference of Agriculturists, at which new machines for reaping were shown ; the Prince Consort's address to the British Agricultural Society, Alice added, lay open on the Committee's table, and was highly thought of ; an asylum for the blind had been started of which she was President.

But this catalogue of engagements failed to convince the Queen that anything should be allowed to interfere with their duty of returning to her in the autumn, and she did not appreciate how natural it was that a young couple should want a home of their own, where, after their five months' absence in England, they could settle down as a married couple should. Darmstadt was evidently threatening to monopolize them as Prussia had monopolized Vicky. But once again Mama's wish was the Queen's will, and leaving the baby behind they came to Balmoral in September for a further stay of six weeks. The Prince and Princess of Wales were at Abergeldie, and Prince Alfred was home on leave, and the Queen had her three youngest daughters with her ; really the family were doing their best that she should not have to " make shift for the day."

Yet still the forward movement of life served only

to unseal for the Queen more memories of the past. She spent an hour or two with the Duchess of Atholl at Blair on the way up to Balmoral, and breakfasted in the same room as on a pleasant never-to-be-forgotten day two years before, when she was there with Albert. The Duke was suffering from a mortal disease, and with a touch of naivest self-revelation, the Queen recorded that her sympathy with him alleviated her own pain in revisiting the house where she had been so happy. She went to the unveiling of a statue of the Prince Consort at Aberdeen, and found it a fearful ordeal. One day, though with a heavy heart, she made a long expedition on Alice's advice, in the manner of old days, lunching on warmed-up broth and potatoes. On the way home the carriage upset. Luckily no one was seriously injured, but John Brown, jumping off the box, hurt his knee, and the Queen sprained her thumb and bruised her face. They sat on the road under the lee of the overturned carriage while ponies were sent for, and the little Malay boy, now christened "Willem," whom Alice had brought to England with her, squatted beside them. The first reaction in the Queen's mind was that it was terrible not to be able to tell Albert about the accident, the second : " I am thankful that it was by no imprudence of mine or the slightest deviation from what my beloved one and I had always been in the habit of doing."[1] After six weeks Alice and Louis went home again to their child and their innumerable duties in Darmstadt. But Alice's heart was torn with tenderness for the beloved mother who was still so inaccessibly

[1] *More Leaves from the Journal of a Life in the Highlands*, pp. 7-11.

PRINCESS ALICE

miserable. She wrote on her journey : " How sad that we should be reduced to writing again. I always feel separation from you so much, for I feel for and with you, more, oh, far more, than I can ever express. I can only say, trust, hope, and be courageous."

But as yet neither sympathy nor devotion nor any external stimulus could rouse a response. The Queen clung, as she had done after the Duchess of Kent's death, to the disabling quality of her bereavement and to the harm she believed it would cause her to make any struggle against it. After one such experience she wrote to Uncle Leopold in pathetic justification of herself:

> " To show how nervous and weak I am, I made the effort to go and visit the truly magnificent Military Hospital at Netley. . . . I went through it all, but I have been ill ever since, bad headache, restless nights and an increase of despair. It shows how shattered I am ! "[1]

[1] *Letters of Queen Victoria,* II, i, p. 84.

CHAPTER III

EARLIER in this year, 1863, Bismarck took an important Fascist step in establishing the autocracy of himself and the Crown by abolishing the freedom of the Press. The Crown Prince and his wife were at Dantzig, on a tour of military inspection, when this was announced. Neither of them had any idea that such a step was contemplated, and she urged him to write to the King, plainly stating that he profoundly disapproved of it, and to send a copy of this protest to Bismarck. The same day the Bürgermeister of Dantzig, a man of strong Liberal views, was to make a speech at the Rathaus, at which the Crown Prince would be present. He suggested that he should allude to this measure in such a way as would give the Crown Prince an opportunity in his reply of saying how repugnant such a step was to his principles, and this suggestion was adopted. The King was justifiably furious at his son's having expressed his personal disapproval of a measure to which he himself had already given his assent and ordered him publicly to withdraw what he had publicly stated. This, with the enthusiastic backing of his wife, he refused to do, and a violent quarrel, which set up a permanent estrangement between father and son, was the result.

The Crown Princess was delighted at her husband's unwise speech: indeed she was responsible for his having made it. She wrote exultantly to her mother; "I did all I *could* to induce Fritz to do so, knowing how necessary it was that he should *once* express his sentiments freely and disclaim having any part in the last measures of the Government." She was convinced that she was right, for this was a splendid opening for him to assert his Liberal principles and oppose such Fascist tyranny in the spirit of the mission with which her father had entrusted her. How it would end she did not know; she thought they might have to leave Prussia for a while, in which case how gratefully would they come to England " the blessed country of peace and happiness." There would be a fight first, for she hoped all Germans of Liberal views would rally round Fritz, " and indeed," she wrote, " I enjoy a pitched battle (when it comes to it) exceedingly."[1] But this enjoyment was denied her, for there was no pitched battle at all. The King wrote a second very angry letter to his son, who had offered to resign all his posts, military and civil, refusing to accept his resignation, and telling him to carry on, but not to make any public speeches whatsoever. Those were his orders: he had approved the measures which his daughter-in-law disapproved, and he happened to be King.

As for Bismarck, who was quite aware that it was she who had encouraged her husband to make this injudicious protest, he contented himself with taking

[1] Ponsonby, *Letters of Empress Frederick*, pp. 41–44.

no notice of the Crown Prince's copy of the letter he had sent his father, and merely made two brief memoranda on the subject. The first referred to his wife : " Either she has herself attained to definite views of her own as to the Government most advantageous for Prussia, or she has succumbed to the concerted influence of the Anglo-Coburg combination. However this may be, she has decided upon a course of opposition to the present Government." He commented on the Crown Prince with the same bleak unconcern. " The pretension that a warning from His Royal Highness should outweigh royal decisions come to after serious and careful consideration attributes undue importance to his own position and experience as compared with those of his Sovereign and father." No more notice was taken of the incident, and there was no question of the Crown Prince and Princess having to leave Germany and take refuge in England. The Crown Princess then thought that another species of punishment might be inflicted on them, and again she wrote to her mother expressing her fears that she and Fritz might not be allowed to visit England in the autumn, lest they should indulge in further mischievous activities there. But these apprehensions were also quite groundless. She had yet to learn, and bitter was the lesson, how impregnable is the defence of an adversary who is armed with indifference. There is no joint in his harness, and it blunts the sharpest arrow-head. Neither Bismarck nor the King made the smallest objection. The Anglo-Coburgs might do whatever they pleased ; they were negligible.

Indeed the Princess's long absence, coupled with the violent attacks on Prussia in the English Press, merely made her more unpopular in Germany, and Bismarck had no objections to that.

The Queen thought that Fritz had been quite right in making this public protest against Bismarck's tyrannical measure, and approved of Vicky's having induced him to do so. That was intelligible enough, for they had acted in accordance with Albert's injunctions to promote a Liberal spirit in Germany. She even interceded with the King of Prussia, begging him not to be too hard on his son, but to give him " reasonable and necessary freedom." He had thought it his duty to express his views; he had no intention of leading an opposition to his father and his father's Government, for he was too good a son for that, and had too much respect for the authority of the Crown.[1] But she did not ask herself what she would have done if an analogous incident had occurred in England, if the Prince of Wales under the influence of his foreign wife had publicly protested, at some Mayoral function in Manchester, against an Act of Parliament which had received her assent. She would doubtless have treated them exactly as her Brother of Prussia had treated his son and daughter-in-law. She would have given the Prince a tremendous wigging, and then have taken no further notice of such a silly prank.

The Schleswig-Holstein question which culminated in the Danish war early in 1864 led to somewhat

[1] Bolitho, *Further Letters of Queen Victoria*, pp. 43-44.

sharp differences of opinion between the Queen and her daughters. Briefly, there were three claimants to the Duchies : the King of Denmark to the throne of which the Princess of Wales's father had now succeeded as King Christian IX : Duke Frederick of Schleswig-Holstein-Sonderburg-Augustenburg: and Prussia in alliance with Austria. Prussia's claim was that Schleswig was mainly German in population and Holstein entirely so, being also a member of the German Confederation. A slight invalidity in the claim of Duke Frederick was that his father had sold (and been paid for) his family rights to the late King of Denmark. The Queen hovered at first between the claims of Prussia and of Duke Frederick, but as the Prince Consort (one of the only three men who had ever understood the question) had decided that neither Denmark nor the Augustenburg family had any rights, she plumped for Prussia. The Crown Prince and Princess on the other hand were supporters of Duke Frederick as was also Liberal feeling in Hanover, Coburg and other German states: Princess Louis, writing to her mother from Darmstadt, told her that all Germany except Prussia felt that his claim was just. Finally the Prince and Princess of Wales, in spite of those quiet conversations at Osborne, were ardent pro-Danes, and English popular sympathy was on their side on the general grounds that a tiny Kingdom was being brutally bullied by two very powerful Kingdoms. When therefore the family was assembled at Windsor in December domestic conversation was animated. The Crown Princess was voluble for Duke Frederick, the

Queen found a memorandum of the Prince Consort's on the subject and was pontifically Prussian, and the Princess of Wales continued to say : " The Duchies belong to Papa." No arguments were of any use, and so the Queen signified that they had better talk about something else. The Crown Princess went back to Berlin unshaken (for the present) in her belief in the Augustenburg claim, and the Princess of Wales, amid national rejoicings, gave birth to a son.

Immediately afterwards Bismarck sent an ultimatum to Denmark to evacuate Schleswig within twenty-four hours : war followed. The Crown Prince went to the front in command of Prussian troops and his wife, veering completely round, abandoned Duke Frederick and, naturally and automatically, became as Prussian as Bismarck himself. To her brilliant, headlong mind the whole rights of this most complicated question were suddenly clear. She jettisoned all her previous convictions and added to the select band of three persons who had hitherto grasped it not only herself but the entire German nation. " It is impossible," she wrote to her mother, " to blame an English person for not understanding the Schleswig-Holstein question—it remains nevertheless to us Germans plain and simple as daylight and one for which we would gladly bring any sacrifice." As for the pro-Danish sympathies expressed in the British Parliament and the Press, she pronounced them " absurd, unjust, rude and violent " : they could only increase the irritation or rather contempt which was felt in Berlin for England's attitude. " The continual meddling and interfering of England with other people's affairs has become *so* ridiculous abroad that it almost ceases to annoy. But to an English heart it is no pleasant sight to see the dignity of one's country so compromised and let down—its influence so completely lost."[1]

This was an ill-considered indictment. Though the Prime Minister, Lord Palmerston, and the Foreign Secretary had expressed their strong sympathy with Denmark and had soundly abused Prussia, if there was one thing on which the Queen and the majority of the Cabinet were determined, it was that England must and should remain absolutely neutral and not interfere in any way. The Queen pointed this out to her daughter, but warned her that if Prussia pursued the career of conquest and attempted to annex Denmark, the feeling of the country against such wanton aggression might become irresistible. But the Crown Princess found fresh causes for scolding : she thought that Sir Andrew Buchanan, whom the Queen had lately appointed British Ambassador in Berlin, was quite unfit for the post and was a great failure, he was most unpopular and without any influence. He could neither speak nor understand the language, nor did he know anything of German affairs, nor listen to those who did understand them. He was thus constantly misinformed, as he " picked up his information from bad sources such as other silly diplomatists."[2] Truly, for the time being at any

[1] Ponsonby, *Letters of the Empress Frederick*, p. 53.
[2] *Ibid.*, p. 54.

rate, she seemed not so much to have left the *Engländerin* behind, as to have sent for her to Berlin and there publicly hanged, drawn and quartered her with every circumstance of ignominy. But this vehemence, this impetuous contempt for meddlesome and ignorant England, this eager identification of herself with Prussian views did not improve her position in Berlin. She continued to be identified, most unjustly, with the rabid hostility of the English Press. Gossip gave to whatever she said or did an English and therefore an anti-Prussian flavour: even her mantles and bonnets betrayed their real sympathies.

Just now the Queen was far better pleased with her daughter-in-law. It was only natural that she should hold that her Papa had been robbed of his Duchies, but, whatever she might say in the privacy of the family circle, she could be perfectly trusted to be discreet in public, and the Queen willingly let her go to Denmark when the war was over to visit her parents, whom she had not seen since her marriage. But the Prince of Wales had been very indiscreet with official personages, he had asked the French Ambassador in London whether France had pro-Prussian leanings, and he had written to various English Ministers rejoicing in small Danish successes. The Queen had already punished him by directing that no despatches from the seat of war should be sent him, so that he knew no more about it than he could read in the public Press, and now she refused to let him go to Denmark with his wife until he solemnly promised to be more careful. Lest Germany should feel slighted, the Queen insisted that they both should visit other relatives there, and after leaving Denmark they stayed with the Prince's cousin, the King of Hanover, and with his sister Alice. They also had a glimpse of Vicky and Fritz at Cologne, but that was less a reunion than an encounter. " It was not pleasant," the Prince wrote to one of his Household, " to see him [the Crown Prince] and his A.D.C. always in Prussian uniform, flaunting before our eyes a most objectionable ribbon which he received for his deeds of valour (???) against the unhappy Danes."[1]

The war, then, caused a good deal of dissension in the Queen's domestic circle. She came out of her seclusion this summer to the extent of holding an extra drawing-room herself in addition to those held by the Prince and Princess of Wales and drove back to Paddington afterwards in an open carriage. She found it " *very painful*," but felt she had pleased her people immensely : they thought it " very kind *of me*." But painful though it was, her reception as she passed through the Park was very gratifying to her, and she wrote about it to Uncle Leopold with quaint complacence : " Everyone says that the difference shown when *I* appear, and when Bertie and Alix drive, is *not* to be described. Naturally for *them* no one stops or *runs* as they always did, and *do* doubly now for *me*." But she felt this was publicity enough for one year, and though *The Times*, feeling that such kindnesses ought to be more frequent, published a

[1] Lee, *Edward VII*, i, p. 256.

strong remonstrance on the third anniversary of the Prince Consort's death about her continued seclusion, she was adamant in refusing to open Parliament next spring. Even when the Prince Consort was with her that ceremony had almost always given her a headache ; without him " any great exertion which would entail a succession of *moral shocks* as well as very great fatigue, which the Queen must avoid as much as possible, would be *totally out of the question.*"[1] It is strange that, though her whole soul was sincerely set on fashioning her life as the Prince Consort would have willed, she conducted it, in this department of her duties as Sovereign, on lines that must have aroused his grave disapproval.

Prince and Princess Louis had spent two months at Balmoral in the autumn before the Danish war broke out, and then she resumed that diligent correspondence with the Queen which contrasts strangely with the bombardments from Berlin which her mother did not wholly relish. " One can say anything to Alice," she once wrote to her great friend Queen Augusta, " which unfortunately is not the case in another quarter." It is easy to see why the Queen set such store on the companionship of this gentle daughter, for her letters show how enchanting her presence must have been. She had the spontaneous pen which portrays and invests the merest trivialities with the thrilled interest she herself took in them. It was a great grief that Baby, on their tempestuous

[1] *Letters of Queen Victoria*, II, i, pp. 233, 245.

crossing, was sick over the shawl that her grandmama had given her. She was busy over Christmas festivities and made a Christmas Tree for her servants, buying their presents and hanging them there herself, and Baby had a small tree of her own, all her very own, at her grandparents' house. A turkey-pie had arrived from Windsor: she and Louis were giving a dinner-party in its honour. There was a long frost and she skated: the only other lady in Darmstadt who could skate at all was a very poor performer. She and Louis went to the theatre three or four times a week—like her mother she loved a play—and had to dine at five in the afternoon. The building of their new house got on apace: she heard of a respectable woman in dire poverty who had just had a baby, so she and her maid stole out incognito, to see what could be done, and she cooked some food for her and tidied up her house. Her mother must keep that item of news to herself, for Darmstadt might think it rather a strange adventure for a Princess. But she felt that she must occasionally get out of "that cold circle of Court people," and see poverty and help it, or "good feelings would dry up." She was learning that to live for others is the only key to happiness, and yet "self constantly turns up like a bad sixpence." And, at every moment, her heart overflowed with tenderness for her mother, remembering the time when first she was "allowed" to be of use to her, on the day when the Duchess of Kent died, and her Papa left them alone together. She treasured that memory "as a sacred request from him to love, cherish, and comfort my darling mother to all the extent of my weak powers. Other things have taken me from being constantly with you, but nothing has lessened my intense love for you and longing to quiet every pain which touches you and to fulfil, even in the distance, his request. Oh, darling Mama, were there words in which I could express to you how much I am bound up with you, how constantly my thoughts and my prayers are yours, I would write them. The sympathies of our souls can only tell each other how tender my love and gratitude to you is, and how vividly I feel every new trial or new thing with you and for you."[1]

For three months from May till the end of August next year, 1864, she and Louis were with the Queen, and then the letters began again with their enchanting jumble of daily topics and the treasures of her heart. Her second daughter Elizabeth, known as Ella, was born in November; there was a momentary disappointment over the sex, but the two little girls would make a very pretty pair. The baby screamed a good deal at her christening, but Sister Victoria behaved beautifully except that she kept tumbling over her footstool every other minute. Hitherto there had been little sympathy between Princess Louis and her mother-in-law, but now a bond of love and comprehension began firmly to forge itself. The Queen had arranged that John Brown should be with her not in Scotland only but at Windsor and Osborne, so that she could ride her pony there with him in attendance. Alice cordially approved : she was so glad her mother had done that, for driving was a

[1] Princess Christian, *Alice*, pp. 89, 90.

very monotonous affair, now she could ride as well, which was good for the nerves. She sent messages of kindly remembrance to him when she wrote : she was delighted to hear that the new arrangement worked so well : it must make Brown very happy to serve so kind a mistress. And for the New Year of 1865 she wrote a gem of a letter, recalling memories of her girlhood :

> " That bright happy past, particularly those last years when I was the eldest at home, and had the privilege of being so much with you both, my own dearly loved parents, is a remembrance deeply graven and with letters of gold upon my heart. All the morning I was telling Louis how it used to be at home, and how we all assembled outside your dressing-room door to scream in chorus ' *Prosit Neujahr !* ' and to give you and Papa our drawings, writings, &c., the busy occupation of previous weeks. Then playing and reciting our pieces where we often stuck fast, and dear Papa bit his lip so as not to laugh ; our walk to the Riding-school (where the alms to the poor of Windsor were distributed) and then to Frogmore. Those were happy days, and the very remembrance of them must bring a gleam of sunshine even to you, dear Mama. . . ."[1]

Constantly she thus dwelt upon the past, always carrying forward into the present its lovely memories, not for lamentation that those days were dead, but for thankfulness that they were still so wondrously alive.

Never in these letters is a word of fault-finding or

[1] *Ibid.*, p. 99.

criticism of others. She was not interested in their failings and futilities : she was alert only for admiration and the instinctive ministries of love : that was the way her mind worked. She and Louis went to stay with her sister in Berlin : the two small daughters accompanied them, Victoria sleeping in her bassinet, and Ella, a bundle of blankets, in her bath. Their hosts were kindness itself, she wrote to her mother, and it did her good to see her father's brilliant intellect reflected in Vicky. And Louis was happy and amused : he would never leave home without her, and a young man of spirit must sometimes find life at Darmstadt rather dull. She regretted that Vicky was alone so much, and it was sad to think that the old family governess, Miss Hildyard, had left her mother, for they were all so fond of her. Perhaps the Queen would invite her to stay at Osborne sometimes, for she had been so devoted to them all.

But in spite of the intense happiness of her married life Princess Louis had gone through disagreeable experiences at Darmstadt during the last two years, analogous to those which her sister had encountered in Berlin, and she felt them bitterly. There was prejudice against her because she was English, and, in especial, because she had been spending so much of the year in her native land. This feeling was not altogether to be wondered at. During the first year of her married life she and her husband had been five months with the Queen, and their first child had been born at Windsor. During the next year they had both been in England for over four months : her lady-in-waiting was English and her private secretary, Dr. Becker, had been librarian to the Prince Consort. The dilemma was similar to her sister's, for Darmstadt suspected Anglicization, while the Queen complained that her daughter and son-in-law should have been with her more. Princess Louis felt torn between opposing forces: she had dedicated herself to her mother's support and consolation, but her husband had duties to Darmstadt that were equally binding. She did all in her power to adjust these conflicting claims, quietly devoting herself to those works of charity and pity in Darmstadt which made her life so busy, and letting them speak for themselves. She wore down those prejudices by dint of that unobtrusive but unremitting service, and now she wrote to her mother of a tribute which had touched and delighted her. Two hundred and fifty women in Darmstadt had subscribed for a present to her, a picture of Loch Katrine by a German artist whom they had sent to Scotland to paint it: " It has given me," she wrote, " so much pleasure—but of all things the feeling that has prompted them to do it, as it shows that, though I have been here so short a time, they have become attached to me, as I am with all my heart to my new home and country."

Then came intimate bereavement. Louis's sister Anna, Grand Duchess of Mecklenburg-Strelitz, died in child-bed, and that was a terrible blow, for she was the darling of her family. Immediately after, his aunt, the Empress Marie of Russia, lost her eldest son, Nicholas, who was about to marry Princess Dagmar of Denmark, sister of the Princess of

Wales. Alice sighed over the brevity and uncertainty of life, for it was the young who were being taken : it made one remember how easy it was to miss opportunities for kindliness and self-denial. . . . Relatives from other parts of Germany and brothers from England came for a brief night or two, but they passed on again on their larger orbits and Darmstadt settled back into the formal monotony of Court life. The children had bad colds, spring was long in coming, she herself was very rheumatic, and her birthday was but a melancholy festival.

But life had its humorous moments also, highly to be cherished. The Queen conferred the Garter on the Grand Duke, and as he was an extremely shy man he begged that the function should take place quietly at Darmstadt ; so instead of his going to Windsor she sent out Prince Alfred with the implements of investiture. On the appointed afternoon Princess Louis drove in State with her suite to the palace, and the Grand Duke received them dressed in shorts. Prince Alfred and Prince Louis (both Knights of the Garter) followed them in a six-horsed carriage with escort, bearing the insignia and wearing full Garter robes. The family, the Court and the *corps diplomatique* were grouped behind the Throne, in front of which stood the recipient. Prince Alfred read his address in English, the Grand Duke replied in German. The investiture then took place : Prince Alfred knelt to buckle on the Garter below the shorts, and with the help of Prince Louis he adjusted the ribbon over the Grand Duke's shoulder, the sword by his side, and the cloak over all. It was a difficult toilet, but they did it beautifully, and retired walking backwards down the Throne-room with many bows. There was a big dinner-party in the evening: the Grand Duke was a very happy man, and, speaking in English, charged Princess Louis to tell her mother that he appreciated this honour " utmostly."[1]

The Queen's third daughter Princess Helena would be nineteen in the spring of 1865, and her mother began to look out for a husband. Two years before she had specified to Uncle Leopold the qualifications she would require for a son-in-law when the time came: she wanted a sensible and moral young prince, not necessarily of a reigning House, who would make his home with her, for she could not part with her daughter. Uncle Leopold who had great experience in match-making (for he had been chief matrimonial agent for the Coburgs since the time when he had been so largely instrumental in marrying his own sister to the Duke of Kent) had suggested a very suitable candidate. This was Prince Christian of Schleswig-Holstein, the younger brother of Duke Frederick who had been one of the claimants for the Duchies. The Danish war and the appropriation of these territories by Austria and Prussia had left the brothers without a country of their own, and Bismarck, who delighted to humiliate fallen foes, however powerless, had deprived them of their commissions in the Prussian army. Prince Christian had already expressed his admiration of Princess Helena, without saying a word to the young lady till her mother was informed of

[1] *Ibid.*, pp. 111-112.

his aspirations, and now the Queen made further inquiries of her eldest daughter, who had already helped in selecting a wife for the Prince of Wales. The Crown Princess gave a most favourable and detailed report. Prince Christian was often in Berlin and was free of their house, coming and going as he liked, and proposing himself to breakfast or to dine. He was " the best creature in the world," amusing when he felt inclined, bald, of good military figure, fond of children, speaking English, and tactful in his difficult position in Berlin. She sent her mother a photograph of him (the Queen had never seen him). Countess Blücher, a great friend of the Crown Princess's, quite agreed as to his suitability, and on these preliminary testimonials the Queen accepted him in principle, and laid her plans to see him herself.

She was not at all pleased with Prussia just now. Bismarck was determined to grab both Duchies, depriving her ally of Holstein, as had been arranged between them by the Convention of Gastein, and the situation, if he persisted, threatened to become extremely dangerous. The Queen's pro-Prussian sympathies had evaporated, for this bellicose, blood-and-iron Prussia, was not the peaceful, powerful but liberally minded Prussia of which Albert had dreamed, and she wrote to her uncle : " Prussia seems inclined to behave as atrociously as possible, and as she *always has done*. Odious people the Prussians are, *that I must say*." The King had also offended her personally ; he had refused to let the Crown Prince and Princess come to stay with her at Balmoral this year in the autumn, though Vicky had made a moving appeal to him. That seemed to the Queen a most tyrannical act, and she intended to write him a very firm letter on the subject. She suspected, too, that her project of marrying her daughter to the brother of the dispossessed Duke Frederick would be interpreted as an open manifestation of her anti-Prussian feelings, but that was quite irrelevant. The marriage concerned nobody but the Family, and indeed it concerned nobody but her daughter and herself. If Princess Helena accepted the proposed bridegroom and if she herself approved of him as a son-in-law, there was nothing more to be said. Her will, always iron, was quite unaffected by her wretched hypochondria, and she meant to settle all matters of the sort as seemed to her wise and good.

The Queen went out to Coburg in August to stay with her brother-in-law for the purpose of unveiling a statue of the Prince Consort, and of seeing the suggested son-in-law. She broke her journey for a couple of nights at Darmstadt, where she occupied the Grand Duke's castle at Kranichstein. The whole family was in Switzerland, and it distressed Princess Louis that they should be away: she thought it looked so odd, but all she could do before she went was to arrange her mother's rooms and order a *menu* of meals which she thought she would like. For this unveiling of the statue the Queen had assembled twenty-four of her German relatives, including the Crown Prince and Princess of Prussia, and she brought Princess Helena with her. She also invited Prince Christian to come to Coburg, and found him " pleasing, gentlemanlike, quiet and distinguished." Princess Helena as yet knew nothing about the matrimonial project, but she was greatly pleased with him, and the Queen asked him to England so that the two should get to know each other better. But she regarded the matter as settled, and felt sure the Prince Consort would have approved. One only had to be firm, and the thing was done : she was delighted also to find that her firm letter to the King of Prussia about Vicky and Fritz coming to Balmoral had been equally successful. He allowed it profusely, and was most anxious to stand well with her, and begged for an interview. She did not want to see him at all, but Queen Augusta strongly urged her, and after an exchange of numerous telegrams which crossed each other in a most provoking manner, she consented to meet him again at the Grand Duke of Hesse's palace at Darmstadt, on her way back to England. The interview was not productive of much, for after he had kept her waiting for half an hour, they talked about the weather for another half-hour. But perhaps that was as well, for there were few important topics on which they took the same views. Albert had held him in high esteem in the old days, and had written him some of his most thoughtful and convincing memoranda on the principles of Liberal Government. But since his accession and the advent of Bismarck that " clever unprincipled man," even his wife, Queen Augusta, found him sadly changed. The weather was the safest subject.

She went back to the dear Highland home : once

more all her daughters were with her, and Princess Helena's engagement was publicly announced. Since the Prince Consort's death the Queen had never opened Parliament, but next year in the spring of 1866 there was a very special reason for her doing so, for she intended to ask her Commons to make provision for her daughter on her marriage, and for her second son Prince Alfred on his coming of age. So strong now was the feeling in the country against her continued seclusion that her Government feared that unless she went in person these grants might be refused, and though she compared the ordeal to being led to execution, she faced it. The usual dowry of £30,000 and an annuity of £6,000 was granted to Princess Helena, and to Prince Alfred—setting a decent precedent for younger sons—an annuity of £15,000. Princess Louis, very highly strung herself, understood her mother better than anybody: she knew what an obsession to her this panic-stricken shrinking from the loneliness of a Sovereign's state appearance had become, and how agonized was the struggle to encounter it. She knew also, as Mr. Disraeli presently learned, her mother's childlike appetite for appreciation, and effusively commended her heroic feat: "It was noble of you, my darling Mamma, and the great effort will bring compensation. Think of the pride and pleasure it would have given darling Papa—the brave example to others not to shrink from their duty; and it has shown that you felt the intense sympathy which the English people evinced, and still evince, in your great misfortune."[1]

[1] *Ibid.*, p. 127.

The war between Prussia and Austria had now been successfully engineered by Bismarck, and it broke out in June. Of the more important northern German States, Saxony, Hesse, and Hanover (the King of which was the blind son of Queen Victoria's Uncle, Ernest, Duke of Cumberland) sided with Austria : other States such as Coburg, Anhalt, and Mecklenburg remained neutral. Austria suffered an overwhelming defeat at Königgrätz on July 3, and there remained the German States to be settled with. The Prussians crossed the Hessian frontier ; there was fighting at Aschaffenburg, and the sound of the guns was heard in Darmstadt. In two days the Hessians lost eight hundred men, but no serious resistance was possible or even contemplated, and they retreated.

On the outbreak of war Princess Louis had sent her two daughters, Victoria and Elizabeth, to England to stay with their grandmother ; they attended their Aunt Helena's wedding, for which the Queen provided them with new frocks. She herself remained at Darmstadt, for, in a few weeks, she was expecting another baby ; she wanted to remain as far as possible in touch with her husband, who was in command of a brigade of Hessian cavalry, and her mother-in-law, whose three sons were all serving, was in sore need of her companionship and support. Equipment was urgently wanted in field-hospitals, for Hesse had been utterly unprepared for war, and Princess Louis was busy collecting sheets, old linen and rags, and making shirts. She begged her mother to send her any discarded stuff from Osborne or Windsor for the need was fearful. Next month she gave birth to a third daughter, but within a few weeks she was visiting the hospitals again, looking after the wounded and the sick.

Before the end of July the Prussian troops entered Darmstadt as conquerors, with bands playing and banners flying, and remained there till an armistice was declared and the terms of peace settled. They paid for nothing, they commandeered whatever they wanted, they forbade any communications with Hessian troops still in the field, and the villages round were in a lamentable plight, for they pillaged right and left. The hospitals were full to overflowing, and there was a great lack of cleanliness and ventilation. Princess Louis's letters to her mother during these weeks were wretchedly unhappy, but Louis, still with his brigade was well and unwounded, and he was idolized by his men for his personal bravery and his cheerful sharing of their privations. And the new baby, to be called Irene, if the Prussians allowed peace to be declared before her christening, was thriving.

An armistice was granted : Louis returned to Darmstadt, and the two daughters from England. The terms of peace were harsh, though less severe than those imposed on Hanover and Saxony. The Grand Duke of Hesse was deprived of the Hinterland and the Domains and the whole of Hesse-Hamburg, and Hesse was terribly impoverished, for the Duchy had to pay an indemnity of three million florins, the postal and telegraph revenues were appropriated by Prussia, and occupying troops had been billeted on the country for six weeks ; to such a small principality that was a terrible drain. But not a hint of bitterness appeared in the Princess's letters. " If only," she wrote, " the other sovereigns (Saxony and Hanover and Hesse Cassel) will forget their antipathies and the wrongs they have suffered from Prussia, and think of the welfare of their people and the universal fatherland, and make those sacrifices which will be necessary to prevent the recurrence of these misfortunes ! " For their own sakes only, she acutely observed, they had better do so, for this enlarged Prussia did not constitute a united Germany. It was an amalgamation effected by force and unless they did their best to make it a union and placed themselves under Prussia " on the next opportunity they will be annexed."

So the new baby was christened Irene, and they settled down to the quiet and much straitened life in Darmstadt. Princess Louis was not well : her confinement and the months of anxiety had tried her strength, and every evening found her desperately tired. She had wanted to get away for a change, but they could not afford the expense. Winter drew on, bringing with it the anniversary of the Prince Consort's death. It was five years now since that terrible fourteenth of December, but the memories of it grew ever more vivid as experience enlightened them. She wondered if her father ever knew how she adored him ; the thought of his example was the star by which she steered the course of her own life. . . . How the leafless trees and the cold light of the winter morning brought back to her those days of anguish when she feared that she might lose her mother as well as him. " Happily married as I am," she wrote, " and with such a good, excellent and loving husband, how far more can I understand *now* the depth of that grief which tore your lives asunder."[1]

The Crown Princess looked on the war at a very different angle from that of her sister : it could not have been otherwise. While Bismarck in the previous spring had been engaged on making trouble with Austria, in order to secure for Prussia the sole possession of the Duchies, she regarded him as a monster. " Not a day passes," she wrote to her mother, " that the wicked man does not with the *greatest* ability counteract and thwart what is good, and drive on towards war, turning and twisting everything to serve his own purpose . . . The tissue of untruths is such that one gets quite perplexed with only listening to them, but the net is cleverly made, and the King, in spite of *all* his reluctance, gets more and more entangled in it without perceiving it."[2] That was a perfectly just view, and she never wavered from it.

Her own husband, like her sister's, was on active service in command of the Silesian army, but while Princess Louis was awaiting her new motherhood a terrible domestic tragedy befell the other, who lost the youngest and best beloved of her children. Sigismund was not yet two years old : from his birth

[1] *Ibid.*, pp. 153, 155.
[2] Ponsonby, *Letters of Empress Frederick*, p. 59.

W. & D. Downey

THE QUEEN WITH HER DOG, SHARP

at Balmoral, about 1866

he had been the treasure of her heart, and the idol and sunbeam of the home. But nothing, even in the darker days that were to come, ever shattered that dauntless courage, and, like her sister, she devoted herself to war-work in the hospitals.

War having once begun with her husband at the front, her sympathies were wholly Prussian. " You will not think it unnatural, I know," she wrote again to her mother, " that my feelings are on the side of my country and my husband, though, of course, one can feel nothing but despair at being obliged to consider other Germans as one's enemies—and wish for their destruction." Swiftly there followed the great victories of her husband's army, and her pride in him was coupled with her admiration of his troops whom the news reported as equally brave and humane against a foe—" the amiable engaging Austrians "— who, so said the Bismarckian Press, had committed the foulest barbarities. " I am *now*," she wrote to the Queen, " every bit as proud of being a Prussian as I am of being an Englishwoman, and that is saying a very great deal, as you know what a John Bull I am and how enthusiastic about my home. I must say the Prussians are a superior race, as regards intelligence and humanity, education and kindheartedness."[1]

She still felt that Bismarck was the sole begetter of this bitter business, and looked forward with dismay to the future if the Government was to remain in those uncontrolled and unprincipled hands, but Prussia had made immense sacrifices and, as victor, must impose harsh terms on the vanquished.

[1] *Ibid.*, p. 65.

She could neither share her mother's sympathy with those German States, which had sided with Austria, nor her indignation at Prussia's appropriations of their territories. She pitied their miserable plight, but it was their own fault. She wrote :

> " At this sad time one *must* separate one's feelings for one's relations quite from one's judgment of political necessities. . . . Those who are now in such precarious positions might *quite well* have foreseen what danger they were running into : *they were told beforehand what they would have to expect* : they *chose* to go with Austria and now they share the sad fate she confers on her Allies. . . . I cannot and will not forget that I am a Prussian but as such I know it is very difficult to make you, or any other non-German, see how our case lies."[1]

But once again this perfect understanding of the true position, similar to that which had enlightened her in the Danish war and equally outside the comprehension of all except Prussians, did not do anything for her in Berlin. Still detesting Bismarck, though enjoying (as a Prussian) the righteous fruits of his iniquity, she fancied that she concealed her feelings towards him by treating him in a semi-jocular manner. Knowing perfectly well that he imposed his will on the King and was indeed the ruler of Prussia, she told him that he would like to be a king, to which he very properly replied that he had no such ambition and was content to serve the King as his faithful subject. He paid no heed to these

[1] *Ibid.*, p. 67.

veiled sarcasms : they were no more to him than the buzzings of a fly round the head of a man who was absorbed in his work. Perhaps they were slightly irritating, but that was all.

In such small ways the Crown Princess, with all her brilliant cleverness, was often unwise : she did not stop to think, nor to weigh the result of acting on impulse. There had arisen a dangerous situation over the Duchy of Luxemburg, which threatened war between Germany and France, but a way out was found at a Conference held in London, and, to celebrate this solution, the Emperor Napoleon asked most of the crowned heads of Europe to attend the International Exhibition at Paris in 1867. Tsar Alexander II was a guest, as were the King and Queen of Prussia, accompanied by the Crown Prince and Princess and Bismarck ; the Sultan of Turkey, the Khedive Ismail of Egypt, and from England, the Prince of Wales : the Emperor of Austria, who had accepted the invitation, was prevented at the last moment by the murder of his brother the Emperor Maximilian of Mexico. The fêtes in order fitly to commemorate the happy occasion were of the most gorgeous description, but in the middle of them the Crown Princess went back to Germany. She could not get over her grief at the death of beloved Sigismund and the pomp and splendour of these great parties were unbearably painful. Her father-in-law urged her to stop for the few days that remained, for her sudden departure must cause much dislocation in these Royal functions, but she refused to do so, and leaving her husband in Paris, she went home.

It was regrettable : her action gave much offence to her hosts.

But whichever way she turned some difficult dilemma, often inseparable from her position, confronted her. In Berlin she was practically forced to approve the harsh fate of the dispossessed German States : had she done otherwise she would only have made more trouble for herself. But in Hanover she was regarded as a Hanoverian Princess, and such sentiments as she had expressed to her mother were deeply resented there. One summer she intended to go to a bathing resort on that coast with her children, but the English Ambassador in Berlin thought that this would be very unwise, for the Hanoverian aristocracy would ignore her and would refuse any hospitality she might offer them. He believed that in days to come she might be of great use in restoring good feeling between Prussia and the outraged Hanoverians, but while there was such bitterness it would be a great mistake to risk the rebuffs that would surely await her.[1]

The years following the Austrian war were harassed times for Princess Louis. Prussians continued to occupy Darmstadt till the indemnity of 3,000,000 florins was paid, and thenceforward half the Hessian troops were under Prussian command : Prince Louis when on military duty was obliged to have a Prussian officer to ride by his side. Perhaps this was the bitterest humiliation of all both for the Grand Duke, lately the head of an independent State, and for him, and

[1] Duke of Argyll, *Passages from the Past*, p. 360.

the knowledge that the Crown Princess considered that they had brought these misfortunes on their own heads did not mend matters, for since they were not Prussians they were incapable of understanding the case. A smaller but irritating confiscation was that of some fine pictures and manuscripts belonging to the State : this was a truly Prussian touch that gave an artistic finish to these cruder indemnities.

Money was certainly scarce in the Royal houses of Darmstadt, for the Duchy had been shorn of substantial revenues, and Princess Louis was one of those imprudent people who cannot see suffering and poverty without giving help, even if it entails personal trouble and self-denial. She wanted a governess for her eldest girl, but she was putting this off for a year, she wrote to her mother, owing to the expense, and taught the child herself. Christmas came round, and Christmas essentially implied a season of treats and presents. There was a Christmas tree for her children, and all her servants' children had gifts off it : for an old and attached retainer lying ill she made a special tree, which was wheeled to his bedside. She bought gifts of the season for all the patients in the Civil hospital and for the sick and wounded in the Military hospital, and distributed them herself; her children made a New Year festival for poor boys and girls in Darmstadt and gave them such of their toys " as did not happen to be broken."

The Queen often sent the family very welcome presents, a turkey pie and other eatables for Christmas, dolls for the little girls and stuff to make their dresses, a great many reproductions of pictures by Winterhalter for Alice, a cheque on one occasion for the layette when she was expecting a baby, and a horse for Louis; but it does not appear that she made any substantial contribution to household expense. No doubt she had excellent reasons. It was a matter of principle with her, as it had been with the Prince Consort, that the country was bound to make proper provision for her daughters on their marriage; Alice had received her dowry and annuity and she must manage on that. Again she may have felt that Alice would only continue to give away more than she could afford, and with such exaggerated charities the Queen had no sympathy. But this habit of Alice's was incurable, for it sprang from love, and she made no attempt to get the better of it.

Sometimes she felt lonely; as often as not Louis was away from early morning until dinner-time, and she had nobody of her own age to talk to or walk with except her one lady-in-waiting, but the daily lesson with Victoria was always a very happy hour in the day. And she contrived a pretty bit of family peace-making. Neither the Prince nor the Princess of Wales had ever forgiven Prussia for the rape of the Duchies of Denmark, and when they came for a few days' visit to Darmstadt Alice arranged that the King of Prussia should look in, and he and the Princess of Wales had a friendly talk. "Very wise of them," thought Alice, "for bearing ill-will is always a mistake, besides its not being right."[1]

Rumours of war between France and Germany

---

[1] Princess Christian, *Alice*, p. 176.

began to flood the French papers, and the thought of that made the heart sick. But neither impoverishment nor the fatigue from which she suffered greatly nor the anxieties for the future clouded the inward sunshine which is the recurring bonus of those who realize themselves in perpetual service to others. She had Louis and her children, and in 1868 she gave birth to a son, Ernest Louis. Next year she had a longer separation from her husband than had ever occurred since their marriage. The Crown Prince of Prussia took him for a tour in the Near East, and the two sisters spent on the Riviera the three months when their husbands were away. On his return, Prince Louis had a bad attack of scarlet fever with diphtheritic symptoms, and while he was still ill, Victoria and the baby caught it. It was an anxious business to have three of the family down, and she feared—that fear was to be tragically renewed nine years later—that the other children might have been infected. But there were no fresh cases, and her invalids recovered well. Life resumed its eager interests and its serenity, and the love that grew ever stronger between her husband and herself made a haven for her that no storm could roughen. And how sweet it was, she wrote to her mother, to confide her troubles to some beloved person like herself : the very telling lightened them.

The Queen took a great interest in her grandchildren. They were extensions of the House of Victoria and Albert, and the territories of the matriarchate were enlarging. When little Victoria had attained the age of six her grandmother suggested that when, later on, Alice and her husband had been paying her a visit with their children, they might leave this daughter in England when they went home again. Alice gladly consented : Victoria had been born at Windsor, and so her grandmama had a particular claim on her. Then the suggestion must have broadened a little. The Queen told Alice that she would like to be able to count upon a grandchild being with her whenever she wished for one. Alice again agreed and sympathized : " I often think so sadly for your dear sake," she wrote, " how lonely it must be when one child after another grows up and leaves home, and, even if they remain, to have no children in the house is most dreary." But perhaps she had some slight uneasiness that Victoria might be kept in England for unreasonably long periods and she added that her mother had now so many grandchildren that there could not be any difficulty about one of them being always with her in the homes where her children had been so happy.[1]

There were, however, questions which affected Princess Louis's own life and the usefulness and duties proper to it, in which she took her own line. One of these was her work in hospitals at Darmstadt. To perform that efficiently she felt bound to acquire solid medical knowledge about the mechanism of the human body, its ailments and their treatment. The Queen did not approve of this ; possibly she said that she thought it " disgusting " ; for Alice answered that she did not find it so ; such knowledge only filled her

[1] *Ibid.*, pp. 198, 199.

with admiring wonder at the ingenious structure and offices of the bodily organs. Besides, in case of sudden illness you could do something useful before the doctor arrived. Of course, when, like her mother one was " surrounded " with eminent doctors, such knowledge was unnecessary, but for others it was most desirable, and she set her own course. She founded a central " Ladies' Union " in Darmstadt with branches throughout Hesse for training of nurses in hospitals and private practice, who in time of war would serve in the military hospitals. She was the head of the Central Committee on which women and doctors sat together.

There was another question, touching herself even more intimately, on which her own conscience must be her only directing authority : neither her mother nor her beloved Louis could give her guidance. She had been brought up to accept the creed of orthodox Christianity without question, and there presently came to her that inward necessity, known to many such, of determining for herself whether her belief was sincere, or whether, in accepting it emotionally, she was not stifling intellectual honesty. Christianity to her was not a profession to be made lightly. If she could not embrace its essential doctrines with her whole soul and without reservation it became a meaningless lip-service which it was a clear duty to abandon. While this struggle to be herself was going on there came to Darmstadt the eminent critic on the historical foundations of Christianity, Frederick David Strauss, with whom she formed a close friendship. He was engaged in writing a series of lectures on Voltaire, and she asked him to read these to her. That a woman in her position should make friends with Strauss was in those days a daring thing to do, for his name was anathema to orthodox Germany, but this inward necessity of being honest with herself overrode any such consideration. She dreaded what the effect on her religious convictions might be, but it was just that which she had to face without flinching, and she went through a miserable period of scepticism. She seems not to have said anything definite to her mother of this experience beyond mentioning that she was reading a great deal of " history and deeper works, was attending some lectures and had one or two acquaintances with whom to read or to have books recommended by." Certainly the Queen would have been terribly distressed if she had known that her daughter was even submitting such questions to the scrutiny of reason, for she held that personally it was impious and officially, as Defender of the Faith, that it was unconstitutional to enquire into the articles of the Christian religion. She took the authority of the Church on these matters as that of an infallible specialist, and if ever any doubts had flickered in her own mind, she would have refused to regard them. Eventually, after this dark night of the soul, the Princess's faith dawned again, and she accepted the creed in which she had been brought up as truth transcending reason. She allowed Strauss to dedicate to her those lectures on Voltaire which had contributed to the temporary loss of her faith. They were to her like the discarded crutches, symbols of halting days, which a cripple dedicates in some shrine of healing to the Power which has made him whole.

Princess Helena's marriage to Prince Christian in 1866 had secured for the Queen the desired son-in-law who would live in England, but the young couple did not make their principal home with her, as she had originally planned, for the rest of her life-time. She gave Frogmore to him and his wife as their residence : it was close to Windsor Castle and her mother, the Duchess of Kent had lived there, and for occupation she made him Ranger of Windsor Park. The Queen had still two daughters living with her, Princess Louise, now eighteen years old and Princess Beatrice, and her youngest son Prince Leopold, a boy whose extreme delicacy precluded any active profession. Twice a year she made long sojourns at Balmoral ; it was there she felt most comfortable, and the remoteness, the brisk air, her drives and her picnics and her sketchings, and the complete freedom from any heartless calls that could be made on her by Prime Ministers who failed to understand her inability to make public appearances were beginning to build up again the nervous system which she was almost anxious to prove was hopelessly shattered. She had a great friend there, Dr. Norman Macleod, the Minister of the Kirk at Crathie who from the time of the Prince Consort's death had been a support and stay. She found his sermons full of consolation, she talked to him intimately about herself : Albert, she said, had worn himself out by never allowing himself any relaxation. Relaxation was necessary for her, and Dr. Macleod very tactfully entreated her always to come to Balmoral to get it. Till his death in 1872 she looked on him as a man on whose understanding and sympathy she could always rely.

Here, as the second volume of her Journal in the Highlands testifies, she began to take pleasure again in the present without seeking to find in it only melancholy reminders of the past. The old glamour of picnics and adventures and explorations began to brighten, and, with her children to accompany her, she started the great expeditions once more, sleeping at some inn or shooting-lodge in the wilds, and again her *Journal* blossoms out into minute accounts of these experiences. Once the luggage went wrong and did not arrive till four in the morning, which was uncomfortable, but her daughter and John Brown made her early coffee beautifully, and Brown helped her over a wall to have tea out of the wind, and she saw eight stags, and the plaids fell out of the carriage, and Brown led her pony so fast that they outdistanced all the others. She built a " compact little house " at Glassault Shiel in a Highland glen two hours' drive from Balmoral, which Albert had marked down as a beautiful site, and thus she was fulfilling his intention. The compact little house could accommodate nineteen persons, and there was a house-warming, and a dance for the servants afterwards which she attended. Brown begged her to drink some whisky-toddy in commemoration of the " fire kindling."

Even while the Queen had been arranging the

marriage of Princess Helena, so that without losing a daughter she might at this second attempt gain a son-in-law who would make his principal home with her, she had recorded what comfort she derived from the constant attendance of John Brown. She wrote to her Uncle Leopold that she had appointed " that excellent Highland servant of mine to attend me ALWAYS and everywhere out of doors, whether riding or driving or on foot, and it is a *real* comfort to me, for he is so devoted to me—so simple, so intelligent, so *unlike* an *ordinary* servant and so cheerful and attentive."[1] He was with her now, as she had told Princess Louis, not at Balmoral only, but at Windsor and Osborne, and the need for a resident son-in-law was less insistent. What she wanted was some active, reliable man without other duties than to attend to her and she found him in this devoted servant without whom she never left the house, and who became a pervasive element in family life, perhaps not always wholly welcome. But he suited her, and she did not for nearly twenty years look out for anyone else.

This satellite-attendance on the Queen of a Highland gillie caused some criticism : there had already been some unfriendly remarks in the Scotch provincial Press about his convivial tendencies which had roused the Queen's indignation. It was thought seemly that on State occasions, as, for instance, when in 1867 she was to hold a Review in Hyde Park, the usual State ceremonial should be observed, in which there was no place, in immediate attendance on

[1] *Letters of Queen Victoria*, II, i, p. 255.

her, for a kilted Highlander. When the proposed arrangements for this review were submitted to her she was much disturbed and poured out on one of her Equerries a flood of indignant and almost incoherent protest of which, however, the general purport was clear enough :

"Lord Charles Fitzroy having always been so kind to the Queen in all that concerns her convenience and comfort, and having only *lately* informed her that the Duke of Beaufort so completely understood her wishes and entered into her feelings respecting her faithful Brown, and having also told her last year that people quite understood his going as an *upper servant with her carriage*, and he [Lord Charles] thinking there should be *no* difference in London to the country, and moreover having taken him everywhere *with her* for *two years* on public as well as private occasions, she is much astonished and shocked at an attempt being made by some people to prevent her faithful servant going with her to the *Review* in Hyde Park, thereby making the poor, nervous, shaken Queen, who is so accustomed to his watchful care and intelligence, terribly nervous and uncomfortable. Whatever can be done the Queen does not know on *this* occasion, or what it all means she does *not* know, but she would be very glad if Lord Charles would come down to-morrow morning any time *before* luncheon, that she may have some conversation with him on this subject, not so much with a view as to what *can* be done on this occasion, but as to what can be done for the *future* to prevent her being teased and plagued with the interference of others, and moreover to make it *completely understood once* and *for all* that her *Upper Highland servant* (whether it be Brown or another, in case he should be *ill*, replaces him) belongs to her *outdoor* attendants on State as well as on private occasions. The Queen will not be dictated to or *made* to *alter* what she has found to answer for her comfort."[1]

Happily the Review was put off, so the question of " what can be done on this occasion " did not arise. But it must be noticed that what evoked this very vigorous protest was the threatened violation of a principle, namely that the arrangements the Queen made for her private comfort and convenience must never be interfered with and she strongly resented being asked to sacrifice any of them. The invariable attendance of Brown had come to be one of these. He was a link with the early happy days at Balmoral, when he had entered her service as the Prince Consort's gillie, and since then he had steadily advanced in her esteem. The constant mention of his name in her second volume *More Leaves from a Journal of a Life in the Highlands*, published after his death, is due to the fact that he as constantly gave her the " watchful care " of which she had spoken. Her *Journal* deals entirely with the private and domestic side of her life, and it was her clear wish and intention that the countless readers of one of the best selling books of the year should be privileged to realize as distinctly as Lord Charles Fitzroy must have done how she valued Brown. The Queen was one of the kindest women in the world to those who looked after her personally, she took the greatest interest in them and their relations and their family history ;

[1] *Ibid.*, II, i, p. 433.

she did not treat them, when once they had earned her confidence, as servants so much as friends, and she regarded the performance of their duties as acts of kindness to herself.

It is the very triviality of the innumerable references to Brown which precisely defines his services to the Queen. He accompanied her everywhere (indeed she stated as a sort of stage-direction that he must always be assumed as being on the box of her carriage, unless she definitely said that he was not) and he walked by her pony when she rode and close at hand when she was on foot. On a day of rain his kilt got wet and chafed his knees behind, and he had to take care of himself, and her doctor ordered him to keep his leg up. The box-seat where he sat was " alarmingly high," though, presumably, it was no higher than that of her coachman. She walked with him through her Palace at Holyrood, and he was much interested in Queen Mary's rooms; afterwards she sat under a hawthorn tree and read the poems of the Ettrick Shepherd from the volume which Brown had given her. On the anniversary of the Prince Consort's birthday, when she made presents to all her upper servants, she gave Brown his present with the rest of them. " The tears," she wrote, " came into his eyes and he said ' It is too much.' God knows it is not for one so devoted and faithful." When, on the resumed great expeditions, the Queen stayed in other houses she always went to see how her servants were lodged : at the inn at Loch Torridon, for instance, one of the party had a very hot room over the kitchen, but Brown's room, though smaller, was very nice and not hot. Again his leg troubled him, and an informative footnote explained, like a bulletin, how he had fallen through a manhole by the turret on the *Thunderer*, when she inspected the ship, and when the knee was getting better he jumped off the box and hurt it again. His mother died, but only a fortnight afterwards he waited on the Queen at a large dinner-party, and again a footnote states that " his sense of duty ever went before every feeling of self." When the Prince of Wales (who detested him) was starting on his Indian tour, Brown shook him by the hand and said, " God Bless Your Royal Highness, and bring you safe back."[1] Nothing can exceed the triviality of such incidents in this book of exclusively trivial events.

The very fact that he was not in the least afraid of the Queen pleased her, for formidable people invariably dislike the timidity which they inspire in others. She appreciated in him the independence of the Highland character which the Prince Consort had so much admired, and she allowed him to treat her with a brusqueness which she would not have permitted from anybody else. He told her to put on her cloak or to sit on a rug, or to make up her mind which way she wanted to drive. At Glassault Shiel she asked for a table at which to sketch : one was too low, another too high, and it looked as if she would never make her sketch at all till Brown told her she must make shift with one of them for they couldn't carpenter a new table for her now. He knew he

[1] *More Leaves from a Journal of a Life in the Highlands, passim.*

was indispensable, and treated her Ministers and her Court with bumpkin familiarity, with daffings and pats on the back if they were respectful to him, and the rudest snubs and contradictions if they failed. Such licence passed unnoticed by the Queen or, at any rate, seemed to her not to signify since she was accustomed to his unceremonious ways herself. If she could put up with them, so could the others. Disraeli was a favourite of his, for he was careful to ask after " Mr. Brown " when he wrote to the Queen, and he made himself very agreeable when they met.

Such in outline is the faithful picture of the part which Brown played in the Queen's domestic life as presented by her in the extracts from her *Journal* which she herself subsequently published. It can only afford food for ridicule to those who fail to understand the candour and homeliness of her character. Below his bad manners and ill bred airs of importance, which undoubtedly caused much annoyance to the family circle, she saw and rightly valued his genuine devotion to herself. Above all he gave her day by day that sense of security and protection of which, as she had intimated to Lord Charles Fitzroy, she stood so sorely in need, and we may regard him as administering to her, by the mere fact of his constant and reliable presence, some sort or rasping yet comforting tonic which without doubt had by degrees the most beneficial effect on that painful hypochondria which caused her seclusion. He helped to build up the confidence which enabled her to face her duties again. Together with this devoted hyperborean practitioner, another physician, suave and Oriental, with more deliberate purpose and subtler technique was treating her on diametrically opposite lines, and while Dr. Brown of Balmoral was short and sharp with her, Dr. Disraeli of Downing Street plied her with fantastic visions of herself as the Faery Queen whose presence in the Isle of Wight caused the primroses to burst into blossom. The treatments were not antagonistic but each supplemented the other. Her recovery owed much to them.

CHAPTER IV

OMINOUS clouds soon gathered up again after the war between Germany and Austria. Bismarck like some baleful invisible witch was brewing them in his vat of blood and iron, and this time he did not intend that any Paris Exhibition and Royal cordialities should disperse them. Early in 1870 the Crown Princess wrote to her mother on a matter which must be kept inviolably secret: nobody knew about it, she said, in Germany save a few of her husband's family. General Prim, who, since the deposition of Queen Isabella of Spain, had been at the head of the Spanish Government, sent a confidential agent to King William of Prussia with the news that Spain was looking out for a Sovereign again and asked him to nominate his kinsman Prince Leopold of Hohenzollern Sigmaringen. His election, said General Prim, would be a certainty. The Prussian Royal Family were against it, since there were legitimate claimants to the throne, but Spain was determined to have no king of Bourbon blood. The Crown Princess wanted to know what her mother thought about it, and she having consulted Lord Clarendon very wisely refused to express any opinion on matters where British interests were not concerned, especially since France would certainly resist the appointment of a Hohenzollern Prince to the throne of Spain to the utmost of her power. Prince Leopold refused to accept this offer, but after it had been renewed several times he finally consented, and King William nominated him. As the Queen had foreseen, France raised the most violent protest, and Prince Leopold withdrew his acceptance.

Throughout these negotiations the Prussian Royal Family had been in complete ignorance of their origin : they believed that this offer was the expression of the wish of the Spanish nation, and had been conveyed by General Prim in confidence to the King. They had not a notion that Bismarck had been at the bottom of it, and that it was he who had urged General Prim to press the offer till it was accepted with the sole object of rousing France to a pitch of fury which, carefully fanned and fostered, might end in war. War, Bismarck knew, was bound to come before long, and the German military machine was ready now, while France, in spite of the prestige of her armies, was unprepared. He hoped that she might find a *casus belli* in this nomination. The withdrawal therefore of Prince Leopold was disappointing, for France had no longer any cause for quarrel. But Bismarck did not give up hope that some awkward incident might yet occur, and France, elated with the withdrawal of the Hohenzollern candidate, which she attributed to the firmness of her Government, made the mistake which served his purpose to a nicety. King William was at Ems, taking his cure, and the French Ambassador in Berlin, instead of using the customary diplomatic channels, obtained an interview with him, and demanded his personal assurance that he would never again put forward Prince Leopold as a candidate for the throne of Spain. That he could give such a guarantee for the future policy of his country was unthinkable: the King told him that this was an outrageous request, and telegraphed an account of the interview to Bismarck. That was the sort of mistake the Chancellor was hoping for. He flooded his Press with exaggerations and misrepresentations of what had occurred, in order to rouse the indignation of Germany, and let loose such a tempest of abuse on the Emperor of the French and his Government and his insolent diplomatic methods, that France, believing her armies to be invincible, promptly declared war. But the most remarkable part of Bismarck's achievement was that not even now had King William or his family the slightest suspicion that it was he who had engineered the whole affair from the beginning.

The declaration of war on July 15, 1870, was received by all Germany, excepting Bismarck and those who knew the stupendous efficiency of his war-machine, with consternation, and the Crown Princess wrote to her mother in incoherent dismay. She believed that the odds were terribly against Germany and that ruin and perhaps annihilation faced her. National feeling there, she said, was that England ought to have prevented war by a strong warning to France that she would not tolerate such unprovoked aggression. In England at the outset indignation against France ran high, as guilty of wantonly breaking the peace of Europe, and the Queen shared these sentiments to the full. "Words are too weak," she wrote to her daughter, "to say *all* I feel for you or what I think of my neighbours! We must remain neutral as long as we can, but no one here conceals their opinion as to the extreme *iniquity* of the war." She was sure that the Prince Consort would have been of the same mind, and she told Mr. Theodore Martin that if he were still living she could not have prevented him from enlisting in the armies of his beloved Fatherland.

This feeling that England ought to have prevented the war, and that her neutrality was not being observed, but that (as King William complained to the Queen) she was furnishing France with horses and coal and millions of cartridges, made the Crown Princess's position in Berlin extremely unpleasant, and a report from Count Bernsdorff, the German Ambassador in London, vastly aggravated it. He informed his Foreign Office that the Prince of Wales, dining at the French Embassy immediately after the declaration of war, expressed to the French Ambassador his hopes for the speedy defeat of Prussia, and that when the Austrian Ambassador, Count Apponyi, hinted at the possibility of Austria's joining France he had shown high satisfaction. This caused the greatest indignation in official circles in Berlin, and though the Prince denied that there was any truth in Bernsdorff's report, Berlin continued to believe it and attributed similar sentiments to the Crown Princess. This was a monstrous injustice, for no one was more whole-heartedly Prussian than she, but she was looked upon with such suspicion that her offers to help in the hospitals at Berlin were refused. Eventually the King allowed her to start a hospital at Homburg at her own expense, in which she insisted on cleanliness and fresh air in the English mode. She was horrified at German notions of hygiene; she sent reports to her mother that most of the doctors were " mischievous, stupid old things," and the nurses (such as they were) " dirty and ignorant and useless." Very likely she offended the susceptibilities of the German doctors by her insistence on the superiority of English methods of hygiene, and presently the King ordered her to leave her hospital and come back to Berlin. " Is it not annoying and provoking," she bitterly wrote, " I never make a plan that is not crossed by the King or Queen, and they invariably disapprove of what I do—it is most disheartening." The Crown Prince, out at the front, was furious at these stupid snubs, and wrote to the King that her hospital at Homburg was a model, and that he hoped others would be conducted on the same lines. The King took no notice of his letter.

The Crown Princess's fears as to the annihilation of the German armies were soon composed. Disaster after disaster overtook the French; during August MacMahon was defeated by the Crown Prince's Southern Army at Weissenberg and Wörth: on September 1 came the battle of Sedan, at which the Emperor Napoleon surrendered, and in October Marshal Bazaine's army of 70,000 men surrendered at Metz. Her wailings of dismay soared into pæans of triumph, and her pride in her husband's victories and in the huge expansion of Prussia allowed her to become a little tactless. She knew that the Prince of Wales had long chafed against the hedonistic idleness enforced on him by his mother, but she sent him her particular love, and was sure that " dear Bertie must envy Fritz who has such a trying but such a useful life " : and she wondered what he and Alix, who had never really forgiven Prussia for the seizure of the Duchies, would say to these wonderful events. All the world, she was convinced, would now acknowledge with pleasure and pride the superiority of the Prussian character, and contrast their hard-working serious life with the habits of Parisians who were so taken up with pleasure that they had no time for self-examination. France would learn (such a downfall was intended to teach deep lessons) what frivolity, conceit and immorality lead to. " Gay and charming Paris," she wrote, " *what* mischief that very Court and that very attractive Paris has done to English Society, to the stage and to literature ! "[1] As for the Emperor Napoleon, how just was her father's estimate of him, when he and the Queen and Bertie and herself paid that State visit to Paris just before she was engaged to Fritz : Papa had never trusted him nor approved of his moral character. Poor Emperor : she pitied him. But he with his dazzling Court had been the corrupter of Europe. He had leisure now in his confinement at Wilhelmshöhe to study the stern lesson that experience had taught him : there were three of his Field-Marshals with him, so they could talk it over.

This enthusiastic belief in the moral as well as the military superiority of the Prussians might have improved her position in Berlin had she not spoiled its

[1] *Letters of Queen Victoria*, II, ii, p. 61.

effect by her inability to control her impetuous tongue. The feeling in Germany, she told her mother, was very hostile to England for not having prevented the war and she now thought that most unjust, so, when she heard criticism of the English, she answered back with vehemence in defence of them. She knew it was unwise, but such comments made her feel " spiteful and savage." Yet while the ink was still wet in her pen, she justified the German bitterness towards England. When the war broke out, Germany, she thought, was quite unprepared (a gross libel on Bismarck's sagacity), and turned to England as her only friend. England declared neutrality and " a cry of disappointment and indignation burst forth from Germany—and the people said ' If we are annihilated England will be the cause. She knows that we have been unfairly and unjustly attacked, and yet she will see us go to the bottom without stirring a little finger to help us. . . . England is growing fat—is too lazy to stir herself, and prefers to let us be ruined rather than say a stern word to France.' "[1] This grievance she thought was well-founded and yet a week ago she had pronounced the feeling against England most unjust ! If her tongue was as inconsistent as her pen and as impetuous it is not much to be wondered at that her German relations found her very bewildering.

The siege of Paris began. Bismarck, backed up by popular feeling in Germany, wanted to bombard the city at once in order to bring the war to an end as speedily as possible. The Crown Prince, on the other hand, knew that the German armies lacked

[1] Ponsonby, *Letters of Empress Frederick*, p. 99.

sufficient siege guns and ammunition to make the bombardment effective. It was a question which concerned the Government and the military authorities, and it would have been wiser of the Crown Princess, surrounded as she was with mischief-makers and ill-wishers, not to have opened her lips on the subject. Instead, she ardently and openly supported her husband's view with the unfortunate but natural result that she was believed to be influencing him, and he recorded in his Diary, a fortnight before the bombardment began : " In Berlin it is now the order of the day to vilify my wife as being mainly responsible for the postponement of the bombardment of Paris and to accuse her of acting under the direction of the Queen of England." English sympathy, now running strongly towards France, after her crushing military disasters and the ruthless thoroughness of German military methods, was further stirred by the iron terms of peace demanded by Germany, and the Queen was blamed for not using her influence with her German relations to procure some mitigation of them. Thus while in England she became very unpopular owing to her pro-German sentiments, it was believed in Berlin that her sympathies were with France.

The family life of the Crown Princess during the war must have been very unpleasant, and she poured out her troubles to the Queen, assuring her that they arose from no fault of hers. With Fritz away she felt utterly alien : the King disliked her, and she often found it impossible to get on with Queen Augusta. It was a very awkward situation, for her mother and Queen Augusta had long been the most devoted friends, and there was no one living with whom the Queen was, inexplicably, on more intimate terms than with this strange hard woman. The Crown Princess protested that she herself was the most dutiful daughter-in-law, but was regarded by her (which was quite true) with cold dislike. She acknowledged and appreciated Queen Augusta's good points, she had always "fought her battles and smoothed her path," and though her mother-in-law often made her very miserable she bore no resentment for that, and only remembered her better and kindlier moods, deeply pitying her for her unhappy temperament. She herself had never a moment's leisure during the day, and she always had to sit with the Queen in the evening. When Fritz came home she would not be able to do this, and she feared that her mother-in-law would make that a further cause of complaint. It was difficult to please such a woman, but she sincerely strove to be patient and forbearing.

A week later she wrote again, and this second letter suggests that her forbearance was not always equal to the strain put upon it. Queen Victoria had lately opened Parliament, and the Crown Princess wrote to tell her how very angry her great friend had been about the speech from the throne. She complained that it flattered the French, that it expressed open sympathy with them, and that the references to Germany were far from civil : certainly it would create a very bad impression in Berlin. She and Queen Augusta had argued about it : they could not agree, and the Crown Princess acknowledged : " Of course I cannot hear a word said against England—and I give it back (I fear not always gently) when I hear sharp words." . . . Yet it is difficult to see what could have been the object of repeating to her mother these disagreeable observations of Queen Augusta, unless it was to shake her confidence in her friend and inspire distrust. Here we touch on a great failing in that noble and impetuous nature : she never had the instincts of the peace-maker. Probably she thought it was her duty to be frank, but though frankness is an admirable quality, some aspects of it are scarcely distinguishable from mischief-making. As she had told her mother years ago, she greatly enjoyed a fight when it came to fighting, but these gratuitous skirmishes with her mother-in-law did not promote that friendship between allied Royal Houses which the Queen held to be conducive to friendship between their nations.

Then for the Crown Princess there was the daily heartache of looking on the cruel maiming through which her eldest son Prince William had come to birth. He was twelve years old now, and the damage seemed irreparable, for his left arm was still powerless and the torturing treatments he had undergone were of no avail. It crippled all his boyish activities, for the withered limb gave him an imperfect balance and he had great difficulty in running or in learning to ride, and his food must be cut up for him. Only by painful effort could he do what came so easily to other boys, and this consciousness of inferiority, so his English tutor feared, was getting more acute as he grew older. But at present she was well-pleased with the affectionate relations between herself and her son. " I am happy to say," she wrote, " that between him and me there is a bond of love and confidence which I feel sure nothing can destroy " : but she did not think much of his abilities, nor of his strength of character. She superintended his education with constant care, and perhaps the Queen remembered that the excessive vigilance that the Prince Consort had imposed upon his eldest son had not produced the effect which was intended, for she warned her daughter that " too much constant watching leads to the very dangers hereafter which one wishes to avoid." She recommended that William should be brought into contact with other classes, and not get to think that because he was a Prince he was of different clay from less exalted folk. Somehow the Crown Princess misunderstood this advice : she wrote back expressing her " horror of low company," and the Queen had to explain that she had not meant " actors, actresses and musicians," as the Princess appeared to think, but such people as her esteemed Highlanders who had great independence of character and noble hearts. Brought up in Prussian traditions of the immense position of Kings and Princes, William, always living in a Palace, would be cut off from such contacts, and he would never find them when he entered on his military training, for soldiers, she had noticed, had no independence of character.

The Princess retorted warmly. Her mother must not think that William only saw Palace folk. When her children were with her in the country they had ample opportunity of going in and out of cottages, as was the habit at Balmoral, but the Prussian peasant, who had lately been the simplest and gentlest of souls, was not at all an amiable person, but obstinate and boorish. In fact the discussion about William's upbringing resolved itself into an irrelevant wrangle about the racial characteristics of Highlanders and Prussians.[1] Both ladies had the same desire that William should grow up to be a good man and a Christian, and as like as possible to his maternal grandfather, but the friendliest advice, even from her mother, for whom the Crown Princess had the deepest regard, always provoked her into argument. Her habit of mind led her to search for points on which to differ, rather than common ground on which to construct. She saw her own point of view so exclusively and supported it so strenuously, that she did not pause to consider if those who did not share it might have sound reasons for disagreeing with her.

The war was over, and the mission with which her father had entrusted her on her marriage was over also : the missioners, for all proselytizing purpose, had been massacred by the chief of the savage tribe which they had hoped to convert. Bismarck had realized the Prince Consort's vision of a vast united Germany, ruled by Prussia, and far exceeding in power and in territory his ideal State, which, in close alliance and amity with England, should bring peace and prosperity to Europe. Blood and iron had accomplished

[1] *Ibid.*, pp. 123, 124.

it; every step of the way had been won by intrigue and aggression and assault. If the Queen was right in pronouncing that, had the Prince Consort been alive when France declared war on his beloved Fatherland, it would have been impossible to prevent his joining Bismarck's armies, what manner of letters would he have written to his wife and his daughter from the front?

At Darmstadt Prince Louis had been called up immediately on the outbreak of war. After dinner one night his wife went with him to the outskirts of the village where his cavalry division was quartered: they stood looking back at each other till the darkness blurred them. The Crown Princess urged her sister to come with her children to Berlin, where they would be safer than in the west of Germany should the French armies invade the Fatherland, and the King offered her the New Palace to live in. But, as before, that was not to be thought of. Louis was at the front in command of his division: he would be in the midst of fierce fighting, and his two brothers were also on active service. It would be a terribly anxious time for their father and mother, and she must remain with them at Darmstadt. It gave the people confidence to see that she stayed here with her family, and as Louis's wife her place was here: it would be desertion of her duties to seek greater comfort and security with her sister in Berlin.

She was busier than ever, looking after the wives and children of soldiers at the front, seeing that the hospitals were ready to receive the wounded and sending out women from her Nurses' Institute to the field-hospitals. The anxiety was frightful, and she had a continual headache, but work was the best palliative for both. She had turned her own house into the headquarters of the Red Cross depot, and lived with her children in the Grand Duke's house at Kranichstein, driving into Darmstadt at half-past eight every morning, returning at mid-day, and coming back again for the afternoon; she hoped her mother would excuse the brevity of her letters, for there were four hospitals she had to visit daily. If it was known there had been an engagement the women crowded round her carriage as she drove from one to another, asking her what regiments had been under fire, and she told them all the news that she could learn. Wounded Germans and French were brought in and the hospitals grew full: " I neither smell nor see," she wrote, " anything but wounds." Her neuralgia grew acute, her eyes suffered and she was expecting another baby before long. The Queen sent out a doctor for her confinement, and a sash for her boy Ernie, and early in October her child was born, another boy, Frederick William. As soon as she recovered she began her work again, for she could not keep from it, but presently her doctor and her mother-in-law insisted on her going away for three weeks, and she joined her sister in Berlin. A quiet time: they spent their evenings together reading and writing, and one day Field-Marshal Wrangel told her what a hero Louis was and how magnificently he had led his troops. " I am very proud of this," she wrote to her mother, " but I am too much a woman not to long above all things to have him safe home again."

Then back she went to Darmstadt, serving with her nurses in the hospitals and meeting trains full of wounded soldiers at the station. Before she left she had been nursing a young man who was desperately ill. She returned to find he was recovering well and the doctors said that she had saved his life : seldom had she felt so pleased. In the town there were many widows and mothers who had lost perhaps an only son. She went to see them all, for sympathy was the only medicine for such grief. Christmas came round : Louis was at Orleans and she decked a minute Christmas tree for him and his staff, and sent him a pair of stockings she had knitted. She distributed her own little gifts at the hospitals and the Queen had sent her two bed-capes which gave great pride to their wearers. She had two wounded officers in her house now, which was a great expense, and this continual assistance to soldiers' widows and to the mothers of infants, whose fathers, like Louis, had never seen the new baby, brought her near the end of her slender resources. But Louis had passed through these months of war unhurt and the children were well and growing fast, and when he came home the joy would be almost too great. How she longed for rest and quiet : perhaps they might be allowed to come to Balmoral with their children in the autumn, for after so long an absence Louis would not like leaving them again so soon. Any odd corners would do for them.

Paris capitulated, and the trains were no longer

full of wounded, but of German soldiers returning from the war, singing and cheering. And at last her Louis came back on leave and for the first time saw his little son. The parents went to Berlin for the entry of the victorious armies with the new German Emperor riding at their head. Watching the triumphant cavalcade Alice's heart ached for the Emperor and Empress to whom France had behaved so shamefully. But they had found a refuge in England and were treated with respect and friendliness.

It is because these letters of Princess Louis to her mother are so devoid of all self-consciousness that they give so vivid a portrait of her. Her nature, warp and woof, was woven of tenderness for others, and that of no sentimental sort but of the strong fibre that manifests itself in self-sacrifice and personal service. Often she speaks of the same topics as those on which the Queen wrote to her sister. They must, for instance, have received very similar letters on the subject of the education of their children, but while one sister picked out side issues to criticize and examine and define, the other seized the essentials with which she was in accord. Of course, she answered, Princes and Princesses must be brought up to know that their position " is *nothing*, save what their personal worth can make it," but, being what they are, they must take extra pains to behave themselves well and modestly and set an example of unselfishness. Princess Louis read the Queen's letter to the governess who had now been engaged, for it would do her good to know that her mother held just the same views as she did. As for England's neutrality in the war, about which Vicky had made some very bitter observations, Alice was content to know that the Queen felt very deeply for Germany and was doing all she could. It was a crime to have caused the war, but there she left it without any recrimination or abuse for the French, and when it was over she drew no moral lessons from the frivolous nation and the Emperor who had corrupted Europe. All she cared to remember was that the war had brought Germany together, and that the resentment in the smaller States over Prussian annexations was dead.

In England meantime the Queen had been much exercised over the marriage of her fourth daughter Princess Louise. She had passed her twenty-first birthday in the Spring of 1869, and was already older than any of her elder sisters had been when they were wed. It would have been in accordance with precedent to have been looking out for some suitable German Prince, but Princess Louise found such a future extremely distasteful. She much preferred to make a British marriage and to spend her life in England. The Queen entirely agreed with her, and when the Crown Princess suggested a marriage with a Prussian Prince, she wrote to her in her firmest style saying that neither she nor Louise would hear of it and the matter " must be considered at an end." That the daughter of a reigning Sovereign should marry a subject was at that time a very startling proposition. Such an alliance had not been contracted in the Royal Family of England since the days of the Plantagenets; so this was a deep well to dip into for precedent. The proposed bridegroom was the Marquis of Lorne, son and heir of the Duke of Argyll.

The Prince of Wales thoroughly disapproved of the idea, and after discussion with his sister wrote to the Queen about it. His main objection was political, for Lord Lorne sat in the House of Commons as a Gladstonian Liberal, and it would give rise to the innuendo that the Crown would be intimately exposed to political influences. He thought also (and this troubled a mind to which orthodoxy of ceremonial and etiquette was so dear) that there would be constant difficulties in assigning correct official rank to the husband and wife. The Queen was particularly anxious that he should see eye to eye with her over his sister's marriage (though she intended in any case to get her way) for some day he would be the head of the family, and she wrote him a remarkable letter which shows how entirely (for the present) her sentiments about foreign marriages for her daughters had altered, and the reasons:

> " Times have much changed; great foreign alliances are looked on as causes of trouble and anxiety, and are of no good. What could be more painful than the position in which our family were placed during the wars with Denmark, and between Prussia and Austria? Every family feeling was rent asunder, and we were powerless. . . . Nothing is more unpopular here or more uncomfortable for *me* and everyone than the long residence of our married daughters from abroad

in my house, with the quantities of foreigners they bring with them, the foreign view they entertain on all subjects, and in beloved Papa's lifetime this was totally different, and besides Prussia had not swallowed everything up. You may not be aware, as I am, with what dislike the marriages of Princesses of the Royal Family with small German Princes (German beggars as they most insultingly were called) were looked on, and how in former days many of our Statesmen like Mr. Fox, Lord Melbourne and Lord Holland abused these marriages and said how wrong it was that alliances with noblemen of high rank and fortune, which had always existed formerly and which are perfectly legal, were no longer allowed by the Sovereign. Now that the Royal family is so large (you have already five, and *what* will these be when your brothers marry?) in these days, when you ask Parliament to give money to all the Princesses to be *spent abroad*, when they could perfectly marry here and the children succeed just as much as if they were the children of a Prince or Princess, we could not maintain this exclusive principle. As to position I see *no* difficulty whatever; Louise remains what she is, and her husband keeps his rank (like the Mensdorffs and Victor Hohenlohe) only being treated in the family as a relation when we are together. . . . It will strengthen the *hold* of the Royal Family, besides infusing new and healthy blood into it, whereas all the Princes abroad are related to one another; and while I could continue these foreign alliances with several members of the family, I feel sure that *new* blood will strengthen the Throne *morally* as well as *physically*."[1]

This letter is of extreme interest. It shows how intolerable to the Queen had become the endless

[1] *Letters of Queen Victoria*, II, i, pp. 632, 633.

By courtesy of Hutchinson & Co.

PRINCESS LOUISE

from PASSAGES FROM THE PAST, by the Duke of Argyll

worries to which the marriages of her two elder daughters, though sanctioned and arranged by the Prince Consort, had given rise. Prussia, Bismarck's Prussia, was the cause of serious discords in domestic harmony, for the Danish war had caused much unpleasantness between Vicky and her brother, and subsequently Prussia, of which Vicky would one day be Queen, had made war on Hesse, of which Alice would be Grand Duchess. Such schisms were inevitably painful, but it is strange to find that the long visits of the Queen's two daughters from Germany had become so distasteful to her. They upset her: she disliked their foreign ways. Once she had bitterly complained that Prussia " monopolized " the Crown Princess and that she saw nothing of her; as for Princess Louis, there was a time when she felt herself stinted and defrauded if she was with her for only five months in the year.

But times were changed, and such were her sentiments now. She had made up her mind, in the capacity both of Queen and mother, that it was far wiser, for national as well as domestic considerations, that Princess Louise should marry this very handsome, able and artistic young man. She had talked the matter over with his father, and next autumn Lord Lorne was asked to stay at Balmoral, even as Prince Frederick of Prussia had been bidden there for a similar purpose in 1855. The procedure of the betrothal was on much the same lines. The Queen drove out in one direction with Princess Beatrice to taste a chalybeate spring and be shown by John Brown the inn where he had once been a servant, while Princess Louise and Lord Lorne, with the Lord Chancellor and Lady Ely drove to Glassault Shiel. The chaperons then effaced themselves, the young people took a walk, and returned to Balmoral with the news for which, as the Queen admitted, she was not unprepared.

She wrote to her friend Queen Augusta about so unusual an alliance, saying that she knew it would cause " sensation and surprise " in Germany, but that she had long thought it very suitable. " Princes of small German houses without fortune," she explained, " are very unpopular here," whereas Lord Lorne was a man of independent fortune and " was really no lower in rank than a minor German royalty."[1] That was indisputably true : the Campbells, of whom Lord Lorne would be the chief, were a clan of far nobler position and tradition than many of the Ducal and Princely houses of Germany which had sought their brides in England, and in permitting and indeed arranging this marriage the Queen renewed a precedent which was very popular in the country. Disraeli wrote to her with elaborate and elegant approval: " Your Majesty has decided, with deep discrimination, to terminate an etiquette become sterile, and the change will be effected under every circumstance that can command the sympathy of the country." He thought the marriage " as wise as it is romantic . . . it would consolidate the happiness of your hearth." He realized how the Queen would feel the parting, but " you will miss her, Madam, only like the stars that

[1] Bolitho, *Further Letters of Queen Victoria*, p. 177.

return in their constant season, and with all their brightness."[1]

The Queen never for a moment contemplated that Princess Louise and her husband should make their principal home with her, as had been her intention in the marriages of two of her elder daughters. As already indicated, she did not now feel the need of a resident son-in-law, and it would have been politically impossible, for the reason advanced by the Prince of Wales. Though it was scarcely conceivable that domestic propinquity would have inclined the Queen towards Gladstonian policies, such an arrangement was out of the question. Moreover one of the main general reasons for the marriage was that her new son-in-law should be an independent British subject, heir to a great estate with solid responsibilities of his own, and not a foreign princeling living in an alien country, where he had no duties except that of being the constant companion of his mother-in-law.

Similar considerations were applicable to the bride. Princess Louise herself was far more suited to be the mistress of a great nobleman's house than the wife of the Queen's resident son-in-law, where her position would have been wholly that of a dependent. She would have been as much out of place there as the Crown Princess herself: temperaments would have clashed. Her individuality was no less strong, and she had the same brilliantly-faceted vitality which those two possessed to a much higher degree than the other sisters, and which was incongruous with the subdued and dominated atmosphere

[1] The Duke of Argyll, *Passages from the Past*, p. 391.

of the Queen's establishments. She was a radiant creature, extremely handsome, genial and ebullient, with little trace of the Teuton in her nature ; and her gay and eager presence, her sense of fun, her exuberant power of enjoyment, her freedom from any conventionally Royal consciousness had a social potency which rivalled her mother's, but with this antipodal difference that the Queen evoked awe and almost paralytic reverence whereas her daughter exhaled a psychical ozone. Like her eldest sister, she, too, inherited from her father an intensely artistic nature and her work in sculpture was far removed from that of the amateur. It was only fit that she should have a wider scope for her gifts and her self-expression than the cloistered home which had been hers since her father's death. How cloistered that was we may gather from the firm refusal that met Mr. Gladstone when he asked the Queen's permission to invite Princess Louise (then twenty years of age) to dine with him one evening when the Prince and Princess of Wales were also honouring him. She thanked him, but Princess Louise never dined out at all except at her brother's house. . . . The Queen communicated the news of the engagement to her Prime Minister with high appreciation of Lord Lorne's superiority in character and ability to the young men of the day, though to lose another daughter would be a fresh pang for her in her " sad forlorn home." But she was convinced that it was her duty to face that, and Mr. Gladstone, approved the revival of the ancient precedent.[1] The Queen little guessed how increasingly

[1] Guedalla, *The Queen and Mr. Gladstone*, i, pp. 226, 258.

this revived precedent for Royal marriages with subjects would be followed during the next sixty years. The Princess Royal of the next generation married a compatriot of Lord Lorne's, and in the generation after the King's only daughter married an Englishman, and two of his sons married ladies of Scottish blood, of whom one is now the Queen of England.

The Queen opened Parliament again in the spring of 1871 ; it was on this occasion that the Speech from the Throne so vexed her friend Queen Augusta. She had performed that ceremony once only in the last five years when Princess Helena was engaged to Prince Christian and Prince Alfred attained his majority. A similar exigency drove her to do so now, for she intended to ask her Commons to make provision for Princess Louise on her marriage. She knew that these grants for her daughters were unpopular in the country, but, as she had written to the Prince of Wales, she ingeniously ascribed that to the fact that English money was spent abroad : on this occasion there could be no complaint on such a score. But Mr. Gladstone was not so easy in his mind as to how the House would receive the request. The cause of the discontent, as he hinted to her, went deeper than any individual grant, and it was " to his agreeable but extreme surprise " that the vote of the usual dowry of £30,000 and an annuity of £6,000 was passed unanimously.[1] But when later in the session a grant to Prince Arthur

[1] *Ibid.*, i, pp. 272, 273.

on his coming of age was brought before the House, it was passed with the expression of the hope that Her Majesty would show herself more frequently to her loving subjects.

Here was the root of the discontent to which Gladstone had darkly referred as going deeper than dowries. He believed that the shattered state of the Queen's nerves which she so often bewailed, was imaginary, and that her doctor, " the feeble-minded Doctor Jenner," was encouraging her to refuse to do anything for which she did not feel inclined ; and now he begged her graciously to postpone her departure for Balmoral till the end of a difficult session, and hold her Council for the Prorogation. Here was one of the encroachments on her private convenience which she always resented. She was so indignant at such a suggestion (perhaps they would next ask her to prorogue Parliament in person !) that she disregarded her Prime Minister altogether and wrote to her Lord Chancellor instead. She told him that she was doing as much as she could, and that, as she grew older, she would not, for the sake of her health, be able to meet the incessant calls. She reminded him that overwork had killed the Prince Consort and Lord Clarendon. She was " driven and abused " ; her private life was being interfered with. As a concession, never to be repeated, she consented to remain at Osborne for three days more, and then, if Parliament had not finished its business, she would wait no longer. She warned him that if this persecution went on, she would have to give up the awful weight of Sovereignty to another, and then perhaps these unpitiful people would be sorry that they had wrecked her health.

The Queen had actually made more public appearances this year than since the Prince Consort's death, but Gladstone's fears for the Throne were by no means fantastic. He knew how strong was the feeling against her seclusion, and, finding that it was impossible to get through Parliamentary business by the hour she had specified as the starting of positively the last train to Balmoral he became both alarmed and disgusted. Personally he was deeply hurt at the Queen's belief that party interests were at the bottom of his anxiety that she should wait for the Prorogation. No such thought had ever entered his mind. He was anxious only for the stability of the Throne, and he regarded her persistence in refusing to put herself to this small inconvenience as the most "sickening piece of experience" he had ever been through in his public life. "Worse things," he wrote to her Secretary "may easily be imagined : but smaller and meaner cause for the decay of Thrones cannot be conceived. It is like the worm which bores the bark of a noble oak tree and so breaks the channel of its life."[1]

In addition, the Queen's German sympathies in the Franco-German war were very unpopular, and the fall of the Monarchy in France, with the establishment of the Republic, had been reflected in England by a strong agitation against the Throne and the prodigious expense of a Sovereign who so rarely appeared, who (it was said) must be annually

[1] *Ibid.*, i, pp. 298–300, 304.

transferring to her own pocket immense sums of money which were granted her by the nation for the purpose of upholding the splendours of the Crown, and who continued to ask her Parliament for substantial grants to her children in spite of the nest egg of the Neild bequest, now cherished for nineteen years and much enriched. On these points Gladstone was her ardent champion. It had always been the custom for the nation to provide for the children of the Sovereign in a suitable manner, and the Queen's official income was her own to save or spend as she pleased. Any prying into that or her other resources was a monstrous intrusion into her private affairs. But her refusal to perform those duties of which he believed her to be perfectly capable might lead to deplorable consequences.

The heir to the throne caused equal dissatisfaction for exactly opposite reasons. Unlike the Queen he was seen too much and always surrounded by frivolous folk; he led a fast and far from edifying existence, and instead of living, like his mother, so substantially within his income he was credited, in spite of his cosy £100,000 a year, with being heavily in debt. He had lately appeared, too, in a horrid public scandal, being subpœnaed in the divorce suit which Sir Charles Mordaunt had brought against his wife, who, he alleged, had confessed to misconduct with the Prince. Two of the Prince's most intimate friends were cited as co-respondents, but there was no evidence of any sort against him, except the alleged statement of a woman who was mentally deranged, and his letters to Lady Mordaunt, which were read by the Judge, contained nothing that could conceivably support the charge. But the fact that he appeared at all in the case caused an ebullition of popular feeling against him and he was hissed when he next appeared at a race-meeting.

These were family affairs which worried the Queen. The Crown Princess wrote to her mother of her horror at this scandal and of the very bad impression it had made in Germany : she was also annoyed with the Prince's openly expressed indignation at the crushing conditions of peace imposed on the French at the conclusion of the war. But the Queen did not intend to allow her children to quarrel, and, in spite of her late assertion that these long visits of her married daughters with their foreign suites were very uncomfortable for her as well as very unpopular in the country, she asked the Crown Princess with her husband and her two eldest sons, to stay with her for the reconciliation of these distressing differences. Germany was as unpopular in England as she was with the Prince of Wales, and when it was known that these Imperial relations were to be the Queen's guests, unpleasant comments were made in the House of Commons. The Queen considered them most impertinent and disrespectful : that her children and grandchildren should come to stay with her concerned only herself and them. Was she to be debarred from seeing her family just because she was Queen ? So they spent a fortnight at the German Embassy in London, and then went down to Osborne for a spell of quiet domestic life. Most mothers, perhaps, would have kept the hot-tempered brother and the argumentative sister apart till they had cooled down a little, but that was not her way: they had got to be friends at once, and she meant to see that they were. Her will triumphed, and what aided much in producing fraternal amity, as once before, was that they all detested Bismarck, and starting from that common ground they got on famously. And Bismarck, they agreed, was " not eternal " nor was his rule of blood and iron. When Fritz became Emperor peace and progress and Liberal policies would dawn again: the sky in the East seemed faintly lit already, for no one supposed that his father would live much longer. Bismarck's rapacities might even be restored to the despoiled nations, and before the family party broke up the Prince of Wales formed the firm impression that Fritz intended to give back part, at any rate, of Alsace and Lorraine to France, and of Hanover to the deposed King.

The Queen did not wait for Parliament to be prorogued, but with the Crown Princess and her children went up to Balmoral. She became really unwell, with an abscess in her arm and most painful rheumatic gout; and these attacks in the Press alarmed and enraged her. The Prince of Wales who had also been a victim, wrote most tactfully to assure her that her people were really loyal, and that the violence of the papers was only an indication, crudely expressed, of their desire to see more of her. But he certainly shared Mr. Gladstone's apprehensions, for he added, " it is feared in these Radical days that, if the Sovereign is not more amongst them and not more seen in London, the loyalty and attachment to the Crown will decrease, which would be naturally much to be deplored ; but I feel at the same time they would not wish you to make such exertions as would be detrimental to your health."[1]

Princess Louis paid the visit to Balmoral to which she had looked forward so much, but it was a sad time, for the Queen was much crippled by this gout and very helpless, unable to walk or even to feed herself. The Princess was most unhappy about her ; she reproached herself, when her month at Balmoral was over, for leaving her when she was still so unwell, but she had promised to pay other visits and was pledged to go to Sandringham for her brother's birthday party in November. She had not spent that day with him since the year before their father died. She, too, was afraid that difficult days were coming, and indeed he was having an unpleasant time now, and she hoped he would be guided wisely and rightly.

The agitation against an invisible and expensive Sovereign and a son who did nothing but amuse himself in so extravagant and unedifying a fashion, still simmered in the Press, and it fairly boiled over when, early in November, Sir Charles Dilke made a most violent anti-Monarchical speech at Newcastle. It contained gross mis-statements : he said for instance, that the Queen paid no income-tax on her vast income and this infuriated her. She urged

[1] *Letters of Queen Victoria*, II, ii, 159.

Mr. Gladstone to contradict on behalf of the Government such atrocious falsehoods, but he refused. Any denial of one point would only shift the attack to a more effective slogan, such as the Queen's seclusion, and further embitter a dangerous controversy.

To what extremes this movement would have gone it is impossible to conjecture. A most fortunate misfortune arrested it for the Prince of Wales was stricken by typhoid fever, and he and the Queen ceased to be a profligate heir and an unfunctioning Sovereign, and became a young man dangerously ill and his miserably anxious mother. Human sympathy with them as such wiped from the slate all the indictments against them, and the most sentimental nation in the world clutched at the first editions of the daily papers to read the latest bulletins. Princess Louis was still staying with her brother when he was taken ill and instantly she became the moral hope and stay of the house, taking charge of her sister-in-law, quiet and confident and responsible, and serving in the sick-room as a trained and competent nurse. The case became critical, and the Queen went to Sandringham where she had never been before, though the Prince had lived there for eight years. The present anxiety ominously linked itself up with the past: the nursing, the symptoms, the attacks of difficult breathing, the rambling voice, all reminded her of the Prince Consort's illness. The patient improved, and she returned to Windsor, but there was a relapse and the doctors told her that she must go back if she wished to see him before the end.

And now the dreadful anniversary of her husband's death, December 14, was approaching and that uneasy fear of fatally ordained coincidences of the calendar, which always lurked in her mind, made her feel certain that she would lose her son on the day she had lost her husband ten years ago. Never since then had she spent that anniversary except at Windsor, sitting for hours alone in the room in which he had died, and it was painful not to be there now. These forebodings were so firmly rooted that when, on that very day, the Prince took a decided turn for the better, she could hardly realize it.

It had been a woeful year, the darkest hour of the Queen's eclipse and the most dangerous for the Monarchy. The long resentment against her seclusion and her personal enrichment from funds granted her for public magnificence had come to a head, and with the energy of the neurasthenic she defended her fancied disabilities. But to her they were not fanciful. There was nothing in her consciousness so solidly real to her. She entirely believed that she was being driven to death with overwork, and that any fresh claim on her or any enquiry into her disposal of the Civil List was an impertinent intrusion into her private life. The Prince's illness caused a truce in the agitation, and when next year it was renewed again its force was spent.

Princess Louis remained with her brother at Sandringham. She was wanted, and that was enough, and till the middle of January she stayed on.

Then she went quietly home to Darmstadt. This had not been the peaceful holiday at Balmoral she had looked forward to with Louis and her children, but her mother had been poorly and very much worried, and her brother like to die.

CHAPTER V

PRINCESS LOUIS'S sixth child, a daughter, was born in the summer of 1872. She proposed to call her Alix, (a variant of her own name, since Germans always pronounced " Alice " so infamously), Helena Louise Beatrice, the names of her sisters. The Queen pointed out that the name of one of her sisters, not to mention her mother, had been omitted, and Victoria was dutifully added. Alix was a " nice little thing," like her sister Ella, but with darker eyes, and her features promised to be good, though it looked as if her nose would be too long. That defect remedied itself, and Alix and Ella grew up to be two of the most beautiful women in Europe. Alix was always laughing, her mother nicknamed her " Sunny," and it is good to know that as a child she was happy. Destiny wove for her imperial splendours, and for them both a doom of Aeschylean tragedy.

Princess Louis was soon engaged again in fresh spheres of service, and again she had to be a little careful as to how she wrote of them to the Queen. A conference on Women's Work and their possible careers beyond marriage and child-bearing and house-keeping was assembling at Darmstadt. Germany, Holland and Switzerland were sending delegates from sympathetic associations, and from England came such distinguished propagandists as Miss Carpenter and Miss Octavia Hill. But the Queen viewed with the deepest distrust movements that threatened any sort of emancipation for her sex. She witheringly alluded to them as " the so-called and most erroneous ' Rights of Women,' " and the idea of women ever being put on the electoral roll was to her an outrage on decency. A nameless (though not unknown) " Lady C——" had once spoken on the subject, and the Queen declared she ought to have " a good whipping." Princess Louis therefore assured her mother that she had taken the utmost pains to rule out all discussion on such repulsive topics, and that the most advanced subjects on the agenda papers of her Conference were girls' schools, the employment of women in postal and telegraph offices, the education of nursery-maids and of young mothers with regard to the care of their babies. She hoped that she would look through the programme and find herself able to be interested in it. But even so the Queen was not quite satisfied: she wanted to know whether Alice's mother-in-law approved of these activities. Alice reassured her. They had talked over all these questions quite freely; where they differed they cordially agreed to differ, and Princess Charles was delighted at the success of the conference. Her work was extending in other directions: she had long been president of the Darmstadt Nurses Institute, and now she was forming an Association for the care of children boarded out by the State. Sometimes they were ill-used, and the whole system needed investigation and reform. Children must be made happy : there was nothing that counted for so much in the formation of character.[1]

There was constant anxiety about the health of her second son Frederick William, known as Frittie, who had been born when his father was serving in the Franco-German war. From birth he had been extremely delicate, and now it became evident that he suffered from that obscure and most dangerous condition called hæmophilia. Pathologically, there is missing from the blood some coagulating constituent in consequence of which a mere scratch on the skin is followed by bleeding which is most difficult to stop. Frittie, now aged two, got a small cut on his ear, and for two days this incessant bleeding continued, till his hair was matted with blood. There was fearful irritation, and the child had to be watched day and night for fear that, when at last the bleeding was arrested with caustic and tight bandages, he should cause it to break out again. And he was so boisterous when he was well, full of tearing spirits : how was it possible to guard against some trivial injury which would cause a further attack ?

Frittie recovered, and his mother and father, travelling incognito to save expense, treated themselves to a tour in Italy. Princess Louis had never been so far south before and instantly the lovely land cast its spell over her : cypresses and stone-pines against the evening sky, the caressing sunshine, a glimpse of the Campagna, a fragment of Roman architecture, an Italian contadino lounging in the

[1] Princess Christian, *Alice*, pp. 250–253.

shade were enchantments hitherto undreamed of. They spent Palm Sunday in Rome : the pictures roused many memories of her father's love for the Primitives, and surely he had in his mind the terraces of the Villa Pamfili when he laid out the grounds and gardens at Osborne. But soon the ache of homesickness gained on her ; she wanted to get back to her children again, for Frittie's illness had shaken her serene confidence in their well-being. Ernie had chosen a china doll in its bath as a birthday present for her. She thought she was a little old for that, for she was thirty, and felt she had said good-bye to youth. It had been a happy time, and she was grateful for the innumerable joys it had brought her, but how fast it had flown ! Good-bye to youth.

There was always great jubilation when she came back from any absence : the children put up wreaths to welcome her and would not leave her for a moment. One morning, a month after her return, her husband had gone off for the day on his military duties, when Ernie and Frittie came romping in to see her while she still lay in bed. The windows of her bedroom, reaching nearly down to the ground, were open, and next door was her sitting-room : this had a projecting bow-window which looked sideways into the bedroom. As the boys ran about playing a game of hide-and-seek, Ernie appeared at this bow-window, and Frittie seeing his brother there, scampered across to the open window of his mother's room. He slipped and fell out on to the stone terrace twenty feet below, and was picked up unconscious. No bones were broken, and at first it was hoped that he was not seriously hurt. All day his mother watched by him, but bleeding on the brain had set in, and in the evening, before her husband returned, the child died.[1]

Princess Louis never got over the shock. There were times when she realised that Frittie had been spared the physical perils and suffering that, had he lived, must always have been his; and now she would cherish till her life's end the image of his flower-like brightness and his love. She tried to make a friend and a dedication of her grief, to fuse it with her love for her dead child, so that it became part of love and part of him, not an agony despairing and separate. Yet she shrank from all that reminded her too poignantly of him. For months after his death she could not touch her piano, for that brought back to her the memory of those baby hands which used to pull hers off the keys, when Frittie wanted her to play with him; and when spring came round again the sight of the early snowdrops wrung her heart, for Frittie loved them. Like her mother, she, only yet thirty, associated with her loss the common sights and sounds of every day, and each hour renewed her loneliness. But she was resolved from the first not to allow her life to become barren and withdrawn or her grief to render her remiss in answering its calls. Life was so short in any case, and she resumed all her work again: the days passed more quickly if she was busy for others. And she devoted herself more closely to the children who were

[1] *Ibid.*, p. 36.

left : they grew up so quickly and she longed that they should take into the world no memory of home that was not charged with happiness. But the family circle, which was the world of her heart, had been broken into by this blind inexplicable stroke, and fear of what the future might hold had entered.

Then there were other hours when solitude and prayer alone could assuage her heartsickness. Early morning was the worst time, when she lay awake waiting for the winter dawn to brighten and the stir of life to begin, knowing that her two small boys could never come romping in and tumble about on her bed, or play hide-and-seek in the corners of the room.

Throughout the year following Frittie's death her letters to the Queen were not less frequent, but the effervescent quality in them died out. They were no longer the sunny vehicles of her own news, nor the sparkling response of the eager writer ; some deepening twilight lay over them. . . . Her mother, evidently with the thought in her mind of the only daughter who now remained unmarried and living with her, wrote about the mistake parents made in bringing their girls up with the thought of marriage only as their future. Alice agreed : she was bringing up her girls not to think of marriage as a thing to be sought : it was but natural and dutiful of a daughter to remain with her parents as long as she was wanted : or she was pleased to hear of her brother Alfred's marriage to so charming a girl as the Grand Duchess Marie, daughter of Tsar Alexander II ; or Louis was reading to her a History of the Indian Mutiny ; or she thanked her mother for sending her a cheque to help her to buy the baby-clothes for the child she was expecting. But she wrote as if these concerns of the outer world were dream-stuff, and her yearning for Frittie, the grief that she loved because it seemed to be part of him were more real to her than they. Ernie missed his brother terribly : he constantly spoke of him. " When I die," he said, " you must die too, and all the others : why can't we all die together ? I don't like to die alone, like Frittie." How that went home to her : it was as if her own heart was crying out through the boy's lips, for it was this remaining behind that was so cruel, not the going away. Or Ernie said to her " Mama, I had a beautiful dream : shall I tell you ? I dreamed that I was dead, and was gone up to Heaven, and there I asked God to let me have Frittie again ; and he came to me and took my hand. You were in bed, and saw a great light, and were so frightened, and I said, ' It is Ernie and Frittie.' You were so astonished. The next night Frittie and I went with a great light to sisters."[1] . . . Yet Ernie was not a boy of morbid fancies, his days were full of fun and robust activity, even as were his mother's of her works of reform and charity. These had to be attended to still, but there was this dream-world, this real world interpenetrating them, and stirring in them as an invisible breeze from the night outside stirs the curtains drawn across the open window. She wondered how long it would be before she herself slipped away into the darkness, and the thought of that hour, perhaps not very far distant,

[1] *Ibid.*, pp. 277, 293.

became familiar to her and unfeared, part of her consciousness. But meantime the duties of life and the calls of love must be answered. " Happy those," she wrote to her mother, " who can lie down to rest having fought their battle well ; or those who have been spared fighting it at all. . . ."

Princess Louis's seventh and youngest child, a daughter, was born on May 24, 1874, the anniversary of the Queen's birthday, and just a year after Frittie's death. Her mother did not wish her to nurse her baby herself, but Princess Louis told her that it was safer to do so. She had no farm in the country which could supply her with fresh cows' milk : besides, in this broiling weather milk would not keep and young babies often got dysentery from being fed with it. She would have liked to go to Scheveningen next month for sea-air and bathing, for she and the children were run down with this heat, but it was too expensive, and they went to Blankenberghe : a single sitting-room served for dining-room and for her husband's dressing-room. Though the bracing air did her good her letters still yearned and wept for Frittie, and her mother in reply to one of these must have advised her to get her nerves in better control, for she answered that it was not her fault that she had that emotional temperament which caused these miseries. She was doing her best to control what she could not alter ; otherwise she would be in a dreadful state. Then there came further criticism about her management of her children, and again she felt this to be unjust. She told her mother that she was not one of those tiresome women who made themselves a nuisance with perpetual baby-worship. Certainly her brothers and sisters had their children less constantly with them than she, but they could afford a staff of trustworthy tutors and governesses. Her motherhood had to be, as in poorer families, of a more companionable kind, and it entailed a good deal of self-denial in other ways.[1]

The first volume of Mr. Theodore Martin's *Life of the Prince Consort* appeared this winter on the thirteenth anniversary of his death. It was the sequel to General Grey's *Early Years of the Prince Consort*, and the Queen had supplied the author with the letters and memoranda on which it was based. By modern standards of biography (whether right or wrong) this substantial volume, the first of five, carried idealism to a point where all impressions of individual portraiture vanish : the Prince appeared to be exempt from any touch of the weaknesses and imperfections otherwise common to humanity ; and whereas now the lapse of so many years since his death would have caused the subject to seem out of date, it was then widely felt that the publication was premature. Princess Louis had received an advance copy from the Queen, and she wrote to her that she found the book interesting, that she was satisfied, that Mr. Martin had done his difficult task feelingly and delicately, that the volume was to her " inexpressibly precious and opens a field for thought in various senses," that " it was touching and fine of

[1] *Ibid.*, pp. 282, 283.

you to allow the world to have so much insight into your private life, and to allow others to have what has been only *your* property and our inheritance." Though the Queen's first selection of *Leaves from the Journal of a Life in the Highlands* had undoubtedly admitted the public to a far greater intimacy into her private life, and though Princess Louis, according to her wont, seized on all possible points for praise, she must also have expressed her regret that the book had been published so soon, for she received a very decided letter to put her right about that:

"DEAREST ALICE,

"Now as regards the book. If you will reflect a few minutes, you will see how I owed it to beloved Papa to let his noble character be known and understood, as it now is, and that to wait longer, when those who knew him best—his own wife, and a few (very few there are) remaining friends—were all gone, or too old or too far removed from that time, to present a really true picture of his most ideal and remarkable character, would have been really wrong.

"He must be known for his own sake, for the good of England and of his family, and of the world at large. . . . And it is already thirteen years since he left us!

"Then you must remember that endless false and untrue things have been written and said about us, public and private, and that in these days people will write and will know; therefore the only way to counteract this is to let the real full truth be known, and as much be told as can be told with prudence and discretion, and then no harm, but good, will be done. Nothing will help me more than that my people should see what I have lost. Numbers of people we knew have had their Lives and Memoirs published, and some beautiful ones : Bunsen's by his wife ; Lord Elgin's by his (very touching and interesting) ; Lord Palmerston's, etc., etc. . . . He [Mr. Theodore Martin] has taken seven years to prepare the whole, supplied by me with every letter and extract ; and a deal of time it took, but I felt it would be a national sacred work. You must, I think, see I am right now ; Papa and I too would have suffered otherwise. I think even the German side of his character will be understood. . . ."[1]

In consequence of the Queen's distaste for long visits from her daughters abroad, Princess Louis had been invited to England of late years less frequently and for shorter periods, but after each there poured out the old spring of tenderest love and gratitude, of the inexpressible joy of having seen her again. Evidently the Queen did not realize that her daughter's health and vital force were ebbing, for before one of these visits Princess Louis warned her how weak she was, and that till the fine air and the quiet of Balmoral restored her, she would be up to very little. She hoped that her mother would not mind her not coming down to dinner at first, for she knew that the Queen disliked any signs of invalidism in her house, and expected people to come down to dinner in spite of their feeling rather poorly. She went alone without either her husband or her children, and she had to break the long journey at Edinburgh. She wrote to Balmoral from there, saying, with a touch of the old thrilled interest in small happenings, how the people in the house

[1] *Ibid.*, pp. 287, 288.

in which she was lodging sent up to know to what church she was going on this Sunday morning, so perhaps she had better go somewhere. But she would see her beloved mother in a day or two, and their meeting would be steeped in that dear love and in the treasured memories of her father which lived on undimmed, though so much of the present seemed to belong to the past. And she was sorry that she was giving so much trouble.

She felt refreshed by her stay at Balmoral, and on her return there was the usual jubilation, the children " eat her up," and when their bedtime came she had to hear all six of them say their prayers and their hymns, and each had secrets to tell her. They were well : Alicky was growing very handsome, and May, the youngest, was enchanting. Then a fresh phase of life with new responsibilities and burdens opened for her and her husband. In the spring of 1877, Louis's father, Prince Charles, died after a short illness, three months later the Grand Duke of Hesse died also, and Louis succeeded his uncle.

There was an overwhelming press of public functions and of business. She was quite unequal to it, and her doctor insisted that she should get away from it all and rest. Louis could not come with her immediately, and she took the children to a remote seaside village on the French coast near Trouville, leaving her husband to follow. The house was very small for such a party, but the place suited her ; it was real country, she bathed in the sea and the absolute quiet did something to arrest the sapping decline of her strength. Then back to Darmstadt, where she and Louis had a tremendous public welcome, and once more she took up her work, with all the duties that her new position entailed. But she was always tired, for she always overtaxed herself; and she hoped that her mother would understand the brevity and infrequency of her letters, for after the day's work was over the fatigue of writing was too much for her. Her doctor forbade her to go to the wedding of her niece, Princess Charlotte of Prussia, and her sister in Berlin was very anxious about her, for she had grown very frail, though that seemed but to enhance her charm and her grace. And always this infinite sadness enveloped her.

She came to England once more in the summer of 1878 with her husband and her children, and spent a month at Eastbourne. Then rest came to that gallant and weary spirit, though preceded by weeks of intolerable grief and anxiety. One morning in November Victoria, the eldest of the six children, fell ill of diphtheria, and four days afterwards Alix was down with it. Early that day the youngest, May, came romping into her room before she got up, as Ernie and Frittie had been used to do, the picture of health and childish high spirits, but when her mother came back a few hours later from her morning's work, it was to find that May had developed the disease in a most virulent form. Next day Irene and Ernie caught it, and now there were five children out of six with diphtheria, and May and Irene were desperately ill. The day after her husband was down with it also, and that night May died. Louis kept asking about the children, and Alice went to tell him.

Ernie's life still hung by a thread, but he began to mend, and he, too, asked after his sisters. One morning he asked his mother to give May a book as a present from him. He could not yet be told that May was dead, and in a reckless impulse of pity for him at the thought of what he must soon know, she kissed him. . . . Sometimes the whole of life seemed to be an agonized dream, sometimes she woke to reality, and then the agony was over, for she consciously accepted the will of God and in His will was peace ; through that complete resignation she could feel gratitude that the others had been spared.

A month passed since the first of her children had been taken ill, and now her husband and those who were left were able to go out again, and she was making arrangements for them to get away for a change of air. All one day she had a very bad headache, and next morning diphtheria developed. At first she felt sure she would never recover, and, not being allowed to speak, she wrote down little messages and directions for her husband. The case was almost hopeless, for the attack was very virulent, and she had no strength with which to fight it, but, as its deadly and most painful inroads progressed she began to think that, after all, she would pull through. Then came a morning when the doctors realized that the end was near, and her husband was told. She was quite conscious, she enjoyed a visit from her mother-in-law, and in the afternoon the Queen's doctor, Sir William Jenner, arrived from England with a letter from her mother, which she read. Her husband came in to wish her good night as usual, and, when he had left her, she said she would go to sleep again. She whispered to herself: " May—dear Papa." She died in her sleep early next morning on the anniversary of her father's death.[1]

NOTE.—Soon after the death of the Grand Duchess a subscription was started at Eastbourne for the foundation of a cottage hospital there in memory of her sympathy with local charitable institutions and of the help she gave them. The " Princess Alice Hospital " was opened by the Prince of Wales in 1883, and has now 120 beds.

[1] *Ibid.*, pp. 51, 52, 309-315.

CHAPTER VI

THE peace of Versailles in 1871 had left Germany satiated with territory, and Bismarck was her dictator. From the beginning of Prussian expansion after the Austrian War the Queen had been bitterly disappointed with the Emperor William's acquiescence in his ruthless policies and she wrote to her daughter comparing the appropriation of the German states with the seizures made in the unification of Italy:

> "To me he [King Victor Emmanuel] has never been the same since he undermined his own uncle's kingdom, and took that, as well as other people's near relations of his own; and it used to be my pride and dear Papa's, to be able to say that your excellent father-in-law never would let himself become a tool of Bismarck's ambition, as the King of Italy had been of Cavour's. Alas! I can say that no longer, and '66 destroyed that bright difference. This does not mean that the uniting of Germany was not right, or not wished for by me and dear Papa. We both earnestly wished for that, for one head, one army, and one diplomacy, but not for dethroning other Princes, and taking their private property and palaces—no, that was and is a grave mistake. And I could never live in these palaces if I was the Emperor or you."[1]

The Crown Princess had already told her mother

[1] *Letters of Queen Victoria*, II, ii, p. 283.

that the smaller German States deserved the punishment that had been inflicted on them for siding with Austria, and that she must keep her sympathy with her relations apart from political exigencies in Germany (which were difficult to explain to anyone except a Prussian) : now she announced that some of these so-called confiscations were in reality purchases of a liberal kind :

" Palaces," she wrote, " my father-in-law never *took* ; he PAID for them and they are legally *his*, and those who sold them had far the *best* of the bargain. We never should have put our foot into a place about which there was the slightest doubt. *Those* in which we *have* been we had as much right to inhabit as you to wear the Kohinoor or place the Indian arms in the Armoury at Windsor. The *Entwickelung* of Germany has *not* taken place in the way I fondly hoped it would, and there are *many* measures which I *cannot* admire or approve of—but I firmly believe that what has been done has been done for the good of Germany and of Europe, as I *also* believe that the unity of Italy is a good and wholesome thing ! Annexations are cruel and painful things and it is most distressing when relations have to take up arms against each other ! The right of conquest is a very hard one.

" *I* am more attached to the cause of liberty and progress than to any other, and I do believe that the events of '66 and '70-'71 are a step in that direction, in SPITE of those who brought them about."[1]

This letter contains admirable instances of a certain lack of logic which sometimes marked the Princess's mental processes. Her father-in-law, she maintained,

[1] *Ibid.*, II, ii, p. 284.

had paid a generous price for the palaces of small German states, and yet they were his by such just right of conquest as had brought the spoils of war to Windsor. She maintained also that the Austrian war which had enabled Germany to grab both the Duchies, one of which had been assigned to Austria by treaty, and that the war with France, which had brought to the German Empire an even more substantial acquisition of territory, were conducive to the cause of liberty and progress. At the same time she deplored the means by which this cause had been so strikingly served. But how else, except by blood and iron, could these blessed results have been obtained? It was hardly likely that Denmark would have surrendered the Duchies or that France would have given up her provinces and paid a huge indemnity for the altruistic privilege of advancing German liberty and progress. The evil tree was bringing forth good fruit, and Germany was gathering grapes of thorns and figs of thistles. Yet immediately afterwards she was telling her mother what a barbarian Bismarck was: he knew little of foreign countries and nothing of England. He was altogether mediæval and the true theories of liberty were Hebrew to him, while simultaneously his mediævalism was working for the causes of which he knew nothing.[1]

The impetuosity of her mind and her over-ready tongue were a grievous handicap to her. The British Press continued to manifest the greatest unfriendliness to Germany, and she could not resist, as she more

[1] Ponsonby, *Letters of Empress Frederick*, p. 139.

THE EMPRESS FREDERICK

from the painting by Heinrich von Angeli

than once acknowledged, replying sharply to any remarks disparaging to England, but her justifications of England, so far from allaying the German rancour against her native country, merely increased the ill-will against the *Engälnderin* who so vigorously championed it. Nor was she yet even beginning to understand that Germany resented any woman, especially a woman in her position, expressing her political views. The Crown Prince shared them, and he had the same love for England and English principles of Government as she, but he was discreet and got on reasonably well with Bismarck, whereas she continually irritated him. Without ceasing to regard her as negligible, he grew thoroughly to dislike her, and lost no casual opportunity of aiding her in rendering her position difficult. Unfortunately, as she recognized herself, Bismarck was omnipotent, and she wrote to the Queen : " I wonder why he does not say straight out, ' As long as I live both the constitution and the Crown are suspended,' because that is the exact state of the matter."

The political complications set up by the revolt of the Balkan provinces, Bosnia, Herzegovina and Servia, from Turkey, and Turkey's declaration of war on them, gave the Crown Princess ample opportunity for advising the Queen on the part that England ought to play. It must be confessed that these extempore exhortations, so vividly expressed, are very bewildering to follow. Brilliant ideas came into her head, and she dashed them off to her mother, confident that each in turn contained the solution to the situation which the Chanceries of Europe found so desperately involved.

The Prince of Wales had once said that in intercourse with Germans his sister was strongly English, and when addressing herself to the English she was strongly German. These letters of hers about the Eastern question show the truth of that observation, and occasionally they caused the Queen great astonishment. The Crown Princess became Bismarckian, and England could do nothing right. At the outset, she maintained, Bismarck would have been only too happy for England to have settled the whole question instead of letting Russia step in and support the Slavs, but now, owing to the hesitancy of England, Russia had the *beau rôle* of championing the Christians against the unspeakable Turks. She grew more Bismarckian yet. She had heard that Bismarck had said that while Russia was advancing on Constantinople, England " ought " to take Egypt, and she hastened to press that singularly typical counsel on the Queen. All lovers of England were agreed that this would be the wisest thing she could do, and nobody could understand why she did not seize this excellent opportunity while Turkey was in such straits. Not only would it immensely strengthen England's position in the East, but it would confer untold benefits on that downtrodden country. Under English rule Egypt would be liberally governed, its trade and commerce would increase, the agriculture of its most fertile soil would be developed. England, in fact, had a great mission in Egypt, and it would be delightful to see it accomplished in the Queen's reign. She was sure that

Bismarck had no other *arrière pensée* in suggesting this, but that he sincerely believed that a strong England would be most useful in Europe. It was most satisfactory that he did so.

It seems strange that the Crown Princess did not know that Bismarck had already made the same suggestion to Lord Salisbury, now British Foreign Minister, and to the British Ambassador in Berlin, or that she did not suspect, from her habitual distrust of him, any *arrière pensée* in Bismarck's benevolence. France, as he certainly foresaw, would have violently opposed (as she subsequently did when the British Expedition for the recovery of the Sudan took place) any extension of British influence there, and to cause dissension between any two Powers was the chief dogma in his political creed, for thereby their possible combination against Germany would be rendered less likely. But she missed that, and the Queen's reply to her letter, containing a severe allusion to Prussian grabbings, supplied the necessary information on that point :

" DEAREST CHILD . . . I will now answer your letter of the 11th (July, 1877) relative to Egypt, the proposal about which *coming from you* has indeed surprised me very much, and seems to be Bismarck's view. Neither *Turkey* or *Egypt* have done *anything* to *offend us*. Why should we make a *wanton* aggression such as the taking of Egypt would be ? It is not *our* custom to annex countries (as it is in *some others*) unless we are obliged and forced to do so, as in the case of the Transvaal Republic. Prince Bismarck would probably like us to seize Egypt as it would be a great slap in the face of

France, and be taking a mean advantage of her inability to protest. It would be a most *greedy* action. I own I can't for a moment understand *your* suggesting it. What *we intend* to do we shall do *without* Prince Bismarck's permission, for he has repeatedly mentioned it to Lord Odo Russell. . . . How can *we* protest against *Russia's* doings, if we do the same ourselves?"[1]

When the Queen wrote in that style, the recipient (with the invariable exception of Mr. Gladstone) experienced a sinking feeling, and those who knew her best sank deepest. This was the effect on the Crown Princess; the mixture of Mamma and Her Majesty, of personality and prestige, produced the desired descent. She hastened to explain that when she said that England in Bismarck's and her opinion " ought " to take Egypt she only meant that she hoped Egypt would soon be " ours." She did not mean that England ought to annex Egypt, but that her influence ought to be " virtually " paramount there, though how and when this should be done was " quite another thing," and about that she had no further suggestion to offer.[2]

During the autumn months the Russian armies marching on Constantinople were held up by the siege of Plevna, but when Plevna fell the way was open. In these five months the Crown Princess recovered her nerve and reversed her policy, no longer exhorting her mother to take Egypt, and thus despoil the Turks of their most important suzerainty, but to support them against Russia by every means in

[1] *Letters of Queen Victoria*, II, ii, pp. 549-550.
[2] Ponsonby, *Letters of Empress Frederick*, pp. 152, 153.

England's power. She longed for " one good roar of the British Lion from the housetops, and for the thunder of a British broadside ! " She tried to rouse the Queen to a sense of " our " duty, by telling her how contemptible England was making herself abroad by her inaction : there was a strong feeling that she was really quite powerless, that she had no army and no statesmen, that her fleet was useless, and that all she cared for was to make money, which, it may be remembered, was the reason the Crown Princess assigned to her neutrality in the Franco-German war. She exhorted her mother to take a worthier view of our responsibilities : " Are not *dignity*, honour and one's reputation things for which a nation like an individual must be ready to sacrifice *ease*, wealth, and even blood and life itself ? " Let England therefore instantly threaten Russia with war if she continued her advance on Constantinople : surely she could bring enough troops from India alone to defeat all the armies of Russia. If she even allowed Russia and Turkey to make peace without consulting her, it would be a fatal blow to English prestige, especially in India, where " eighty millions of fighting *men* " would scorn her European insignificance. A careful study of continental conditions and politics had produced in her " the firm conviction that *England* is *far* in advance of all other countries in the whole scale of civilization and progress, the only one that understands Liberty and *possesses* Liberty, and above all the only *really humane country*." She was " a country vastly superior to all others in every sense " ;[1]

[1] *Ibid.*, p. 156.

though only lately Prussia was superior to all the world in " intelligence, humanity, education and kindheartedness." And the Crown Princess strenuously denied that, as the Queen had written to her, Bismarck wanted to see all the Powers quarrelling with each other. In refutation of such a view she assured her that the last thing in the world that Bismarck wanted was that Germany should quarrel with Russia. But that, though undoubtedly true, was no refutation at all. Once again, as when Bismarck was in favour of England annexing Egypt, she had missed the point of his policy. Nothing was further from his thoughts than that Germany should quarrel with Russia, but nothing was nearer to his heart than to see other Powers quarrelling with each other.

It is impossible not to admire the vigour and enthusiasm of these counsels. The Crown Princess, as she herself acknowledged, was in a " perpetually pugilistic frame of mind " and found it almost more than she could bear to have to listen to criticism of England without the satisfaction of knocking somebody down. She swept all difficulties aside, she scarcely admitted that any existed. The Queen, on this occasion, was entirely with her on the main point, and did not need the goad of those stinging warnings that Europe believed England to be decadent and powerless and intent only on making money. The only difference between her and her impetuous counsellor was that she, in her more responsible position, had to reckon with these difficulties. No one was more alive to the importance of stopping Russia's advance, and incessantly she harried Lord Beaconsfield on the subject, insisting that the Tsar must be told that England " will not *allow* her to go to Constantinople, and that that would be a *casus belli*." Something must be done at once, or England would be too late, and Russia would " crow over " her. But it was her Government, not she, who were undecided : Lord Derby and Lord Carnarvon were against supporting Turkey, and Gladstone had emerged from his retirement and swept over England in a hurricane campaign in which he hailed Russia as a Crusader dedicating herself to defend the Christian peoples of these provinces against the appalling persecution of the Moslem tyrant : Turkey must be turned out of Europe " bag and baggage." Lord Beaconsfield dismissed this movement as a " sentimental eccentricity " and " coffee-house babble," but it could not be disposed of by a phrase, however elegantly contemptuous, and the whole country, as well as the Cabinet, was deeply divided.

Gladstone's campaign had a disagreeable reaction on the relations between the Queen and her connections by marriage, for one of his most fervent supporters was Princess Louise's father-in-law, the Duke of Argyll, who had been a member of the late Government, and the Queen felt obliged to express herself quite clearly about his conduct. She told Princess Louise (who personally thought that Gladstone was out of his mind) that this campaign had done untold mischief in encouraging all Europe to believe that England would never bring herself to make a stand against Russia's arrogance, and continued: "And I can't overlook the way in which those who hold the language (from which I am sorry to say I can't exempt your father-in-law) have *played* the honour and interests of this country into the hands of Russia. . . . To me it is, I must say, utterly inexplicable and totally at variance with usage, for statesmen who have been in high office and who have *known* all the difficulties and anxieties of Government to behave as they have done."

Possibly these firm statements were not conveyed to the Duke. At any rate he did not mend his ways, and the Queen wrote to him direct:

"I do not wish or intend to touch on politics, but I *cannot* conclude without a few words of *earnest* warning. Though you may refuse to believe statements made by official people, you will not refuse to believe *mine*: I wish therefore to state *solemnly*, that I know that this war and the fearful consequences which it may have, might, and it is my firm conviction *would* have been *prevented*, had Russia not been *encouraged* in the strongest manner by the extraordinary, and, to me, *utterly* incomprehensible agitation carried on by some Members, and especially by one of my late Government, to believe that she could do what she liked without meeting with opposition. I know this to be true! Let me add that it is not too late now to act a patriotic part and to desist from so lamentable a course."[1]

It was a disagreeable situation. Only the autumn before the Queen had spent a week at Inverary as

[1] *Letters of Queen Victoria*, II, ii, pp. 498, 538.

the guest of the Duke's, and little had she thought that within a few months it would be her painful duty to address her host in such terms. But she had no such complaints against her son-in-law, and when next year Lord Beaconsfield consulted her about appointing Lord Lorne Governor General of Canada she sanctioned the offer being made, though she wished it to come from the Prime Minister and not direct from herself. Possibly Princess Louise would not like to be away from England for five years, and that was a long parting for herself as well, but it would be a great distinction for him and a " fine independent position " for her. Lord Lorne asked for time to consider it and to get his wife's views and then accepted it. . . . He related a curious story that before he had any inkling of what was coming he had a clairvoyant vision of an interview taking place between Lord Beaconsfield and himself which was fulfilled down to small details when the actual interview took place.

The Queen had thus two daughters left her in England, Princess Christian, now the mother of four children, and her inseparable companion Princess Beatrice, who led the same withdrawn life as her mother. Of all the Queen's daughters Princess Christian was the best-known and the busiest. She was not of the intellectual brilliance of her eldest sister, but she had a genius for geniality and kindliness. Like her sister Alice she supported a hundred charitable and industrial institutions and presided at their committees with incomparable tact and authority : and it was as if there was nothing in the world that she enjoyed more than to open bazaars and exhibitions of needlework and to visit hospitals. She and the Princess of Wales made a new profession for Royal ladies out of such functions and activities; constant journeys and work and withal a beaming demeanour were necessary, and their daughters and nieces were brought up in that tradition. There had never been anything like it before : with what incredulous dismay would the last adult Royal Family, daughters and daughters-in-law of George III have seen a list of the yearly engagements voluntarily undertaken by a succeeding generation !

As the years went on the Queen's relations with her daughters spread to their growing families, and her grandchildren in Germany from their early years were made reverentially aware through their mothers of that shrouded but august figure whose wishes must always be consulted in everything that concerned them. For the Crown Princess's eldest son, Prince William, his grandmother had always had a special tenderness, and William's character, as he developed through boyhood into manhood towards his imperial destiny, would certainly become of the greatest moment to Europe in the future. The Crown Princess told the Queen that the Emperor's influence over him was very hurtful; the most poignant memories of William's childhood were the triumphant re-entries into Berlin of German armies after three swiftly successful wars, and his grandfather encouraged him to look on the attainment of military glory as the noblest of human ambitions. To counteract this the Crown Princess had hatched a scheme with the boy's tutor that, after his confirmation at the age of fifteen, he and his brother Henry should spend three years at the grammar school at Cassel, where, far away from the pageantry of Berlin, they would steep themselves in culture and scholarship. No doubt the system of education devised by the Prince Consort for the Prince of Wales, who was sent to Oxford and Cambridge for three years, was in her mind; and this therefore was a proper training for the heir to a throne. But it was a most unusual course of education for Princes of the House of Hohenzollern, there was much opposition in the family, and William himself greatly disliked the idea of having to compete with other boys on equal terms and perhaps " come out lower on the list." But his mother got her way and for these three years, till William came officially of age on his eighteenth birthday, he was a school-boy. The Queen had intended to make him a Grand Commander of the Bath on this occasion, but the Crown Princess persuaded her to give him the Garter, which William also thought more suitable. Then his military education began, and for two years he was with his regiment.

In 1878 the Crown Princess's eldest daughter, Charlotte, was married to Prince Bernhard of Saxe-Meiningen, heir to the Duchy. Her mother thought she seemed very unconcerned at leaving her home, but for her it was a bitter wrench to part with a child whom she had brought with anguish into the world, and now must resign to another. Then there came further bereavements, for in the winter her sister Alice, to whom, in spite of certain misunderstandings, she was devotedly attached, died of diphtheria, and in the following spring she lost her youngest son Waldemar, at the age of ten. Like his cousin Frittie, he had been from birth extremely delicate, and he died of hæmophilia. A couple of months afterwards Princess Charlotte gave birth to a daughter, and the Queen at the age of sixty became a great-grandmother.

Prince William's return from his military training marked the end of his loving relations with his father and mother which had been so great a happiness to them both, and for her it was the opening of the domestic tragedy that ended only with her death. He came back soaked through and through with militarism and highly contemptuous of his parents' liberal principles. Intellectually he resembled his mother in many points, he had her quickness of perception, her decisiveness, her impetuosity, and her combativeness. These similarities between them were of the quality which rouses disagreement rather than harmony, for they were instinctively disposed to differ and both were disputatious: their very points in common sundered them. In character they were poles apart, for nothing was more foreign to her than his arrogance once assumed as a cloak for his sense of inferiority but now grown aggressive. It provoked from her sharp rebukes which might have been better left unuttered, for they only stung him to retort. He was a man now, and it could hardly be expected that he should receive with a child's submissive silence reprimands, however well deserved.

His father distrusted him as profoundly as he trusted his wife, and the domestic circle was an arena of incessant wrangles. Then, without consulting either his parents or his grandparents, Prince William engaged himself in 1880 to Princess Augusta Victoria of Schleswig-Holstein-Sonderburg-Augustenburg, daughter of Duke Frederick, whose claims to the Duchy of Holstein had once been so strongly upheld by the Crown Princess ; Princess Augusta was also the grand-daughter of the Queen's half-sister Feodore who had shared her unhappy childhood at Kensington. The Crown Princess sent the news to her mother before the engagement was announced, and the Queen, since this came within the jurisdiction of her matriarchate, as greatly concerning the welfare of a grandson and of a great-niece, at once invited the prospective bride to Windsor to be inspected. Princess Augusta had not seen her future parents-in-law since her engagement, but this summons to England took precedence of all other calls. Fortunately the Queen approved of her : she found her " gentle and amiable and sweet." Such qualities were more likely to be of value to her than mental brilliance, which Dona decidedly lacked, for ability was a handicap rather than an asset in one who would be Empress of Germany. The Crown Princess also liked her for the same qualities as the Queen : " her smile and her manners and expression " she wrote " must disarm even the bristly, thorny people of Berlin with their sharp tongues, their cutting sarcasm about everybody and everything." Bitter memories of her own troubles when she herself came as a bride to Berlin at so early an age were in her mind, and she thought Dona lucky in being twenty-two, not seventeen, when she entered those censorious circles. As for William, she was sorry that he had not seen more of the world before he settled down, but he had no taste for travelling, and never looked at a guide-book nor appreciated the beauties of Art and Nature, so where was the use? In view of William's subsequent developments that was not a very discerning criticism, for presently he was to be known as the Reise-Kaiser, and he composed music and painted (or at least designed) large rancid allegorical cartoons and excavated Greek antiquities. But it is easy to understand her depreciation, for he made a point of disagreeing with his mother, and it was sufficient for her to invoke his admiration for a masterpiece of Art or a panorama of fine scenery, or to claim his interest in some historical monument, to ensure his indifference. . . . The night before his wedding she mourned over the thought that he would never sleep under his parents' roof again : she was inconveniently soft-hearted, she told her mother, and William thought her absurdly sentimental, for what did it matter where he slept? But her regrets were more for the vanished love and confidence which had once existed between him and herself and for the years in which bitter seed had been sown, than for the fact that her eldest son had a wife and an establishment of his own.[1]

[1] Ponsonby, *Letters of Empress Frederick*, pp. 179, 183.

The Congress of Berlin in 1878, had not, as had been hoped, settled the Eastern question. Bulgaria had been declared an independent state under the suzerainty of the Sultan, and Prince Alexander of Battenberg, first cousin of the Grand Duke Louis of Hesse, whom Russia had put forward as her candidate for the throne, had been made Prince of the new realm. The Sultan had promised protection to his Christian subjects and general internal reforms, but he was not carrying out any of these obligations, nor had he made those rectifications of frontiers to which he had agreed. A Conference of Powers was summoned at London two years later in order to convince the Sultan that he must do as he was told, and the Crown Princess again warned her mother that energetic and immediate action must be taken, and that England must do her duty without delay. It was Russia, she told her, who was now encouraging the Turks to defy the decrees of Europe with the intention of dismembering Turkey and getting Constantinople for herself. The only Power again that could prevent this was England, who must instantly —in a few weeks it would be too late—send her fleet into the Dardanelles ; otherwise " torpedoes " (mines ?) would be placed in the Straits. Turkey had been given every chance of establishing a firm and reformed system of Government but she was incapable of it and she could not be allowed—even her best friends admitted it—to remain a Power in Europe any more. She must be turned out " bag and baggage," even as Gladstone had demanded, but most emphatically not through the agency of a

Christian Crusading Russia. England must commit this "*douce violence*" of occupying the Golden Horn with her ships, must make a military convention with the Sultan, and put Mr. Goschen in charge of Turkish Finance : the Sultan himself could go to live at Smyrna. This was the only way to prevent war, and she trusted that " there may be enough *energy* and *decision* at the (English) Foreign Office to *take* the right step and *not* to wait or hesitate." She felt sure that the other Powers would support this programme.

She sketched the happy result of this astonishing gesture. An independent State would develop out of the British occupation, and it would need a Sovereign. There was no one more suitable than one of her brothers. Perhaps the Duke of Edinburgh would not be available as he would one day be Duke of Coburg, but the Duke of Connaught would be very proper, or her youngest brother Prince Leopold. If not, there was the Duke of Genoa, or Prince Waldemar of Denmark, or other German Princes. That could be considered later, but just now time was precious : " Not another *moment* should be lost and a bold *coup* made. The details of *how*, I am sure there are clever heads in the Cabinet enough to make out ! "[1] But the requisite energy and decision were lacking in the English Cabinet : they were not clever enough to see how to substitute for Turkey in Europe this new England in Turkey. Bismarck might not have been sorry to see England attempt it, for that would surely have involved her in trouble

[1] *Ibid.*, pp. 189, 190.

with Russia. But the expression of such views in Berlin could only have the most disastrous consequences for the Crown Princess. Bismarck's distrust of her, knowing as he did her influence over her husband, became active rather than contemptuously passive and he introduced into their official household as Court Marshal to the Crown Prince Count Radolin-Radolinsky whose business was to counteract her influence with her husband and act as a spy upon her.

An even more useful instrument to Bismarck's hand was Prince William, now an independent married man, who despised the Liberal views of his parents and detested their English leanings. Bismarck made much of him and influenced the Emperor, now growing very old, to employ him on missions which should properly have fallen to the Crown Prince. He sent him to Russia for the official coming of age of the Tsarevitch Nicholas and William told the Tsar that the Prince of Wales and the Queen and his mother were doing their best to induce Germany to ally herself with England against Russia, but that these conspirators had forgotten about the existence of Prince William of Prussia. He solemnly promised to look after the Tsar's interests. Then there was a meeting between the Emperors of Germany and Austria at Gastein, for the restoration of imperial and national cordiality, and it was William who attended his grandfather. Immediately afterwards the Tsar was holding a Military Review at Brest-Litovsk and once more William was sent to represent the Emperor. His mother was horrified at the thought of the mischief he might make. She wrote to the Queen : " William is as blind and green, wrong-headed and violent in politics as can be." William was charged to tell the Tsar that, if he chose to take Constantinople, Germany would make no protest, but that was not well received : the Tsar answered that if he wished to do so, he would not ask Prince Bismarck's leave. Just so, some years before, Bismarck had said that he would allow England to take Egypt, and had received precisely the same reply. His object then was to brew trouble between England and France : now, to brew trouble between England and Russia. Finally Bismarck asked the Emperor to let Wiiliam work under him in the Foreign Office. The Emperor, with a gibe at the Crown Prince and his wife, at once consented, in order that William's " young soul may be guarded against errors," such errors, of course, being the Liberal heresies of his father and mother. The Empress Augusta, now coldly hostile to them both, approved.

Bismarck gave notice of this intention to the Crown Prince, who formally protested in terms practically identical with his wife's criticisms of William to the Queen : " In view of the immaturity as well as the inexperience of my eldest son together with his tendency to overbearingness and conceit, I cannot but frankly regard it as dangerous to allow him at present to take part in foreign affairs."[1] No doubt they believed it to be their duty to state in these emphatic terms their opinion of the appointment thus formally notified to them, but they must have

[1] Emil Ludwig, *Kaiser Wilhelm II*, p. 21.

known that their protest would be useless. Just so, with untoward consequences, the Crown Prince with his wife's support had protested against Bismarck's abolition of the freedom of the Press when it had received his father's assent. The same thing happened now. Bismarck replied that such was the Emperor's pleasure and showed William what his father had written about him.

There was no mistaking the intention of these missions and offices bestowed upon William. They were designed and deliberate obliterations of his father. The Crown Princess recognized them as such, and, as such, she resented them for her husband's sake. Such obliterations, now manifest for the first time were to prove, in the years to come, the chief source of her most bitter experiences.

CHAPTER VII

JOHN BROWN died at Windsor in the spring of 1883. It was perfectly natural and proper that the Queen should wish the world to know what this loss meant to her. Half a column of Court Circular appeared in the Press, describing the course of his illness and giving a summary of his life. He had become a gillie at Balmoral in 1849, he rose in 1858 to be the Queen's personal servant in Scotland, and in 1864 he became her personal attendant wherever she was. During the last eighteen and a half years he had never absented himself from duty for a single day. " He has accompanied the Queen in her daily walks and drives, and all her journeys and expeditions as well as personally waiting on her at banquets &c. . . . To Her Majesty the loss is irreparable, and the death of this truly devoted and faithful servant has been a grievous shock to the Queen."

At Osborne she put up to his memory a seat of solid Aberdeen granite, and at Balmoral a statue for which her Poet Laureate devised an inscription which, though just in sentiment, cannot rank among his finer lines.

Friend more than servant, loyal, truthful, brave :
Self less than duty ever to the grave.

She sent a photograph of him to the Empress

Augusta, promising that further ones should follow, and she dedicated to him *More Leaves from a Journal of a Life in the Highlands* which appeared the year after his death. Her grief for his loss was profound, and it can only add to our respect and sympathy for her that she expressed it with the simplicity and sincerity that were so characteristic of her. Not for many years had she suffered a bereavement which affected the trivialities of her daily life, which to her were matters of great moment, so intimately. She had a devoted family, but none of them ministered to her comfort and sense of security as he had done. In her " sad isolated position " which sometimes she found so intolerable, it was the companionship of a man, who treated her as he would have treated any other indulgent mistress, that she valued so highly. He understood that very well and had bridged, by means of that knowledge, the chasm that lay between her and the innumerable multitude of her subjects. Her friendship with Lord Beaconsfield who had died two years before had had a touch of the same personal intimacy. Deprived of the two who had done so much to restore her self-confidence she felt lonely again, for her youngest son, the Duke of Albany, had married and no longer lived with her, and like every other normal woman she missed the daily companionship of a man whom she trusted and relied upon. Once more she bethought herself of that arrangement, which years ago had seemed so essential for her comfort, of having with her a permanently resident son-in-law.

She had long taken a great interest in the family

of Battenberg, the handsome and charming sons of Prince Alexander of Hesse, uncle of the present Grand Duke Louis. Prince Alexander had morganatically married a Polish Countess, Julia Theresa von Hauke, who had been created Countess of Battenberg, a small Hessian district. Of his four sons the eldest, Prince Louis, had entered the British Navy as a midshipman in 1868, and, as a naturalised Englishman, had married Princess Victoria of Hesse, the eldest daughter of Princess Alice, and grand-daughter of the Queen. The second son Prince Alexander had in 1879 been elected Prince of the independent State of Bulgaria. He wanted to marry Princess Victoria of Prussia, the daughter of the Crown Princess, and though no formal betrothal had taken place, her parents were both in favour of the match, and so also was the Queen. The third son Prince Henry was yet unmarried, and the year after John Brown's death, he met Princess Beatrice at Darmstadt, where she had gone with her mother. The Queen looked with great approval on the mutual attraction of the two, and when he came to stay with his brother Louis in England for Christmas, he asked her permission, confident of obtaining it, to propose marriage. That was exactly what she had hoped; he was a charming young man, she felt for him just that affection which she had felt for Prince Louis when he came a-wooing Princess Alice, and he fulfilled all the required conditions. It is true that in the case of Princess Louise, thirteen years ago, she had strongly discountenanced a marriage with a penniless Prince of a small German House, partly because she no longer liked prolonged visits from daughters living abroad with their husbands and their foreign suites, partly because Parliament did not like granting dowries and annuities which would be spent out of England, but there were no such objections now involved. Prince Henry had no duties to perform in any Foreign Principality, he was content to make his permanent and only home with her, and the post of resident son-in-law would at last be perfectly filled. The Queen wrote in high satisfaction to the Duke of Grafton who knew what a devoted daughter Princess Beatrice had always been to her : " He can therefore understand that it would have been *quite out of the question* for her ever to have left the Queen ; and *she* would *never* have *wished* it herself, knowing well how *impossible* it was for her to leave her Mother. . . . Prince Henry of Battenberg is, however, ready to make England his home, and the Princess will continue with the Queen as heretofore. He is very amiable, very unassuming and sensible, and in addition very goodlooking."[1]

Two of the Battenberg brothers were therefore married, the younger to the Queen's youngest daughter, the other to her grand-daughter, Princess Victoria of Hesse, but there were political difficulties in the way of the marriage of Prince Alexander to this second German grand-daughter, Princess Victoria of Prussia. Bismarck came to hear of it and of the Queen's approval, and fixed on her as being the chief and the most formidable promoter. He saw in

[1] *Letters of Queen Victoria*, II, iii, p. 593.

it a deep-laid scheme of hers for alienating Russia and Germany. As he judged her by the principles that directed his own foreign policy that was no matter for wonder : it was strictly in accordance with what he himself would have done if he had been Queen of England. For Prince Alexander had made up his mind from the first that he would not, as Prince of Bulgaria, let himself be Russia's tool, and he had been very unwilling, after his appointment, to accept the Tsar's invitation to visit him at Livadia, for fear he should give the impression that he had gone there to get his instructions. Since then he had shown that he had no intention of letting Bulgaria become a mere province of Russia, and Bismarck argued that, if he was permitted to marry the daughter of the future German Emperor, Russia would consider that Germany approved and supported his independence. He at once got the Emperor William to refuse his consent to the match on these grounds. But he was afraid that the Queen, who was possibly coming to Berlin for her daughter's birthday, might manage it. " There would be the greatest danger," he said, with an elephantine jocosity that masked his genuine misgiving, " that she would get her way. In family matters she is not accustomed to contradiction and would immediately bring the parson with her in her travelling-bag and the bridegroom in her trunk and the marriage would come off at once." [1] Prince William, it is unnecessary to state, sided with his grandfather and Bismarck, and the most violent quarrel took place between him and

[1] Busch, *Bismarck*, III, p. 174.

his mother. But the Queen did not come to Berlin, and next year (1886) Prince Alexander was kidnapped in Sofia by Russian officers and forced to abdicate. He went back to his home at Darmstadt, and there for the present the question of his marriage stayed, to be raised again two years afterwards in tragic circumstances.

The Emperor William was in his ninetieth year: his son was a very healthy man in the middle fifties. It looked as if his succession could not be far off, and he might reasonably expect a reign of fifteen or twenty years, during which Germany would be freed from the oppression of Bismarck and led, like the enslaved Israelites, into the Promised Land, surveyed as from Pisgah, by the Prince Consort. Before William succeeded, it might be hoped that he would learn discretion and wisdom, and at any rate he would for this period be powerless. At present, in Imperial affairs his parents counted for nothing: it was as if William, bitterly opposed to them, and backed up by Bismarck and his grandfather, stood next the throne.

In the winter of 1886-1887 the Crown Prince suffered from a very obstinate sore throat and loss of voice. Various remedies were tried without success, and there appeared on one of his vocal cords a growth which the German doctors feared was malignant. They advised an operation for its removal, but wished first to call in some foreign specialist for consultation, and unanimously decided on Dr. Morell Mackenzie, who at once went out from London to Berlin. He insisted that Professor Virchow, the most eminent pathologist in Europe, should examine fragments removed from this growth, and on his diagnosis that they showed no signs of cancerous structure, it was decided that Mackenzie should treat the Prince at his clinic in England, where he and his wife and Prince William were invited to attend the Queen's Jubilee in June. They would thus be away from Germany for some months, and (so highly did they rate Bismarck's unscrupulousness) they thought it wiser to take with them boxes of private papers, including volumes of the Prince's diary, for safe storage at Buckingham Palace, as there were many pages in it which would be of great interest to the Chancellor. Before they left Berlin, Mackenzie submitted to Virchow further fragments of the growth in the Prince's throat. Virchow reported that he could still find nothing that indicated malignant disease.

They had hardly left Germany before Berlin began to seethe with scandalous suggestions against the Crown Princess and the part she had played in these decisions. It was said that she had caused Mackenzie to be sent for from England, whereas it was the German doctors who had unanimously asked for him. It was said that she had induced him to pronounce that the growth was not malignant because, according to the laws of the House of Hohenzollern, a Prince suffering from a malignant disease could not ascend the throne, and thus she would never be Empress. This suggestion was as groundless as the other, because there was no such law.

The Crown Prince attended the Queen's Jubilee, riding in the procession of Princes to the Abbey, and afterwards stayed in England till early in September for the treatment recommended by Mackenzie. Though the trouble in his throat was not cured, it was no worse, and it was felt in Berlin that he ought to return there. He had been able to attend the Queen's Jubilee, and now his place was at home, for the Emperor was very frail, and had frequent attacks which incapacitated him from doing work which required his personal attention, and which was therefore left undone or entrusted to Prince William. Such sentiments were in no way unfriendly to the Crown Prince : it was reasonable to ask that the heir to the throne should undertake the duties which were definitely his, if he could perform them without serious risk to himself. But the Crown Princess resolved to resist his return " by tooth and nail." She believed him (trusting to Mackenzie) to be on the road to recovery, and therefore it would be madness to retard his progress by the exertions and fatigues and the use of his voice which this would entail : he must husband his strength by rest and quiet for the sake of his complete cure.[1] There was no need, however, for " tooth and nail " : the Emperor and Empress and Bismarck were all agreed that his recovery was the first consideration, and, on the advice of Mackenzie, she took him, after leaving England, to spend the early autumn in the pinewoods of Toblach. From there they went to Venice, where the dustless thoroughfares would not irritate

[1] Ponsonby, *Letters of Empress Frederick*, p. 242.

his throat and to the mild warmth of the Italian lakes.

But she was most anxious that William should leave Berlin too, and this was not so reasonable, for while the Crown Prince was abroad it was only right that his eldest son should represent him. She thought that it was bad for him to be always with the Bismarcks and the Emperor who spoilt and flattered him, and she was jealous for her husband's sake that William was taking his place, continuing the process of his obliteration. And what a fuss, she wrote to her mother, Germany was making over the celebrations for Bismarck's completion of twenty-five years of office! No doubt he had done great things for the Fatherland, but she had always considered him a man belonging to the dark Middle Ages to whom force was everything. It was pitiable to see how the young generation worshipped him.

Official Germany soon began to murmur again at the Crown Prince's prolonged absence, and now all the blame of that, so Count Radolin-Radolinsky amiably informed the Crown Princess, was put on her. That was cruelly unfair: and she told him that such criticism was "as unjust and ignorant as it was spiteful and impertinent," for it had been agreed that this régime promised best for her husband's recovery. It was personal hostility to her, she well knew, such as had pursued her ever since she came to Germany, that prompted their malice. "I am an English woman," she wrote to a friend, "suspected of Liberal, of free-thinking and artistic tendencies; of cosmopolitan and humanitarian sentiments and the like abominations in the eyes of Bismarck; so I am labelled 'suspicious' and 'dangerous' by the clique who are all-powerful now." . . . And then the true nobility and bigness of her nature reasserted itself. She brushed all personal bitterness aside and added: "After all it is only *sometimes* that I boil over with annoyance, as I usually feel how much greater and better and more useful people than I am have been continually attacked and abused more from ignorance than evil intention. So one ought to make every allowance for people's different tactics, views and opinions. *Tout comprendre c'est tout pardonner*, and one *must* learn the hard lesson of being tolerant to the intolerant, which I try very hard to learn."[1]

Throughout September and October the Crown Prince held his own. Mackenzie told his wife that he was satisfied with his progress and that if he obeyed orders, avoiding cold and damp and using his voice as little as possible, he might be quite well in three or four months. But it is doubtful whether at heart she shared this optimism. She would have cared very little for what Berlin was saying about her, if she had been convinced that by following Mackenzie's treatment he would soon be a strong and healthy man again.

They moved from the Italian lakes to San Remo, and at once a new growth appeared in the Crown Prince's throat. Mackenzie was sent for and told him that it looked malignant. The news was telegraphed to Berlin and the Emperor sent Prince William with

[1] Mary Ponsonby, p. 259.

two German doctors to San Remo to consult with the doctors there and send him their joint report. A dreadful scene took place at the meeting of mother and son. They wrangled as to which of them should send this report to the Emperor; William was rude, and the Crown Princess threatened to ask his father to forbid him to come into the house. Nothing could more tragically reveal the relations between the two than that, on the threshold of the room where William's father had just been told what he had to face, they should in the presence of others thus storm at each other. Such a meeting might have held for them both the chance of reconciliation: instead it only rendered reconciliation far more remote.

William presided at the Conference of doctors, and, as ordered by his grandfather, sent their findings to Berlin. Mackenzie concurred with the others in their verdict that the Crown Prince was suffering from cancer. When that was known there broke on the Crown Princess the full tempest of malevolence from the German press and from the multitude of her ill-wishers, but for the devoted wife they had no word of sympathy. His life, they said, might have been prolonged for many years yet by a timely operation, had not she, trusting to the verdict of an ignorant doctor of her own selection, persuaded him against it: her son Henry told her so to her face. They said he was far worse than he really was (the wish, she bitterly commented, was father to the thought) and that he ought at once to resign the succession. It would be far better that William should succeed his grandfather, who was fast failing, than a man stricken with mortal disease, which had now progressed beyond possibility of cure. By dint of her own admirable courage, she kept her husband from sinking into despair, and then it was reported in Berlin that she was concealing from him the seriousness of his condition. Sometimes she refused to believe it herself; she thought that the doctors might still be wrong, for doctors had been known to make the strangest mistakes, or, even if they were right, the progress of the disease might be arrested. Though Mackenzie at this Conference of doctors had agreed that the Crown Prince was suffering from cancer, he reported to Queen Victoria that there was still a hope that it was not so, and when he came to England in January, he was even more decided, for he told her that " though he fully believed there was nothing malignant, he could not say so positively for another six months," and that the Crown Prince was in no danger. Clinging to this hope, consoling herself with the reflection that the German doctors could not " give him a disease he has not got," his wife poured scorn on their ignorance and their pessimism. William came to see his father again, and gave himself tremendous airs, as if he was Emperor already, but for her he showed neither sympathy nor affection. Surrounded by quarrelling doctors, outraged by the ruthless publicity given to her privacy by the fantastic reports published daily in the German Press, gallantly suppressing the secret despair that gnawed at her heart, she found her only refuge in her husband's reliance on her and in his unshaken devotion. . . . But the iron had entered into her soul.

The Emperor William died on March 9, 1888, and the Emperor Frederick III at once returned to Berlin. The Empress found it grievous to have to leave the sun and the south, when a few weeks more might have done him so much good; but, while refusing to give up hope she felt it " an inestimable blessing to be relieved from the thraldom and tyranny which was exercised over us in the poor Emperor's name, as now the right thing can be done for Fritz's health."[1] The hour had struck for which, throughout the thirty years of their marriage she and her husband had devotedly prepared themselves, when his Liberal rule would be realized and the power of Bismarck shattered. But they both knew that it was too late: the aspirations once green and vigorous in that remote spring-time lay withered round them, smitten by the incurable frost, and the Emperor confirmed Bismarck in his Chancellorship since his dismissal could only uselessly dislocate the Imperial Government and suspend for a month or two the administration which would so soon be restored again. "People in general," the Empress wrote to her mother, "consider us a mere passing shadow soon to be replaced by reality in the shape of William." Fate would have been less cruelly ironical if this day had never dawned.

A family matter called for immediate settlement. The Emperor William I had forbidden the marriage of Prince Alexander of Battenberg to his granddaughter Princess Victoria, but the new Emperor and Empress wished the formal engagement to take

[1] Ponsonby, *Letters of the Empress Frederick*, p. 293.

GROUP AT BALMORAL, 1896

ht to left: Princess Margaret of Connaught, the Duchess of Connaught, the Tsarina, the Duchess Fife (daughter of Prince of Wales), Queen Victoria, Princess Patricia of Connaught and the Tsar of Russia.

place. Prince Alexander had been forced to abdicate from the throne of Bulgaria two years before, but Bismarck was still violently opposed to the marriage, for it was possible that there might be a reaction in his favour in Sofia, and an attempt be made to restore him: the notorious Madame Novikoff announced in the English Press that the Queen would be willing to go to war with Russia for that end.[1] Bismarck's political objection to the marriage was therefore as strong as ever, and he told the British Ambassador in Berlin that he would resign if the engagement was permitted. But now the Queen, who had previously favoured it, changed her mind. Crown Prince William sided with Bismarck, and his opposition had become far more weighty than it had been when the late Emperor forbade it, for then his father had been a hale man with the expectation of a long reign before him: now it could be only a few months at the most before William would succeed, and, whether his sister was engaged or not, he would certainly forbid the marriage. The Queen was in Florence, intending to go to Berlin to see her son-in-law for the last time, when Lord Salisbury told her of these rumours of the approaching engagement, and in her firmest matriarchal manner she telegraphed to the Empress not to permit it, unless William gave his consent: that now had become essential. But as for Bismarck's contention that Russia would object to the marriage, she pronounced it "impudent and impertinent beyond measure" that Russia or Bismarck should presume

[1] *Letters of Queen Victoria*, III, i, p. 259.

to interfere in a matter that only concerned her family.

The Chancellor was still under the impression that the Queen encouraged the Battenberg marriage, and his fears revived that (as he had humorously expressed himself before) she would bring the parson and the bridegroom in her luggage, and insist on the marriage taking place. He had therefore been inflaming public opinion in the Press, directly inspiring articles which denounced foreign interference in the domestic affairs of the German Royal Family, and his papers had been full of such insulting language about the Queen that Lord Salisbury feared she would have a cold if not a hostile reception in Berlin, and he tried to dissuade her from going. He was also uneasy about her meeting Crown Prince William. Count Hatzfeldt, German Ambassador in London, had conveyed to him that the Crown Prince's head had been turned by the prospect that his father's fatal illness opened, and might give himself such imperial airs that Her Majesty would feel obliged to reprove him. If he took such reproof ill, and allowed it to rankle in his mind the effect on the relations between England and Germany would be deplorable, for " his impulses, however blameable and unreasonable will henceforth be political causes of enormous potency." These dissuasions, as might perhaps have been expected, had not the slightest effect on the Queen beyond making her very angry at any attempt to interfere with her plans.[1]

Lord Salisbury's fears about the Queen's reception

[1] *Ibid.*, III, i, p. 398.

in Berlin proved to be quite unfounded. Just as the anti-monarchical agitation in England died completely down when, in 1871, the Prince of Wales lay desperately ill of typhoid fever, so now Berlin gave a welcome of warm sympathy to the old lady who had come to say farewell to her beloved son-in-law, and to give comfort and support to her daughter. Bismarck's campaign in the Press was an entire failure, but for himself, in compensation, there was a very pleasant surprise. She willingly gave him the interview he asked for, and though when she was in England he could be jocose about the authoritative power of her will, he was in considerable awe of her personally and was very nervous about this dialogue. To his great relief he found that she cordially agreed with him about the impossibility of the marriage. They agreed also that William was most ignorant of foreign affairs, and Bismarck assured her that he should never be Regent while his father lived, and that he would stand by the Empress in the days that were coming.

The Queen had gone to Berlin to make things easier for her daughter, and she had a grandmotherly talk to William : he promised that he would behave better to his mother. But with her departure to England, all the wretched wrangles broke out more violently than ever. The German surgeon Bergmann, by some incredible awkwardness caused fresh damage to the Emperor's throat, and Mackenzie threatened that if he was allowed to touch the patient again, he himself would have nothing more to do with the case. Bergmann retired and William took up the quarrel on his behalf, showing him marked attention. He behaved as if he had come to the throne already in direct succession to his grandfather, and his arrogance exasperated his mother beyond endurance. She realised now that the end was very near, and all she could do for her husband was to keep him shielded, as far as possible, from worries, but she was surrounded by hostile eyes and scandalous tongues, which twisted into fresh malevolence towards her every incident of those despairing days. The Emperor insisted on attending the marriage of his second son Prince Henry with Princess Irene of Hesse, another of the Queen's grandchildren, and the word was whispered that the Empress had given him some powerful stimulant that carried him through the ceremony but was followed by complete collapse afterwards. Or, if he was not seen of a morning sitting in the garden at Charlottenburg, he was said to be dead, and that she concealed it in order to be Empress for yet another day. He was moved by water to the New Palace at Berlin where he had been born, and entering it for the last time, said that he wished it to be known for the future as Friedrichskron. He died there on June 15, 1888, within a year of the Queen's Jubilee at which he had been the most gallant figure in the escort of Princes who rode to the Abbey.

The Empress Frederick at her husband's death was only forty-seven years old, and just when her vigour of mind, her self-confidence and her combativeness were at their height the call for their employment was over. The task for which she and her husband had so long made ready would have been arduous, for it meant the essential reversal of all that Bismarck stood for. But without doubt a very large volume of educated opinion in Germany believed that her true expansion lay in Liberal Government and in industries and the arts of peace, and with the Emperor Frederick on the throne for a reasonable length of years this might have been realized. But his accession which they had both looked on for thirty years as the sunrise of their day had proved its brief and tortured sunset : all would move on again without pause, without break as if he had never reigned. Those ninety days had no political significance and left no mark on the future or the fortunes of Germany.

The new Emperor did things that wounded his mother deeply and intimately, and the unhappy relations which had so long existed between them precluded any approach from either side which might have explained or extenuated them. He ordered that Friedrichskron should become the New Palace again. He consented to a post-mortem examination of his father's body and a publication of its findings. She regarded this as an outrage, forgetting that almost throughout her husband's illness she had staked her faith on Mackenzie's diagnosis that malignant disease was not present, and that the German doctors, who had declared from the first that it was, were entitled to this official acknowledgment. He promised in his speech to Parliament " to follow the same path by which my deceased grandfather won the confidence of his allies, the love of the German people, and the goodwill of foreign countries," omitting his father's name. Then once more there came up the question of his sister Victoria's marriage to Prince Alexander. The Emperor Frederick had made his will two months before his death and in it he had written (addressing his son) : " In case I am summoned hence I wish to have it set in evidence as my unbiased personal opinion that I entirely acquiesce in the betrothal of your second sister with the Prince Alexander of Battenberg. I charge you as a filial duty with the accomplishment of this my desire, which your sister Victoria for so many years has cherished in her heart. I count upon your fulfilling your duty as a son by a precise attention to my wishes, and as a brother by your not withdrawing your co-operation with your sister." Two days after his father's death the Emperor William wrote to Prince Alexander that the marriage must be given up " owing to the profound conviction previously held by my late deceased grandfather and father."[1] At first sight that seems like a deliberate falsification of his father's express wishes, but that was not quite the case. Since the Emperor Frederick had written those words, the whole situation had changed. The Queen in her last visit to Berlin had convinced her daughter and son-in-law that if William was against the marriage it would be a fatal mistake, and they had acquiesced. And Prince Alexander no longer wished to marry Princess Victoria. As Prince of Bulgaria such an alliance might have been of great

[1] Ludwig, *Kaiser Wilhelm II*, p. 56.

use to him politically, as strengthening his hand against Russia, but his abdication had cancelled any such consideration. Eight months afterwards, to the horrified amazement of the Queen, he married the opera singer Fräulein Loisinger.

The Empress Frederick regarded such actions as insolent and deliberate obliterations of her and her husband : she had suffered from such before in his life-time. But what was the chief cause of her wretchedness, apart from her overwhelming sorrow at his death, and of her resentment, was her inability to accept the change in her position for which her widowhood was alone responsible. She rebelled fiercely against the inevitable. " I close my eyes and ears," she wrote to the Queen, " and find it the only way not to feel the profoundest irritation with William. I am only too ready to make all allowance for him when I think of the deplorable friends he has had, and all the nonsense with which his head has been so systematically stuffed." But indeed in the anguish of her heart and the wreck of all her noble ambitions she was too raw with the sense of outrage to make allowance for anybody. She could not bear to see William and his wife with their Court round them in the places where she and Fritz should have been : " the sooner he is forgotten the better, therefore the sooner his widow disappears the better also. . . . I am glad to see and hear of it all as little as possible, and am very nearly indifferent to all this, so deep and intense is my disgust and contempt for these people and their doings." She saw in the tragedy which fate alone had decreed for her the culminating victory of the Bismarckian party, which years ago had set William against his parents. The Empress Augusta, she wrote, had worked hard for that, and now was the hour of her triumph.[1]

The Prince of Wales had been at the funeral of the Emperor Frederick, and he brought back to the Queen a piteous account of his sister, nervous and distracted, seeing ingratitude and insult everywhere, and of a conversation he had held with William, who struck him as very reasonable and anxious to do what was right.

Years before the Empress had said to her son, " If your father should die before I do, I shall leave at once. I will not stay in a country where I have had nothing but hatred, not one spark of affection." But even if she had seriously intended to do that, it was impossible, for there were three unmarried daughters who must be brought up under her care in Germany. It was naturally her immediate concern to know what home of her own William would offer her. The Prince of Wales said that he was proposing to assign her the Villa Liegnitz in Berlin, and this gave the Queen a good opportunity to write William a letter of grandmotherly counsel in this and other matters.

The Villa Liegnitz, she wrote, was far too small for his mother, who was Dowager Empress of Germany and who in England was, as her eldest daughter, the second Princess in the land. Could he not let her remain for the present at Friedrichskron ?

A more important point followed arising from the

[1] Ponsonby, *Letters of Empress Frederick*, pp. 322, 326, 329.

Prince of Wales's report. "Let me also ask you," she wrote, "to bear with poor Mamma if she is sometimes irritated and excited. She does not mean it so : think what months of agony and suspense and watching with broken and sleepless nights she has gone through, and *don't mind it.* I am so anxious that all should go smoothly that I write thus openly in the interests of both."

A third point. She had heard that William was about to start immediately on official visits to other Sovereigns. She begged him to postpone these, for his father had died only three weeks ago.

The letter did not have the authoritative effect the Queen intended. William, in his reply, first set her right about the question of a home for his mother : Uncle Bertie was misinformed. He was doing everything to meet her wishes. He had already asked her to stay on at Friedrichskron for a year, and as for the Villa Liegnitz, which the Queen thought not up to her Imperial dignity, she had herself told the Emperor Frederick that she only wanted a *pied à terre* in Berlin, and specifically asked him to leave her the Villa, which he had done. Moreover when she told William that she would like a house on the Rhine he had offered to supply the capital. As to his visiting other Sovereigns he intended to meet the Tsar in the Baltic in a few weeks. He and Bismarck were agreed that national interests demanded it, and that these could not wait " till the etiquette of Court mourning has been fulfilled." " I deem it necessary," he wrote, giving out his key as on a tuning-fork, "that monarchs should meet often and confer together to look out for dangers which threaten the Monarchical principle from democratical and republican parties in all parts of the world. It is far better that we Emperors keep firm together."[1] . . . He had already remarked and resented that his uncle treated him as if he was any ordinary nephew and forgot that he was an Imperial Majesty, and it seemed necessary to remind his revered grandmamma also of that. Though the Emperor subsequently stated in his *Memoirs* that the Queen saw that she had been wanting in respect and mended her ways, the effect of this reminder was, as very soon appeared, precisely the opposite.

The Queen's appeal to William to overlook his mother's irritability shows that she recognized that the Empress was not making things easy for him, and when her sister Princess Christian went to stay with her in Berlin she came to much the same conclusion. William's conduct, she reported, often pained his mother, but his fault was thoughtlessness, and certainly he was not guilty of the intention she attributed to him of insulting and humiliating her. She heard on all sides that he wished to be kind and considerate, and her own observation had confirmed that. With a wisdom that showed how very well she understood her nephew Princess Christian begged the Empress " to take him into her confidence as much as she can by consulting him about trifles. That would flatter and please him—and she would unconsciously gain a far greater influence than she at

[1] *Letters of Queen Victoria*, III, i, pp. 423-425.

present has any idea of."[1] That was admirable advice, but it was just that which the Empress could not bring herself to do, and she did not attempt a single gesture of approach. She had made up her mind that William and the Bismarcks were leagued to calumniate and persecute her till all memory of her and her husband was obliterated. Over and over again in her letters to her mother she went through the terrible year of his illness, framing fresh indictments against the German doctors for all his sufferings, and now she felt sure that it was the worry that William's undutiful conduct had caused him, previous to his illness, that had predisposed him to it, and that Gerhardt and Bergmann had developed it by their rough treatment. Bergmann, she was told, had killed a patient of his by similar roughness; he was vindictive, a notorious liar and a Russian intriguer. Mackenzie published his account of the case: it was extremely polemical and violently attacked the German doctors for their fatal mismanagement of their patient. Naturally this provoked a counter-attack on him in the German Press, and the tragic history was again argued and advertised from the German medical standpoint with repetition of the gross falsehood that it was the Empress who had insisted on calling in Mackenzie whose failure or refusal to recognise malignant disease was held responsible for the Emperor's death. The whole controversy was excruciatingly painful to her and utterly useless: sometimes she almost believed that the campaign was a plot against her, organized

[1] Ponsonby, *Letters of Empress Frederick*, p. 327.

perhaps by Bismarck himself with the idea of driving her out of Germany altogether. She listened also to mere gossip brought to her knowledge by injudicious well-wishers and even while some friends were telling her that Bismarck's aim was to make her leave Germany, others reported that her son-in-law Prince Bernhard of Saxe-Meiningen was saying that he hoped she would not be allowed to leave Germany at all, for if she went to England she would intrigue against the German Government.

William, dizzy with the arrogance of power, had from the first been thoughtless of his mother's feelings, while Bismarck, in spite of his assurance to Queen Victoria that he would stand by the Empress, never stirred a finger nor spoke a word to help her: indeed her husband's death was to him and his son the removal of an incubus, and with it she passed out of such compassion as he was capable of. Her desolation and the collapse of all that she lived for unbalanced her judgment, and for a while it was a fixed idea with her to find nothing but malice and deliberate insult to herself wherever conjecture could imagine it. There came out, for instance, in the *Deutsche Rundschau*, unauthorized extracts from the Diary which the Emperor Frederick had kept during the Franco-German War. He had lent this diary, fifteen years before, to his legal adviser and friend Professor Geffcken, who had copied out certain portions of it, and, now that the Emperor was dead, he anonymously published some of these extracts, containing information about the creation of the German Empire and the consequent title of Emperor for the King of Prussia; these showed that this was not solely the work of Bismarck, but, primarily, of the then Crown Prince. Such publication was quite illegal: as long as the Emperor Frederick was alive these papers were his own property, and on his death the copyright was his heir's, and no publication of them could be made without his consent. Alternatively they had become State papers, the publication of which was a very serious offence. Bismarck first took the line that they were forgeries, but he knew very well that they were genuine, so also, of course, did the Empress, who was familiar with her husband's diary, though the form in which the extracts appeared, their collocation and arrangement, was new to her. She had not the slightest notion who could have published them, and thought such publication most indiscreet. The rumours therefore put about by her enemies that it was she who had given them to the Press in order to revenge herself on Bismarck were as false as they were cruel.

Bismarck made investigation, and, having found that it was Geffcken who had caused these extracts to be published, he prosecuted him for high treason. But the Empress could not see that this prosecution was perfectly proper. She insisted that it was a piece of Bismarckian fury at the publication of anything that hindered the obliteration of her husband's deeds. Bismarck wanted, she wrote, ", to terrorize all people who might be inclined to speak a word of truth and to raise their voices for Fritz and me. . . . ; Prince Bismarck wishes to strike terror and show that if anyone dares to have been friends with the Emperor Frederick or me, they must be held up to the public as dangerous, as enemies to Germany and the Empire ! ! and liable to be put in prison." She thought of prosecuting him for libel, but in her deep mourning it would not be right to appear before the public and perhaps the Procurator General would refuse to let the case come on, and that would be another insult. And William, in consenting to Geffcken's prosecution, was actuated, she felt sure, by his desire never to hear his father's or her name again. The Bismarcks, she repeated, had " stuffed his head full of rubbish—mingling flattery with accusations against his parents—*il gobe tout*, because he is so green and so suspicious and prejudiced."[1] Sometimes, in what must almost be called saner moments, the Empress allowed that William did not mean to distress and wound her, but even so he was like a child who pulls off a fly's wings ; it did not occur to him that the fly would suffer.

She did not make the best of her cruel position, but indeed the ignorings, the unfounded slanders, and above all the cold hostility which surrounded her might have driven a less forcible nature to the resignation of despair. That they did not break her was due to her invincible will not to be beaten and the furious courage with which she stood up to them. She was often apt to take too personal a view, to imagine deliberate slights where none were intended, but, on the other hand, never were her lamentations and her invectives those of a self-centred woman ;

[1] *Ibid.*, pp. 352-363.

what gave these slights their intolerable smart was that they were aimed at her husband and were inflicted on her by his son and hers. Her widowhood involved far larger issues than her mother's, who, on the Prince Consort's death, was still Queen of England, and, in following his counsels and his policies, could feel that she was continuing his work. With the Empress the tragedy went much deeper, for the Emperor's death implied the annihilation of all their noble ambitions in directing the destinies of their country, and she, ignored and powerless, foresaw the doom which must be the result of William's chauvinistic megalomania. In her eyes, Germany under her hotheaded charioteer was being whirled along the road to ruin. Her husband had shared her forebodings: in his last illness he had said to her: " I must not die ; what would become of Germany ? "

Meanwhile the Emperor had got into his grandmother's black books for other family reasons. The Prince of Wales when attending the Emperor Frederick's funeral, had asked Count Herbert Bismarck whether, had the Emperor lived, he would have wished to give back to France part at any rate of the provinces of Alsace and Lorraine : since the peace of Versailles the Prince had believed that it was his intention to do so. But it was a very tactless question for the heir to the English throne to put, however conversationally, to the German Foreign Minister, and various similar indiscretions as to the return of North Schleswig to Denmark, and the restoration of the ex-King of Hanover had been tacked on to it by the time it reached Emperor William's ears. His annoyance was perfectly natural and he pounced on the incident as an opportunity to put his uncle in his place. At his request Bismarck sent a formal despatch of complaint to the German Ambassador in London, with the Emperor's further grievance that the Prince did not treat him with the respect due to Imperial Majesty. This letter was passed on to Lord Salisbury, who conveyed it to the Queen.

She was already very indignant with William for his treatment of his mother and vexed with him for not having taken her advice about postponing his Royal visits. She thought it " sickening " of him to strut about Europe so soon after his father's death, and hoped that the Princess of Wales's parents, whom he was visiting at Copenhagen, would be no more than civil. This complaint that his uncle did not recognize that he was an Emperor as well as his nephew roused her special fury, and she wrote to Lord Salisbury : " This is really too *vulgar* and too absurd, as well as untrue, almost *to be believed*. We have always been very intimate with our grandson and nephew, and to pretend that he is to be treated in *private* as well as in public as ' his Imperial Majesty ' is *perfect madness*. . . . If he has such notions he had better *never* come *here*. The Queen will not swallow this affront."[1] With the Prince's other delinquencies William dealt in his own manner. The two were shortly going to Vienna as guests of the Emperor Francis Joseph, and when the Prince of Wales wrote

[1] *Letters of Queen Victoria*, III, i, p. 440.

to his nephew that he hoped their visits would coincide, William did not answer his letter, but signified to their host that he wished no other Royal personages to be his guests when he was there. In consequence the Prince had to leave Vienna before his Imperial Majesty arrived. William continued the chastisement in a speech he made when he unveiled a statue of his cousin the late Prince Frederick Charles, in which he referred to " people who have the audacity to maintain that my father would have been willing to part with what he, in conjunction with the late Prince, gained on the battlefield." Then turning to one of his staff he said, " I hope my uncle will understand that." Finally Bismarck joined in and started an Anglophobe campaign in his Press against English interferences in internal German affairs. He suggested that it was the Empress Frederick who had prompted her brother to make those tactless inquiries which had caused all the mischief, and by an ingenious perversion of the facts accused the Prince of deliberate incivility to William in leaving Vienna on the eve of his arrival there.

It seems to us now like a page of mediæval history or, even more, like some incredible farce that personal quarrels between irascible members of Royal Families could endanger international relations. The situation had its comical side : there was the Queen at Balmoral boiling with unsuppressed fury and underlinings at her grandson's insane and vulgar and scarcely credible pompousness, and writing to her Prime Minister about him in such terms as she had never previously used to a subject about a member of the Family : there was the Prince of Wales, equally angry, cutting short his stay in Vienna and fleeing into Rumania in order not to be on Austrian soil when his nephew arrived, and there was Emperor William, as he unveiled a statue at Frankfort, accusing his uncle of audaciously slandering his father. But these Royal wranglings had, at that time, a serious side, and Lord Salisbury, who was not easily alarmed, expressed to the Queen his misgivings that they might lead to perilous consequences. She agreed that if possible they must not be allowed to, but feared that " with such a hot-headed, conceited and wrong-headed young man (William) this might at ANY moment become *impossible*." But whatever the consequences might be, she was determined to manage the affairs of her Family (Emperors or whoever) exactly as she chose, without advice from anybody, and her way was not to propitiate William but to put him in his place. He must be at once and unmistakably shown what she thought of his conduct to his unhappy mother and of his rudeness to his uncle, and she asked the Empress and her three unmarried daughters to come and spend three months in England with her. Both Lord Salisbury and the Prince thought this was going too far : the Emperor would take it as aimed at him, which was precisely what the Queen intended. Lord Salisbury therefore in their joint names asked the Queen to postpone the Empress's visit. He got a remarkable telegram in reply, telling him that no doubt he meant well, but the Queen would not dream of doing so : " It would be no use, and only encourage the Emperor and the Bismarcks more against us. You all seem frightened of them, which is not the way to make them better. Tell the Prince of Wales this, and that his persecuted and calumniated sister has been for months looking forward to this time of quietness. Please let no one mention this again. It would be fatal and must not be."[1]

William went to the station to see his mother off to England and bade her an affectionate farewell. He had not treated her to such attention for months : perhaps his grandmother's firmness was already beginning to make him better. The Queen sent the Prince of Wales across to Flushing to meet her in the *Victoria and Albert.* It was over thirty years now since she had sailed for Germany in that yacht, a young bride of seventeen with an adoring husband. Her mother came from Windsor to welcome her on landing at Port Victoria : never before had she gone farther than her own front door to receive the most exalted guest, and William would certainly take notice of this peculiar honour. The Family assembled for the Empress's forty-eighth birthday two days later, and, as in the years of childhood, her " present table " was covered with gifts. The entire staff of the German Embassy came down to offer their congratulations.

The Empress with her daughters remained in England for three months, and the Queen, with a Sovereign's escort, drove with her to Charing Cross to

[1] *Ibid.,* III, i, p. 443.

see her off. The Queen had begged her not to listen to mischievous tales brought to her about William, but in this self-torturing mood she could not resist hearing them and retorting with bitter criticism of him, and on her return to Germany the mischief went on as before. It was still the obliteration of her husband's memory that wounded her so deeply. She thought it heartless of William to move into Friedrichskron and occupy the rooms she and her husband had used : he ought to have left the house empty for a year. It was agony to her to go there and see their old servants still in their places, and the life of the younger generations flowing on uninterrupted : the room where her husband had died was used as a passage-room, and strangers passed through it, laughing and chattering. The anniversary of his death came round, and she could neither forgive nor forget the callous disregard of his wishes, the heartlessness, the treacheries, the indignities. And the sense of her own loneliness overwhelmed her, a few friends remained loyal and her three younger daughters, but her elder children had been brought to believe that she was "a conspirator against Germany and a traitor to her country."

The Empress's long stay in England with its special honours had been an adequate object-lesson to William as to his grandmother's sympathy with her, and now in view of the serious ill-feeling between Germany and England, the Queen was persuaded to let him pay her a visit. She was most reluctant ; she thought that he would not have a very cordial reception, that he ought to apologize first for his odious rudeness to the Prince of Wales over the Vienna incident, and she would have liked to put off his visit for another year. But he was extremely anxious to be taken back into her good graces, and Lord Salisbury was very urgent that he should be forgiven. He believed that he had now " thoroughly awakened from the temporary intoxication of last summer. It is your Majesty's interest to make his penitential return as easy to him as possible." The Emperor, though tactfully approached by Prince Christian as a mediator between him and his uncle, refused to apologize, preferring to say that there had been no Vienna incident, and this condition was withdrawn. The Queen invited him for the Cowes week in August, and the Family hatchet was magnificently interred. She created William Admiral of the British Fleet, and invested his brother Henry with the Garter. In return her gratified grandson appointed her Colonel-in-Chief of his First Dragoon Guards, and gave his cousin, Prince George of Wales, the Order of the Black Eagle.

The Empress Frederick understood that, for the sake of restoring cordial relations between the countries, William's visit was wise, but she could not easily overcome the personal bitterness of knowing that he had been taken into favour again by her mother with all the insults he had showered on her unregretted and unatoned. The Bismarckian Press was highly exultant at the popular welcome he had received in England ; it took this welcome as a sign that the British public did not believe a word regarding his supposedly cruel treatment of her, but considered it a spiteful invention of her own. She even regretted that *The Times* had become friendlier, for it would only make William think himself more perfect than ever. Once more she reiterated to her mother in detail all the wrongs and the insults she had suffered at his hands during the last year; they could only be forgiven when he asked her pardon. " Some day," she concluded, " I must be righted in the eyes of Germany, and the calumnies must be refuted which are still believed and which William chooses to believe to a great extent."[1] She had made that resolve, as will be seen later, soon after her husband's death, and it remained with her unshaken till the end of her life.

Early in January, 1890, the Empress Augusta died. Since the Franco-German war she had been head of the Red Cross Society, and the Crown Prince Frederick had told his wife, now twenty years ago, that he hoped that she would take his mother's place if she gave this work up or in case of her death. But now when she said to William that she was ready to do so, she found that it had been arranged a year ago that the present Empress should be appointed. She was terribly hurt: she felt that once more her husband's wishes had been brushed aside, and that this was a plot, to which the Empress Augusta had been privy, to ignore her and to prevent her holding any position of influence. But it was very unlikely that anything of the sort had been intended, or that the Crown Prince Frederick's wishes had been

---

[1] Ponsonby, *Letters of Empress Frederick*, pp. 385, 386.

disregarded. His mother had held this place as Empress, and it was really only reasonable that the present Empress should succeed her. But the Empress Frederick could not see it like that.

She came back from Italy for the funeral and went to look once more on the face of her mother-in-law as she lay in her coffin. For forty years the Empress Augusta had been one of the Queen's most intimate friends, she had visited her alone at Windsor and Osborne in the secluded years succeeding the Prince Consort's death, and there had been a close and constant correspondence between them. But after the Emperor Frederick's death the Queen wrote no more : possibly her silence sprang from sympathy with her daughter, for Augusta had behaved to her with cold, compassionless hostility. This seems borne out by the Empress's letter to her mother, for it contains no word of condolence with her on the loss of one who had been a friend for so many years. It is written with complete emotional detachment :

"The poor Empress lay in her coffin which looked like a bed as it was so covered with flowers. You would have thought she was just going to a fête, or a soirée, her face was so calm and peaceful and had grown younger. There seemed not a wrinkle, and the eyes that used to stare so and look one through and through were closed, which gave her a gentler expression than I ever saw in life. Her false hair in ringlets on her brow, the line of the eyebrows and eyelashes carefully painted as in life—a golden myrtle wreath on her head and an ample tulle veil, very well arranged, flowing and curling about her head and neck and shoulders hiding her chin, her hands folded, her bracelets on and her wedding ring. The cloth of gold train lined and trimmed with ermine which she wore for her golden wedding was very well folded and composed about her person and over her feet, and flowed far down the steps in front. She looked wonderfully well and really almost like a young person. I felt that if she could have seen herself she would have been pleased. She was 'the Empress' even in death and surrounded with all the stiff pomp and ceremony she loved so much."

Then just one sentence betrayed the soul-anguish that lay below this impersonal observation. It half killed her to remember that this was the mother of her own angel-husband. . . . "He would have felt his poor mother's death terribly. His kind and tender heart gave more affection than he received."[1]

The Empress had always held that Bismarck, in spite of his vast achievements, had in reality been the evil genius of Germany, and that it was he who from the first and continually thereafter had alienated William from his parents and roused his contempt for their Liberal views. While her husband was still a man with the prospect of a long reign before him, she would have hailed Bismarck's resignation of the Chancellorship as a cause for national rejoicing, but when in 1890 the Emperor forced it on him she sincerely regretted it. William gave various reasons for parting with him: he told the Queen that he accepted his retirement with tears and sorrowful

[1] *Ibid.*, pp. 399, 400.

embraces, but that Bismarck would break down if he continued in office, and that he released him in order to preserve his services as "international European capital" instead of letting him fritter his powers away in the rough and tumble of the Reichstag : he told the British Ambassador in Berlin that he was afraid Bismarck would lose his self-control and throw the inkstand at his head : he told the Tsar that he refused to obey his orders, which was nearer the truth, and was the explanation which the Empress accepted. Bismarck, she wrote to her mother, was remarkably well and vigorous, and William had made him resign because he himself was a thorough despot, and wanted nobody in his Government who would oppose his will. Though, time and again, she had execrated Bismarck's ingenuity in procuring causes for war, she believed that in spite of the corrupt system he had created " his genius and prestige might still have been useful and valuable for Germany and for the cause of peace, especially with so inexperienced and imprudent a Sovereign."
. . . Caprivi succeeded him as Chancellor : no doubt, she said, that was because he knew nothing about politics. She outlined for her mother the sort of Government which would suit William's tastes. Jules Verne, Lord Randolph Churchill and Lord Charles Beresford would form a steadying nucleus against his impetuosity, and General Boulanger, some African explorers and Richard Wagner (had he been alive) would supply the more adventurous and imaginative element. She did not know whether to laugh or cry over William's Imperial

flamboyance, and that very admission testified to a change in herself.[1]

The fierceness of her resentment against insult and obliteration, against the cruel destiny which had deprived her of her husband and the fulfilment of all her hopes grew less bitter. She still saw herself as the last champion of his aspirations for Germany, but the persecution of her as such was dying down: they thought her—William and Dona—a harmless survival, so long as she made no attempt to secure influence for herself, nor criticized their imperial pranks. All she had suffered became part of the irrevocable past instead of an ever present outrage, and the tastes and interests of that vivid and brilliant mind asserted themselves again. Art with her was a passion: she had for it the reverence and ardour of the initiate. Lord Leighton once described her painting as the work of " a second-rate artist," but he hastened to explain that he judged it not as that of an amateur at all, but as that of a trained and capable professional, who had devoted her life to it. She had built herself a house at Cronberg, and surrounded by beautiful possessions, pictures and furniture and antiques, she found that "*consolation des arts*," which can palliate or even heal the hearts of those whom life has deeply wounded. Little gibes at William spurted forth now and again, but these were only the last flicker of the tragic flame that had once enveloped and agonized her: the core of heat was cooling under the ashes. She was aghast sometimes at the imprudence of his swashbuckling speeches

[1] *Ibid.*, p. 414.

(and there indeed were ample occasions for dismay) and sometimes she harked back to the machinations of his grandfather and the Empress Augusta who had first set him against his parents. She still deplored German policy : William's craze for colonies, for instance, was great rubbish ; he had got the idea from Bismarck who always wanted them in order to bring England to terms when he needed her support, and as for his dream of building up a navy more powerful than England's, it was pure madness, and perhaps in time he would come to understand that. He should have taken up the noble legacy his father had bequeathed him, and worked for Germany's manumission from the slavery of militarism, instead of weaving fantastic dreams of becoming a Peter the Great or a Frederick the Great. He was inconceivably rash : he formed his opinions without reflection, and instantly acted on them, and criticism only irritated him. But there came a marked softening of the violent terms in which she wrote of him, regret took the place of indignation. She assured her mother that William thought he was being a good son to her, and she acquitted those who had always worked against her husband and herself of the malevolence she had previously attributed to them : in their blind mistaken way they thought they were behaving patriotically. She wished she could put a padlock on William's mouth whenever he made a public speech, yet in spite of his rashness and his conceit he was just " a big baby," and there was no one—certainly not his wife who thought him perfect—who could open his eyes to the grievous harm wrought by his imprudence, for the press seized on these speeches to encourage the vanity and chauvinism of Germany. But the anger and bitterness were transmuted into anxiety and pity for the big baby crippled from birth. A certain tenderness, long dormant, revived.[1]

Ibid., pp. 435, 440.

CHAPTER VIII

THE QUEEN had passed through her hours of twilight and eclipse while still in middle-life, and the approach of old age was more like the breaking of dawn than the closing of day, for it came with sun renewed and with serenity. In the years when the autocratic are apt to turn adamantine or querulous, she became far kindlier and more content. She was happier in her domestic life than she had been since the Prince Consort died, and what chiefly contributed to that was the marriage of her youngest daughter, Princess Beatrice, in the year 1885. She and Prince Henry of Battenberg, permanently resident with her, brought gaiety back to her and the power of spontaneous enjoyment, and the thought of her approaching Jubilee, which not many years ago would have appeared an unspeakable, a paralysing ordeal, now kindled her vitality. She opened the People's Palace, she visited Buffalo Bill's "Wild West" ("most extraordinary!"), she went to a garden-party at Hatfield, and held one herself at Buckingham Palace; she received innumerable addresses and deputations, and though a few years ago she had been totally incapable of entertaining any Royal visitor, save near relations, she had a houseful of Kings and Princes as her guests. She found that her old taste for the theatre and the opera, which had furnished bright spots in her sad childhood, but which had lain hibernating through her widowhood, was alive again; companies came down from London to perform in the Waterloo chamber, or she had a concert, "a great treat," with Edouard and Jean de Reszke and Melba to sing to her. Guests to dine and sleep were constant visitors at Windsor and at Osborne where for so many years such entertainment had been scanty. She took immense pride in the title Lord Beaconsfield had with difficulty procured for her from a very disrespectful Parliament, and as Empress of India she felt she ought to learn Hindustani. For this purpose she procured an Indian, Abdul Karim, the son of a native doctor, to give her daily lessons, and when Indian Princes visited her she took a childlike pleasure in speaking a few words to them in their own tongue. Originally Abdul Karim's office had been to wait behind her chair at table, but so servile a task, even though he waited on Her, would have meant loss of caste, so she made him Munshi Abdul Karim, Indian secretary and tutor to Her Majesty. He lived at Frogmore Cottage when she was at Windsor, and had quarters of his own at Balmoral and Osborne. He became a person of considerable importance, and when Lord Wolseley, as Commander-in-Chief, was bidden to Balmoral, he was rather surprised, as he drove from Ballater in a station-cab, to meet the Munshi taking the air in a Royal carriage. Besides this tutor she had other Indian attendants of lower caste, who propelled her wheeled chair along the corridors and waited on her at meals. This service of Indians was sometimes slightly misinterpreted by foreign guests. Prince von Bülow, for instance, on a visit to Windsor with the Kaiser, described as an eye witness how the Queen was carried into dinner in a " priceless litter " borne by four Indians, the sons of native Princes, clad in rich bejewelled silk, who stood behind her as she dined.[1] . . . Her rejuvenation was amazing : she lived again with zest, instead of dwelling with widowed melancholy on the past, and in the eyes of her subjects age brought apotheosis.

Once more small feet scampered down the corridors, and small grandchildren trotted into her bedroom of a morning to say " Good morning, Gangan," and tumbled off their ponies on their rides about the Park as their uncles and aunts had done nearly forty years ago. Her " poor old birthday," as she now called it, came round, and her " present table " was laid out for her laden with gifts thought suitable by children, and in the evening they requested her presence in the Indian room at Osborne. Greatly mystified she obeyed the summons, and they showed her, for her amusement and edification, just such a series of tableaux as those with which Vicky and Bertie and Alice and Alfie and Lenchen had astonished her and the Prince Consort in the years before their mother and father were born.

Instead of closing in the horizons were opening out all round her, and her matriarchal dominion was extending like her Empire. Elder grandsons and grand-daughters had long been married : she had

[1] Prince von Bülow, *Memoirs 1897–1903*, p. 306.

great-grandchildren in Germany, and in 1894 a direct heir of the fourth generation was born to the English throne. She went to Coburg this spring for another marriage between grandchildren: Ernest, the elder son of Princess Louis was now Grand Duke of Hesse and he was marrying Princess Victoria of Coburg, daughter of the Queen's sailor son Alfred, Duke of Coburg. A galaxy of Princes and Princesses, so many that the Queen gave up the task of enumerating them all in her *Journal*, awaited her. Among them was the Tsarevitch Nicholas, son of Tsar Alexander III and the Princess of Wales's sister, and Princess Alix of Hesse, the sister of the bridegroom. She was now a young woman of twenty-two, shy and reserved, but of very notable beauty. For the last four years Nicholas had been in love with her, but his father had refused his sanction. What his reasons were is conjectural: he may have thought on general grounds that she was not a suitable woman for the position that would be hers, and he must also have known that her young brother Frederick William had suffered from hæmophilia, and that Princess Alix might transmit it to any son of hers: this unhappily proved true. But now, knowing that he himself had not got long to live, the Tsar gave his consent, and Nicholas had come to Coburg with the intention of winning her. At first she was as obdurate as his father had been. She wept, she declared it was impossible, for she was very unwilling to make the necessary change in her religion and become of the Russian Orthodox Church. Here Nicholas's mother, who was in favour of the marriage, could help him, for she had made the same change herself and he gave Alix the letter the Tsarina had written to her begging her to marry him. The struggle was hard : she was deeply religious and loyal to her own faith, but she yielded.

So the morning after Ernest's wedding the two came hand in hand to the Queen and told her they were engaged to be married. The Queen expressed herself as " quite thunderstruck." But she had long known that Nicholas was in love with her granddaughter, and this bolt from the blue must have been her surprise that the Tsar had given his consent or that Alix had got over her religious objections. In any case the thunderbolt gave her great gratification, and she was so interested in it that she omitted in her *Journal* to say anything about the wedding which had brought her to Coburg : it eclipsed everything else. She had always been very fond of her Hesse grand-daughters who had lost their mother in that tragic visitation of diphtheria sixteen years ago, and they had often stayed with her in England. But now " sweet gentle Alicky," chosen for the dazzling destiny of being the " great Empress of all the Russias," became the object of the Queen's special regard, affection and even reverence. This was not to be wondered at. The Tsarevitch adored her, his father could not live long, and the girl held in her hands the potentiality of immense influence. For years the international relations between Russia and England had been deplorably bad, more than once the countries had been on the verge of war, and both the Queen and her Prime Minister, Lord Rosebery, saw in this marriage of her grand-daughter to the heir to the throne of Russia a most hopeful prospect of restoring friendship between the countries. As for the young man's father, Tsar Alexander III, she had, till now, never forgiven him for forcing Prince Alexander of Battenberg to abdicate from the throne of Bulgaria, and she had used the very strongest expressions to the Prince about him : " My indignation," she wrote, " against your barbaric, Asiatic, tyrannical cousin is so great that I cannot trust myself to write about it." But that was long ago and now she told the barbarous Asiatic how gratified she was at this betrothal.

Before leaving Coburg the Queen arranged that Princess Alix should stay with her in England during the summer for two solid months, and for a month Nicholas was there also : they brought with them the Russian priest who was preparing her for her reception into the Orthodox Church. After the iron etiquette of the Romanoffs the Tsarevitch was astonished at the freedom the Queen permitted : she allowed him, he told his mother, to go for drives with Alix without a chaperon. Not less astonishing to him was the democratic atmosphere of Sandringham. The Prince of Wales was having a sale of horses, and the house-party consisted chiefly of horse-dealers quite unknown to his Aunt Alix ; there was even a Jew among them which perhaps was the oddest experience of all for a member of the Russian Royal Family. His cousins teased him about his " efforts to keep away from these queer guests and to avoid talking to them."[1] He perceived, perhaps with a touch of ironical amusement, how warm was the welcome with which he was received into the English Royal Family, for he was to dine one night at Windsor, at the officers' mess of the Guards, but, he reported, " I couldn't give a definite answer because Granny loves me so, and doesn't like me missing dinner."

Though many years later, the Emperor William claimed to have had a hand in promoting the match he did not at all like it, for the prospect of England and Russia becoming friends was one of his chronic Imperial nightmares. Nor did he like the slightly possessive affection which his grandmother lavished on the engaged couple. Princess Alix had only just left when he arrived for his yachting week at Cowes, and his perturbation expressed itself characteristically in the letter he wrote to thank the Queen for his pleasant visit. Russia, he told her, was contemplating a military advance towards India, and was massing troops on the Eastern German frontier, so that he would be unable to go to the aid of " anybody " she was intending to attack. But the Queen was not alarmed by this kindly warning; she construed it quite correctly. William, she believed, was truly anxious to be friends with England, but a *sine qua non* condition of that friendship was that England must have no other friends but Germany. She, too, was always most anxious to be friends with Germany, but just now there were other claims on her attention.

[1] *Letters of Tsar Nicholas and Empress Marie*, p. 84.

The marriage then held tremendous possibilities, and the Queen with her habitual dominance in family affairs was determined to make the most of them. She and the Prince Consort, nearly forty years ago, had foreseen for their eldest daughter a very similar mission in Prussia, when they married her to Prince Frederick, as she now projected for Princess Alix. She remembered also how before the marriage of the Prince of Wales to Princess Alix of Denmark she had sent for the girl to spend some days alone with her for instruction in the duties and the tact necessary for young ladies about to marry heirs-apparent to foreign thrones, and what marvellous fruit that tuition had borne : how completely her daughter-in-law had merged herself in her new nationality ! Grand-daughter Alix must follow that example : she must shed her German nationality, and, though becoming a true Russian, must never forget that she was the grand-daughter of the Queen of England. So before they parted in July, it was settled that she should come back again in the winter, before her marriage, and spend a few quiet days with her as Alix of Denmark had done.

But this visit never took place. Before the winter Tsar Alexander III died, and Nicholas was Tsar of all the Russias. Princess Alix was received at once into the Russian Church, and it was arranged that as soon as the prodigious funeral ceremonies were over the marriage should take place, for otherwise it must be postponed for months, since, according to the traditions of the Russian Church, it could not be performed between Christmas and Easter. This meant the abandonment of the Princess's promised visit to her grandmother, and it was a daring thing to upset her arrangements for whatever reason. Alix and her sister Ella, Grand Duchess Serge, both telegraphed to her that they were sure she would understand, and that all the Imperial Family and indeed the whole of Russia wished the marriage to take place now. The Queen was not pleased : she felt it to be a " shock and a great disappointment " not to see Alicky again before her marriage, but allowed that nothing " could be said or done."

The Prince and Princess of Wales (she to be with her widowed sister) had already gone to Russia, and they accompanied the funeral train from Livadia, where the Tsar had died, to St. Petersburg, where after a fortnight of daily ceremonies his body was interred. The Duke of York joined his father there, and the Queen made the new Tsar Colonel-in-Chief of the Scots Greys, the most intimate military honour she could bestow. All these attentions had their political significance ; not for nothing would the Prince of Wales have gone through these appalling obsequies, and now he waited till his niece's wedding had taken place. On that day the Queen gave a large dinner at Windsor, and herself proposed the health of their Majesties the Emperor and Empress of Russia, " my dear grandchildren," and remained standing while the Russian National Anthem was played. " How I thought of darling Alicky," she wrote in her *Journal*, " and how impossible it seemed that gentle little simple Alicky should be the great Empress of Russia. . . . She is so dear and good and a real daughter to me."[1] The Prince of Wales returned after spending more than a month in Russia, with very good news of them both. The Tsar had begun his reign very well, he was absolutely devoted to his bride, and Lord Rosebery made the Prince his congratulations on the success of his mission.

So now this lovely girl, so pious and so stupid, and so obstinate for all her gentleness was the great Empress, and the last, of all the Russias, and next time that she and her grandmother met they would curtsey to each other in the correct mode between Sovereigns and go to the door side by side, where the Queen would draw back a shade, and let her sister and grand-daughter pass out first.

The Emperor William came to Cowes again in 1895. The long and fervent cordialities between his uncle and the Tsar had profoundly displeased him; they had aroused, as Pepys would have diagnosed, "a mighty chagrin humour," which sought self-expression in the most disagreeable antics. In his naval escort was the cruiser *Wörth*, and on the anniversary of the German victory in the Franco-German war after which she was named, he addressed her crew in terms which, considering that he was the guest of a country in friendly relations with the French, were deliberately insulting. He scratched his yacht, the *Meteor*, in the race for the Queen's cup because he thought she was unfairly handicapped; he arrived an hour late for a dinner the Queen gave in his

[1] *Letters of Queen Victoria*, III, ii, p. 454.

honour; he was incredibly rude to his uncle, and he left, after a visit of six days, saying that he had done with England. The Queen, who had already asked her Ambassador in Berlin to convey a hint to him that she would not take it much amiss if his visits to Cowes ceased to be annual fixtures suggested by himself, found him a most fatiguing guest, and it was a great relief when his stay was over, and she could take her breakfast again in tranquillity, under the immense green umbrella in the garden. She read the contents of her daily despatch-boxes, and had her lesson in Hindustani from the Munshi, and the grandchildren played with her dogs, and then her pony-chair came round and she went for her morning drive with her daughter or her son-in-law to keep her company.

They were with her always; for Prince Henry there was shooting or hunting at Windsor, and deer-stalking at Balmoral, and at Osborne sailing in the Solent in the schooner-yacht she had given him, and they accompanied her on her annual spring holiday abroad. But his only office was to be a family man with wife and children living with the Queen of England without any further occupations or responsibilities of his own. A few weeks intermittently of such a life would have been a most recuperative existence for a man taking a well-earned rest after a prolonged period of hard work, or for one regaining his strength after a severe illness. But he was in the youthful prime of life, and the horizons of recuperation stretched away into the unforeseen. Yet the very contract of his marriage provided that he should bear the burden of perpetual leisure, without the relaxation of the employment that should have been his, and once only did he obtain leave of substantial absence, and went out on his yacht, *en garçon*, to the Mediterranean. It can scarcely have occurred to the Queen that, in order to supply her with this ideal domestic companionship, now at last so perfectly realized, she was sterilizing the natural expansions and activities of a very energetic man not yet forty years of age. Moreover the Prince of Wales was not very friendly towards his young brother-in-law, seventeen years his junior. He thought that the Queen discussed matters of national importance with Liko, while he himself was rarely consulted by her, and her warm affection for her son-in-law unreasonably displaced him.

For ten years this matriarchal régime continued till, in the autumn of 1895, the Government decided to send out an expedition to Ashanti to stop the raids which King Prempeh, in spite of a warning ultimatum, persisted in making into the Gold Coast, for the purpose of kidnapping its inhabitants and selling them for slaves. Volunteers were asked to join it : the eldest son of Prince Christian in the Rifle Brigade had applied, and his parents and the Queen consented to his going. A few days afterwards Prince Henry, to the Queen's astonishment and dismay, asked her leave to volunteer also. She refused, and told her doctor, Sir James Reid, to back her up, and insist on the inadvisability of the Prince risking himself in so unhealthy climate. For once, in a domestic matter which affected her intimately, she did not get her way. Princess Henry agreed with her husband, and put their case to the Queen. He smarted under this enforced idleness : he was a soldier's son, his brothers had seen active service, and it would be a reproach to him now and to his children hereafter that he should continue to lead this idle and unmanly life, when there was so admirable an opportunity for his serving his adopted country : volunteers were asked for, and he would not be taking any other man's place. They had talked it over together and they both thought it was his duty to go. The Queen yielded, and within a few weeks of Prince Henry's arrival on the Gold Coast he was stricken with the deadly fever of the country. He was invalided home, and died on the voyage.

The Queen felt his death, not only for her daughter's sake, but for her own, more acutely and personally than any loss that had befallen her since the Prince Consort's death. She had the greatest affection for him, he had been " our help, the bright sunshine of our home " : he ought never to have been allowed to go on the Ashanti expedition. Princess Henry would not hear of that : it had been right for him to go, and the tragic consequences must be accepted as the Will of God. But Osborne was steeped for her in memories of him who had been her very life, and she took her four children to Cimiez, where the Queen would come a month later for her spring holiday. Never before, since the days of her early childhood, had this most devoted of daughters been separated from her mother for so long, and never till the final separation was there to be a similar parting.

The Queen had had great hopes of better relations between England and Russia owing to the marriage of her grand-daughter with Tsar Nicholas II. They sent her messages of tenderest love on all suitable family occasions, but otherwise the results were at present disappointing. A series of articles violently hostile to England had appeared in the Russian Press by a writer who was credited with being in the Tsar's confidence, and these, translated into English and published in the Press, had roused strong resentment. The Queen wrote direct to the Tsar asking him to repudiate them, but though " Granny loved him so " he seems to have taken no notice of this request, for neither he nor his Government nor indeed his wife found the slightest obligation inherent in his marriage to love England. This unfriendliness was accentuated by the appointment this year of Prince Lobanoff, a rabid Anglophobe, as Russian Foreign Minister. He soon had an opportunity for making trouble, for early in 1896 the British-Egyptian Expedition started up the Nile in order to reconquer the Sudan, which, since the death of General Gordon, had been in the hands of the Mahdi and of the Khalifa who succeeded him. A convenient pretext for this move was offered by the plight of a small Italian force at Kassala. They had been defeated at Adowa by the Abyssinians, who threatened their base, and a British-Egyptian advance to Dongola would relieve the pressure. The Queen was all in favour of " helping the poor Italians," but this piece of altruism deceived nobody and it was no secret that the Sudan was the real objective. France had no illusions about it, and looked upon the project with a most disapproving eye. Prince Lobanoff, with the knowledge of the Tsar, was doing all he could to encourage her to make some counter-move, for though nominally (leaving the poor Italians out of the question) England's only purpose in conquering the Sudan was to restore it to Egypt, its recovery would vastly increase the English sphere of influence.

The Queen considered this situation as coming well within the territory of her enlarged matriarchate : private conversations with her Russian grandchildren ought to bear good fruit. She asked them to stay with her quietly for ten days at Balmoral, bringing with them their baby girl. It was to be a purely domestic visit, and she counted on the Tsar's regard for his grandmother's wishes being an influential factor in counteracting Russia's hostility to England, and in his disassociating himself from the unfriendliness of the French. A propitious circumstance was that Prince Lobanoff, who would have accompanied the Tsar, died suddenly just before their visit.

The Queen had gathered the whole Royal clan about her at Balmoral : the fourth generation was represented in the person of Prince Edward of York. The Family was displayed, as her Navy might have been assembled at some Review, to personify England, but with this difference that whereas the Navy would have been decked with flags and loud with salutes, domestic informality was the key to this more subtle demonstration in the Highlands. But, as the Tsar's letters to his mother show, this personification made no impression on him : it looked as if he had made up his mind to be on the defensive, or at the most to preserve a strict neutrality. He did not feel at all English : he found it unpleasant to say goodbye to the officers and crew of his yacht at Leith, clad in his foreign uniform with the bearskin of the Scots Greys, which had been intended to be so signal an honour ; he disliked the drive through the streets of Edinburgh in an open carriage under pouring rain, and the special train to Balmoral rocked so violently that Alix was nearly sick. An escort of Scots Greys and pipers and torchbearers met them at Ballater, and their grandmother received them at the door of her Castle : she seemed to him smaller than ever, but very amiable. He did not enjoy himself at all : Uncle Bertie insisted on his going out stalking all day in torrents of rain and gales of wind, and he never got a stag. He was glad when Uncle Bertie went to Newmarket for some race meeting, for then he need not go stalking any more. Surrounded by this clan of his wife's aunts and uncles and cousins, he hardly saw his beloved Alix at all ; indeed he complained that he saw less of her than when he was at home and occupied with the business of State.

Once before when, in the early days of the Queen's reign, Tsar Nicholas I stayed with her at Windsor, it had seemed like a dream to be breakfasting and strolling with " this greatest of all earthly Potentates," and she had been overwhelmed by the compliment he had paid her by his visit ; and now again it seemed like a dream to be entertaining Tsar Nicholas II and his wife, her dear grandchildren, in this informal manner, driving with them in the rain and having tea in bothies. But as for the intimate conversations from which she had expected so much, they produced nothing; he made himself a bland and impenetrable mask. No one could have been more charming or more amiable, but no one could have been more deliberately evasive. Never did she obtain from him any direct expression of his personal views, and the most tactful cross-examination failed to show that he had any. She spoke to him of the critical state of affairs in Turkey and of the possibility of deposing the Sultan : he quietly agreed that affairs were critical but thought that to depose the Sultan might lead to dangerous complications. He was sorry that William was so injudicious and so unfriendly to England. He seemed to have no objection to the British-Egyptian expedition for the recovery of the Sudan, but she could not be quite sure about that. More than once she intimated how important it was that Russia and England should stand together, for they were the most powerful Empires and there would be peace as long as they were friends, but even that failed to secure any very sympathetic assent. He seemed to think this and he seemed to feel that, but he completely baffled her efforts to get anything definite from him. Lord Salisbury fared no better : the Tsar had wished to see him, and they had two long conversations together. The Tsar, commenting on these to his mother said that it was " good for Lord Salisbury at least to learn from the source what the opinions and views of Russia are," but Lord Salisbury confessed that he had learned practically nothing of what these opinions were.[1] For instance, he understood the Tsar to say that he did not object to the English occupation of Egypt, but then he stopped and changed the subject, as if he were being indiscreet.

Trees were planted to commemorate the visit, a moving picture was taken by the new and marvellous cinematograph process to show the family strolling on the terrace with the Queen in her wheeled chair, and after ten days of this domestic life the Tsar and the Tsarina left for a State visit to Paris. Most affectionate were the farewells, but the Queen, conscious of having accomplished nothing, instantly sent a letter after him asking him to make it clear to the French Government that he disapproved of their hostility to England, especially with regard to Egypt, and yet once more she stressed the importance of Russia and England being on very friendly terms. His answer was as non-committal as his share in their conversations had been. Though he had told his grandmother, to her high approbation, that he disliked having to visit so dreadfully irreligious a town as Paris, he enjoyed himself there extremely. The weather was good, everything was beautifully arranged, the welcome he received was tremendous; he was touched and delighted with the enthusiasm of the crowds, and much impressed by the French military review. The bonds of friendship between Russia and France were immensely strengthened, whereas the visit to Balmoral, as regards international rapprochement, was a fiasco. Certainly he was

[1] *Letters of the Tsar Nicholas and Empress Marie*, pp. 118-120.

devoted to Alicky, but the marriage from which the Queen had anticipated such magnificent results might just as well have ended in a divorce. Never in the years to come did the Tsarina influence him in the ways of wisdom, but rather in those of ruinous folly. She encouraged him to hold fast to the principles of autocracy which eventually wrecked Russia, and to seek in religion the quackeries of magic.

The Empress Frederick emerged from her retirement at Cronberg in the spring of 1897 to make one more excursion into international politics over the Greco-Turkish war. Family reasons prompted it, for her daughter Sophy had married Constantine, Crown Prince of Greece. The trouble began in Crete where the Greeks, who formed a majority of the population, started a guerrilla warfare of murder and pillage as a protest against Turkish oppression. The Mohammedans put up an effective resistance and the Greeks appealed to their mother country to help them. King George, the Princess of Wales's brother, yielded to the popular clamour in Athens, and allowed regular troops to be sent to Crete, which (as it was part of the Turkish Empire) was an act of war. The Powers, with the consent of Turkey, were willing to grant autonomy to Crete, but refused to allow Greece to annex it, or to intervene in any way until the Greek troops had been withdrawn. King George, fearing that he would lose his throne if he stood out against national feeling, declined to do so, and Turkey very properly declared war.

The Empress had already been making frantic

appeals to the Queen to procure the intervention of the Powers in order to save Greece from invasion and inevitable defeat. It was useless to appeal to her son, for he, quite rightly, insisted that if Greece desired intervention she must accept the terms of the interveners, and it was not just to attribute to him, as she did, a brutal callousness to the fate of Greece because he personally disliked the King and had quarrelled with his sister for having been received on her marriage into the Greek Church. But the Empress did not fully appreciate the difficulties in the way of England's intervention. The Queen had already asked the Tsar to intervene, but neither Russia nor Austria would move without Germany, France would not move without Russia, and Turkey, who regarded England as her bitterest enemy, would certainly not obey any orders coming from her if unsupported by other Powers. Rather illogically the Empress bewailed that the three Emperors were " on the WRONG tack," yet any other tack was tantamount to allowing Greece to commit acts of war against Turkey and forbidding Turkey to retaliate.

Turkey, having declared war, invaded Thessaly, and encountered no real opposition from the Greek troops, of which the Crown Prince was the Commander-in-Chief. They retreated before them unsteadily and speedily. The Empress then suggested to the Queen that England should reorganize the Greek army, but not only was that a perfectly hopeless task, owing to its chaotic disintegration, but, as Lord Salisbury pointed out, to have attempted it would have been equivalent to taking part in the war, and there were few people in the country so Hellenically minded as to approve of that. Within three weeks from the beginning of the war Thessaly was in the hands of the Turks and the way to Athens was open.

The Emperor William held the key to the situation, for Russia and Austria would follow him, and the Queen (it must have been a bitter pill) had to appeal to him to insist on an armistice ; simultaneously she sent a message to the King of Greece that he must obey the conditions laid down by the Powers, if he wanted the intervention which alone could save Greece. Greece could no longer resist and the troops from Crete were withdrawn. And William had the intense satisfaction of informing his grandmother that the King of Greece had begged for his intervention and accepted his terms. He had great pleasure in bringing the war to an end. That was the object in view, but the Queen found it difficult to bear William's " grandiloquent " telegrams, not even sent in cipher, imperially informing her what he had done.

This happy conclusion had been arrived at before the Queen's Diamond Jubilee in June, 1897. A full six months earlier she had decreed that no reigning Sovereigns should be invited. She was old, and did not feel up to the fatigue of entertaining them ; heirs-apparent and collaterals would not need such personal efforts. Ambassadors of foreign Powers were duly informed of this exclusiveness, and the

King of Siam, who had already announced his intention of coming, was recommended to change his mind. But William, though he knew this decree, and had been told that the Crown Prince would be welcome, was extremely anxious to come himself. He was a grandson, he thought that blood was thicker than Crowns, and he got his mother to write to the Prince of Wales to ask if he could not obtain an invitation for him. He could not have chosen a less zealous advocate. His uncle was seized with panic. William would bring an enormous suite and he would want to run the whole show, and he expressed to the Queen, in case the Empress had written to her also, his earnest hope that she would not be persuaded. The Queen reassured him: on no account would she ask William, and she was surprised that his mother should have suggested it. So she gave no more thought to him and other baffled crowned heads. This was to be a festival of Empire, and it was her own people who occupied her. She was very anxious about the stability of small houses in poorer quarters on the route of the drive she was to take on Jubilee day. The roofs would be crowded with people to see her pass and she trusted that the London County Council would make sure that the parapets were strong. She spent her " poor old birthday " at Balmoral and went to see her first wardrobe-maid, Annie Macdonald, who had been with her for forty years. Annie had been ill and was much upset at the thought that she might not be well enough to be at her post on the great day.[1]

[1] *Letters of Queen Victoria*, III, iii, p. 268.

The Empress Frederick came with three of her daughters. Ten years ago she had attended her mother's first Jubilee, as Crown Princess of Prussia, and her husband and William had been with her. She had not then been alarmed about the Crown Prince,[1] for she had firm faith in Morell Mackenzie, and looked forward to his swift recovery. For the Queen these ten years had garnered rich harvests of Imperial Sovereignty and invested her with a personal apotheosis unparalleled in the annals of the monarchy; for her daughter there were only the memories of blanched banners and of dreams long dead. To-day she was the most exalted of that huge assembly of her mother's children and grandchildren, all those heirs to foreign thrones, the Archduke Franz Ferdinand of Austria, the Prince of Naples and the Prince of Persia, and to all these the future beckoned with promise; for her the future was peopled with the spectres of the past.

She came to England only once more when in the autumn of next year she stayed with the Queen at Balmoral. There it was that forty-two years ago her Fritz had been permitted to give her the sprig of white heather and " make an allusion to his hopes," and that moment had laid down the lines of her life. Never had a woman a better-loved and more loving husband, but apart from him her days had been woven of hostilities and bitter disappointment, without ever a spell of tranquil happiness. She was not wholly blameless: too often she had approached the

[1] Ponsonby, *Letters of Empress Frederick*, p. 333.

immense and probably insuperable difficulties of her position with pugnacity rather than patience, but such faults had been visited with a malice that was cruelly unjust. Her noble qualities had been rendered barren of fruit and her brilliant abilities forged into a sword in the hand of ruthless enemies. But never had she suffered the fine fire of her high ideals to be quenched, and throughout the months of physical anguish which she had still to endure it burned with undiminished brightness. " So one lives on," she wrote to her most intimate friend, " a diminished and crippled existence, but still ready to do what is possible for the happiness of others, and still able to rejoice in what is beautiful and great and true and noble ; still anxious for ideals to be realised and eager to see the right triumph and truth to be recognised, wrongs redressed and suffering relieved as much as can be." Nor did she lose her sense of the infinite harm Bismarck had wrought for thirty years in fostering bad relations between the countries of her birth and her adoption. The seed he had sown continued to spring up after his death, and she attributed to it the rancour of Germany towards England in the South African War. Her spirit was still superbly unbroken : the abuse of "*everything* English *every* day makes me so savage that it scatters all my tolerance, philosophy and patience to the winds, and I long to be a man sometimes, and *knock somebody down.* . . ."[1]

But her struggles and her suffering, and the sense of failure and obliteration which had followed her

[1] Mary Ponsonby, pp. 284, 286.

husband's death had made her a most unhappy woman, unhappy in the very fibre of her being.

The Queen's contributions to the voluminous correspondence with her daughter, covering the period from the birth of William till when, forty years later, the Empress was stricken with the same fatal malady as her husband, have, with the exception of a few letters, never seen the light. It is, however, easy to conjecture in many cases from allusions made in answer, what the tenor of them was. Her sympathy with her daughter was constant and wholehearted, and she execrated the campaign of calumny of which she was the victim. But again and again there are clear indications that she thought the Empress was making the worst of her woes, and she urged her not to listen to the tongues of mischiefmakers, and to put away from her mind the offences she found it so impossible to forgive instead of dwelling on them.

It would, however, be most erroneous to interpret the Empress's letters to her mother, with their reiterated catalogues of the insults showered on her, as merely or primarily the grievances of a bitterly wounded woman. She had a further definite object in putting them down in writing, for she meant, using these letters as material, some day to compile a life of her husband which would do him justice, and restore to him his proper place in the history of his time. Three months after his death, when they were fullest of the obliteration of his memory and the misrepresentation of his aims, she sent a memorandum to the Queen telling her of this intention, and asking her if she would get Sir Theodore Martin, who had written the official life of the Prince Consort, to make extracts from those that concerned the political and domestic history of her married life, with a view to their being translated into German. Life was uncertain, "but the truth which is being so systematically smothered and twisted must be put down somewhere whether it is published in my life-time or not." She had no other record of these years, since she did not keep a diary, and thus this correspondence, written while current events were still fresh in her memory, constituted her sole mine of material. The Queen must have approved, and possibly she suggested that she should herself make these selections, for shortly after sending this memorandum the Empress wrote again: "The work of making extracts from my letters to you will be immense, perhaps you could find someone else to help also? as Sir Th. Martin will not do."[1] She therefore contemplated this business of selection being begun more than ten years before her death, while her letters were still in the Queen's possession. The intention remained with her, for a year afterwards she wrote again: "It will be my duty some day to endeavour to let the truth go down to history, and not the lies that suit Prince Bismarck and the Government and all those who court its favour." This intention therefore was formed before the publication of Bismarck's *Reminiscences*, and the reiterations in her letters to the Queen were due to her desire to

[1] Ponsonby, *Letters of the Empress Frederick*, pp. xviii, 341.

have the *dossier* complete without chance of omissions. It was the material on which she meant to base her justification of her husband and herself. These letters would be safe among the Queen's papers at Windsor till the time was ripe for their embodiment in her projected book.

This book was never written, and the letters themselves were kept at Windsor, where the last of the series was sent in the autumn of 1900. The Queen died in January, 1901, and next month King Edward VII, with Sir Frederick Ponsonby accompanying him as secretary, went to his sister's house at Cronberg, where she was dying of cancer, to see her for the last time. This collection of her letters, as was presently apparent, was then in her possession, and it seems a certain inference that she had asked for them to be sent her after her mother's death (when, as the writer of them, they would on request be returned to her), in order that she might begin to go through them herself for the compilation of the life of her husband which should be a refutation of Bismarck's lies.

She was in constant and agonizing pain, relieved only by injections of morphia, after which there were periods when she was herself again. In one of these remissions she sent for her godson, Sir Frederick Ponsonby, talked to him for a while with eager animation and then suddenly asked him to take her letters back with him to England. She charged him to tell nobody of this : it was above all important that her son should not get hold of them nor know what had happened to them. Sir Frederick promised to do what she wished, and she said she would send these letters to his room at one o'clock that night when the house was asleep. At that hour four servants came silently into his room, bearing a couple of large boxes. They deposited them and vanished again. He had expected some small packet, and the appearance of these bulky boxes was a complete surprise to him. But there was no doubt that they contained the letters she had spoken of, and all that concerned him was to carry out the promise he had made.

Sir Frederick did not see the Empress again before he left Cronberg, and he returned to England with these boxes, labelled as his, among the King's luggage. He received no further instructions from her, and arrived at a probable inference of her wishes about what was to be done with the contents by an elimination of what she assuredly did not wish. She could not intend him to destroy them, for they had been in her possession since she had sent for them from Windsor after the Queen's death, and she would have done so herself if she had wished them to perish. He argued also that if she meant them to be returned to the archives at Windsor where they had been accumulating for forty years she would have entrusted them to the King.[1] He might also have justly made this further inference that, if they had gone back there, they would on the Empress's death have been asked for by her son who as his mother's heir would have been entitled to them unless she had devised them otherwise. They would thus have gone back to him, which, as the Empress had expressly told Sir Frederick, must not be their fate. She had

[1] *Ibid.*, pp. ix–xvii.

provided against that by giving them during her lifetime to him.

When these boxes were safe in Sir Frederick's own house he opened them, and found the memorandum already quoted, written by the Empress to her mother, asking her to get extracts made from her letters, under Sir Theodore Martin's supervision, which should form the basis for her book. A letter had closely followed this, replying evidently to an answer from the Queen, that, as Sir Theodore Martin " would not do " and the work of making extracts would be very great, the Queen might get someone else to help. The possibility therefore arises that this selection was in process, under the Queen's supervision, while the letters were in England, for Sir Frederick found that whole pages had been blackened out by erasures. He concluded that the Empress had been through them all and had made these erasures herself. But it must be remembered that when they were returned to her after the Queen's death life was already a torment of agony, and it would seem unlikely that she was capable of such application. Indeed her sister, Princess Henry of Battenberg, had been to stay with her a couple of months before the Queen's death and found her unable to use her hands, and her only occupation was reading or being read to.[2] The manual labour, therefore, of going through her letters and making these extensive erasures may be considered impossible. It seems therefore probable that the Queen, as her daughter had suggested over ten years ago, had been through them herself,

[2] *Letters of Queen Victoria*, III, iii, p. 629.

and that the erasures were hers or had been made under her direction.

The steps which the Empress had taken to prevent her letters falling into her son's hands (in which case he would certainly have destroyed them), proved to have been necessary. She died at Cronberg five months later, and instantly the Emperor ordered that the house should be searched for her papers, while a guard surrounded the place to see that nothing was smuggled out. He had taken similar precautions after his father's death, searching through Friedrichskron for the papers which, as Crown Prince, he had taken with him to England at the time of the Queen's Jubilee. Sir Frederick went with the King to the Empress's funeral, and at the Emperor's request applied to the Keeper of the Archives at Windsor to know if these papers were there. As they were in his private possession the search among the archives was as vain as the search at Cronberg had been, and, in view of the injunction laid on him by the Empress that they must not fall into William's hands, there can be no question that he was right not to disclose that he held them. Twenty-seven years later he published a substantial selection of the letters that had been entrusted to him in such strange and dramatic circumstances. Legally it may be argued that the right of publication belonged to the Emperor, but there can be no doubt that, short of definite instructions, Sir Frederick carried out the Empress's wishes. She had repeatedly stated that she meant to do her husband justice by producing a book, founded on her letters which, whether published in her lifetime or not, should accomplish this. If Sir Frederick was right in supposing that the erasures in these letters were made by her own hand, it is evident that she was preparing her manuscript for publication, when she entrusted him with it : if these erasures were made by the Queen or under her supervision, it is equally evident that she approved of the material which she allowed to stand. It is impossible to tell what form the book would have taken if she had lived to write it herself or superintended its compilation, but there can be no doubt that these letters constitute the basis and synopsis of the tragic history she would have therein disclosed.

CHAPTER IX

DURING the later years of her life the Queen looked upon Osborne as the home most intimately bound up with her domestic life. She still went to Balmoral twice in the twelvemonth, but its early charms, the Great Expeditions, with nights spent in remote inns, the rides on her pony, the sketchings, the picnics and teas on the hillside had long since ceased, and now the old folk to whom she used to distribute petticoats and tobacco were all dead : there was no one left who was associated with the wonderful years. But Osborne had been Albert's first creation of a home outside the impersonal splendours of official residences, and by degrees it had grown into a vast museum of family relics. There was a regiment of busts and statues, representing members of the family in bronze or marble by eminent Victorian sculptors whose industry much exceeded their inspiration. There were endless family pictures and family groups by Winterhalter, and many masterpieces by Landseer, and great frescoes by W. Dyce, R.A. Fathomless cupboards were full of peculiarly personal property ; there were dozens of china plates and plaques with views of Coburg and Rosenau, where Albert was born, painted below glaze, or with portraits of the Queen's dogs, Sharp and Noble and others of the canine dynasty, and portfolios full of lithographs of family pictures, and there were effigies in marble of the infant hands and feet of the Queen's children. Lares and Penates had accumulated here in enormous quantities and these material mementoes of imperishable memories held for the Queen something of the sacredness of what they commemorated. Never in the life-time of its original owner had any house been so enriched with records of its contemporary history.

To her, too, the Hanoverian dynasty, of which she was the sixth representative, was extinct : the dynasty of Victoria and Albert had replaced it, and this was the house which had been designed and decorated in accordance with the founder's own taste ; the Clock Tower and the Flag Tower and the huge stables and the terrace where even in midwinter she could enjoy the mellow maritime air, and the winding walks through the ilex-trees were his : Osborne was the great private house of the new dynasty. Since those days it had been greatly enlarged, a wing had been built out from the original Pavilion, and for Princess Beatrice a smaller wing. The Queen had also given her a house with a garden of its own near by in the Park, and to Princess Louise another establishment, Kent House, on the estate, so that her daughters could have adjacent homes of their own. These two houses, like dower houses, depended for their amenities on the big house being in possession of the Family : it was the centre of this Royal colony of private life, holding it all together. Like Balmoral it was the personal property of the Queen, and in her will she devised it to her eldest son, with the reservation of these two other houses to her daughters. The beloved place, Albert's creation, would thus become the private ancestral home of his descendants. She figured it as continuing to be just what it had been to her, a home of withdrawal from the pomp and trappings of official residences, and her son, after her death would find seclusion and refreshment here, and so from generation to generation it would pass on, always in private possession of the dynasty.

For many years the Queen had gone abroad in the spring for a month's holiday, but in 1900 she went to Ireland instead. The war in South Africa had raised the bitterest hostility to England on the Continent, and particularly in France. The French papers took her as the personification of English aggression and brutality, and were full of vile caricatures of her. She did not wish to pass through France, far less to spend her holiday on the Riviera. With two of her daughters, Princess Christian and Princess Henry of Battenberg she went to Dublin, staying at the Viceregal Lodge. It was a gallant expedition for an old lady of eighty years, but she wanted to mark her appreciation of the services of the Irish regiments in South Africa : also she had not been to Ireland since she was there forty years ago with the Prince Consort to see the Prince of Wales at the Curragh. But this visit could scarcely be described as a holiday : day after day she inspected convents and churches and schools and troops, she gave dinners at the Viceregal Lodge, and she came back, immensely gratified with the enthusiastic loyalty of her people, but tired out.

It had been a drain on her vitality, which the failing powers of old age could not make good. Anxiety about the war weighed heavily on her, and there were grievous family bereavements to be borne. The only son of Alfred, Duke of Coburg, died, and his death was followed by that of his father. Young Prince Christian, who had gone out on the Ashanti expedition with Prince Henry of Battenberg succumbed to an attack of typhoid in South Africa. Of her eldest daughter, there was the worst of news : she had been suffering for months from agonising pain, supposed at first to be lumbago, which would not yield to any treatment, and now the German doctors had pronounced the sentence which thirteen years ago they had passed on her husband.

All these were heavy burdens for one over eighty years old, and her physical infirmities increased as her life-force ebbed. She grew very blind, and could barely read the despatches. Her appetite failed, she had wakeful nights, and when morning came and she wanted to attend to her work she would drop asleep. But still she stuck to her duties, seeing her Ministers, and inspecting troops who had returned from the war. Once more the anniversary of the Prince Consort's death came round : then she left Windsor for Osborne, and at Christmas there came yet another bereavement which touched her daily life very intimately, for Lady Churchill, who had been with her for fifty years, died in her sleep. The Queen could no longer see to write in that *Journal* which she had begun at her mother's desire nearly seventy years ago, but she dictated it to a grand-daughter, Princess Helena Victoria, who was now constantly with her. She invested Lord Roberts, returned from South Africa, with the Garter, she saw Mr. Chamberlain, her Colonial Minister. She went daily drives with one daughter or another : sometimes she thought that her annual holiday abroad, when the spring came, would restore her strength.

The Queen died on January 22, 1901. As we have seen, she had given two of her daughters houses of their own on the Osborne estate, but she had left that estate and the estate and Castle at Balmoral to the new King. Balmoral was a pleasant possession : there was good sport to be had, and for many years he had spent a few weeks near by at Abergeldie. But Osborne was a different matter. Ever since his marriage he had had his own country house at Sandringham ; he would certainly spend much more time at Buckingham Palace than his mother had ever done, and Osborne, as a residence, was perfectly useless to him. It was an immense house with large gardens and stables and a Park of 2,000 acres, and the upkeep was very expensive. He had no intention of ever occupying it, and his son, to whom it would eventually pass, said that under no circumstances would he do so. The King consulted his lawyers as to whether, in these circumstances, he had the power to dispose of it, and found that if he and his son were both agreed, there was nothing in the actual terms of his mother's will which would forbid it. It had been left to him, and if he had wished, he could have sold the Park for building land.

Coincidentally there arose two national needs which it might meet. The ancient ship *Britannia* moored at Dartmouth had hitherto been a school for naval cadets : both the King's sons and his brother Alfred had been trained there. But the *Britannia* was inconvenient and obsolete, and the Admiralty was looking out for some other site for this school. It was suggested to the King by Lord Esher that the stables at Osborne, with a substantial slice of land added for playground, might be replaced by school buildings, erected at the Admiralty's expense : the proximity to the sea rendered it an ideal site. The second national need was for a convalescent home for officers in the Army or Navy invalided from foreign service. No such existed ; there were only the naval and military hospitals for hospital cases. The big wing of Osborne House could be easily converted into such a home. The King approved both these suggestions. As for the Pavilion or central portion of the house, he kept the rooms on the first floor, where his father and mother had their private apartments, as a memorial shrine to them. They were left exactly as they had been during the Queen's life-time, but the State-rooms on the ground floor, with the immense Indian or Durbar room, were to be treated like the State-rooms at Windsor, and to be open to the public on certain days.

But though these arrangements did not contravene the provisions of the Queen's will, they certainly disregarded her intention, which was that Osborne

House should be an appanage of the Crown, to be used as a residence by her eldest son and those who succeeded him, while two of her daughters should live in the houses on the estate which she had given them. But with the stables converted into a school for Naval Cadets, with a wing of the house occupied by convalescent officers, with the rooms used by the Queen and the Prince Consort closed, and with the State-rooms periodically open to the public, the whole character of Osborne, as she had meant it to be, was radically and ruinously changed. Convalescent officers would be sunning themselves on its terraces and strolling in its gardens, small boys would be riotous in the barrack-like building erected on the site of the stables and in the playground. She had intended to give Princess Henry and Princess Louise quiet country houses here, just as she had given Frogmore House and subsequently Cumberland Lodge in Windsor Park to Princess Christian, the third daughter who lived in England, and these changes nullified the spirit, if observing the letter, of her will. King Edward offered to extend the ground attached to Princess Henry's residence, ensuring her a bigger privacy, but it was childish to imagine that any such extension could compensate the effect of the main conversion, which rendered the houses which the Queen had given her daughters undesirable residences. A conversation took place in the garden at Osborne between the two sisters and their brother, and on the day of his Coronation the King informed his Prime Minister of the magnificent gifts he had made to his people.

With the death of Queen Victoria the sixty years story of her and her five daughters comes to its close. Since the early days of their happy childhood when the eldest observed " *le tableau qui se déroule à mes pieds* " there had been dark waters of trouble to be passed through, and bereavements grievous in themselves and bitter in their consequences, but all alike had found in their mother firm and unfailing comfort. In turn they had rendered her the eager obedience of devotion to one who was not only their loving mother but their Queen. Again and again in the letters of the two eldest daughters this double aspect is apparent. They thank her, with recognition of the honour done them for some deed of kindness to them or theirs, and " kiss her dear hands." This was no empty phrase, nor a mere formula to express the dutiful respect with which the daughters of that day were taught to regard their parents. The reverence was real, and so far from imposing formality on filial affection, it enhanced it. The two emotions were fused together and the conscious sense of loyalty was one with love.

INDEX

A

Abdul Karim, 246
Aberdeen, 88
Adelaide, Queen, 10-11
Albany, Duke of, *see* Leopold, Prince
Albert, Prince-Regent, early life of, 1-3 ; meets Victoria, 9, 16-17 ; marriage of, 17 ; is nominated Regent, 18 ; his part in affairs of State, 20, 31-2 ; and his children's education, 21 ; rebuilds Osborne, 24 ; visits Coburg, 26 ; relations of, with his children, 27-31, 102 ; rebuilds Balmoral, 33 ; his organization of expenditure, 33, 83 ; visits Paris, 34-5 ; on future of Prussia, 38-9, 145-6, 182 ; his influence over Princess Victoria, 39-40, 43-5, 49, 59 ; chooses bride for Bertie, 51, 56, 63 ; on Louis of Hesse, 54, 59 ; in Ireland, 62 ; arranges wedding of Alice, 65-6 ; death of, 68 ; and Schleswig-Holstein question, 82, 94 ; unveiling of statue to, 108 ; and William I, 109 ; publication of *Life* of, 175-7

Alexander, Prince, of Battenberg, made Prince of Bulgaria, 199, 208 ; seeks hand of Princess Victoria of Prussia, 206-9, 216-18, 222 ; forced to abdicate, 209, 217, 250 ; marriage of, 223
Alexander, Prince, of Hesse, 206
Alexander, Prince, of Orange, 8-9
Alexander II, Tsar of Russia, 117
Alexander III, Tsar of Russia, 248, 250, 252
Alexandra, Princess of Wales (Alix), 56, 63-5 ; engagement of, 78-9 ; receives premarital advice from Victoria, 80-3, 252 ; wedding of, 83-4 ; on Schleswig-Holstein question, 94-5 ; birth of son to, 95 ; visits Denmark, 97 ; charitable activities of, 194 ; goes to Russia, 253
Alfred, Prince (Duke of Edinburgh, Duke of Coburg), 87 ; childhood of, 25-6, 29 ; joins the Navy, 52-3 ; at Alice's wedding, 76 ; illness of, 84 ; invests Grand Duke of Hesse with Garter, 105-6 ; annuity for, 110 ; marriage of, 172 ; death of, 279

INDEX

Alice, Princess (Princess Louis of Hesse), 51-2, 108; birth of, 25; childhood of, 28-9; meets Prince Louis, 53-4; engagement of, 57-9, 65-6; dowry of, 60; her mother's comforter, 61-2, 68-9, 72, 78, 100-1; marriage of, 74-7, 114; letters of, 77, 86, 89, 99-105, 110, 112-14, 122, 147-50, 172-8; visits England, 82-3, 84-5, 87-8, 99, 101, 103, 163-6, 177-9; birth of children to, 85, 101, 111-12, 121, 147, 167, 174; duties of, in Darmstadt, 86-7, 104, 111, 122, 167-9; on Schleswig-Holstein question, 94; visits Vicky, 103, 147; prejudice against, 103-4; at investiture of Grand Duke with Garter, 105-6; on war against Prussia, 113; ill-health of, 113; on her father, 113-14; comparative poverty of, 119-20; generosity of, 119-20; hospital work of, 122-3, 146-8; religious doubts of, 123-5; her nature revealed in her letters, 149-50; nurses her brother, 164; visits Italy, 169-70; death of child of, 170-74, 180; on *Life of the Prince Consort*, 175-6; failing health of, 177, 179; death of, 180-1, 196

Alix, Princess, of Hesse (Alicky) later Empress of Russia, 178; birth of, 167; illness of, 179; marriage of, 248-9, 252-4; visits England, 250-2, 259; bad influence of, 263

Alsace-Lorraine, question of return of, 162, 231
Apponyi, Count, 137
Argyll, Duke of, Victoria's reproof to, 191-3
Arthur, Prince (Duke of Connaught), 26, 157, 200
Ashanti War, 256-7
Atholl, Duke and Duchess of, 88
Augusta, Queen of Prussia (later Empress), 99, 109, 157, 202; relations of, with Crown Princess, 141-2, 224; Victoria's friendship with, 142-3, 239; death of, 238-240
Augusta Victoria, Princess, of Prussia (Dona), later Empress, marriage of, 197-8; head of Red Cross Society, 238-9
Augustus, Prince, of Saxe-Coburg, 75
Austria, seeks Holstein, 81, 94, 107; at war with Prussia, 111, 184

B

Balmoral, 26, 32, 246, 280; rebuilding of, 33; visits to, 35, 63-4, 78, 87-8, 99, 109, 125-6, 153-4, 163-4, 177-8, 267, 276; memorial to John Brown at, 204; Tsar visits, 259-62
Beaconsfield, Lord, 110, 193, 246; his relationship with Victoria, 132-3, 205; on marriage of Princess Louise, 154-5; and Russo-Turkish War, 191

INDEX

Beatrice, Princess (Princess Henry of Battenberg), 55, 125, 278; birth of, 26; marriage of, 206-7, 245; in devoted attendance on Victoria, 207, 255, 257; death of husband of, 257; visits Vicky, 273; house of, at Osborne, 277, 282
Bergmann, Dr., 219-20, 227
Berlin, Congress of, 199
Bernard, Prince, of Saxe-Meiningen, 195, 228
Bernsdorff, Count, 137
Bismarck, Prince, 106, 117; attitude of, to Princess Victoria, 44, 79-80, 91-3, 116-117, 185, 201, 228; autocratic rule of, 79-80, 90; attitude of, to Crown Prince, 92; sends ultimatum to Denmark, 95; and war with Austria, 167, 114-15; engineers war with France, 134-6; press campaigns of, 136, 218-19, 233; and bombardment of Paris, 140; achieves unification of Prussia, 145, 182; dislike of English Royal family for, 162; seeks to divide other Powers, 186-8, 190, 202; and William II, 201-3; opposes Battenberg marriage, 207-8, 217-18; on Queen Victoria, 208; meeting of, with Victoria, 219; and publication of Frederick's diary, 229-30; resignation of, 240-1; colonial policy of, 243; results of policy of, 268
Bloomfield, Lord, 41

Blücher, Countess, 107
Brown, John, 64, 88, 126, 153; Victoria's dependence on, 101-2; brusqueness of, 131-3; death of, 204-5
Bruce, General, Governor to Prince of Wales, 51, 53, 57, 65, 68, 73-4
Buccleuch, Duke of, 43
Buchanan, Sir Andrew, 96
Bulgaria, attains independence, 199; Alexander forced to abdicate throne of, 209, 217
Bülow, Prince von, 247

C

Carnarvon, Lord, 191
Chamberlain, Joseph, 280
Charles, Prince, of Hesse, 53, 178
Charles, Princess, of Hesse, 54, 101, 111, 168
Charlotte, Princess, of Prussia, marriage of, 179, 195; child born to, 196
Christian IX, King of Denmark, 81, 83; and Schleswig-Holstein question, 94-5
Christian, Prince, son of Princess Helena, 257, 279
Christian, Prince, of Schleswig-Holstein, 106-9; marriage of, 111, 125
Christian, Princess, *see* Helena, Princess
Churchill, Lady, 279
Claremont, 10, 22
Clarendon, Lord, 37, 134, 158; on difficult position of Princess Victoria, 48-9; his appreciation of Princess Victoria, 66-7

INDEX

Clark, Sir James, 47
Coburg, Dowager Duchess of, 4, 55-6
Connaught, Duke of, *see* Arthur, Prince
Conroy, Sir John, 4-8, 10, 12, 14
Constantinople, Russian march on, 188-9, 191 ; Russia incited to take, 202
Conyngham, Lord, 12
Crete, occupation of, 263-5
Cronberg, 242, 271, 274

D

Dagmar, Princess, of Denmark, 104
Dantzig, 90
Darmstadt, 86-7, 100 ; Victoria in, 108-9 ; Prussian occupation of, 112-13, 118-119 ; hospital work in, 122-3, 146-8 ; conference on Women's Work in, 167-8
De Ros, Captain, 47
Denmark, quarrel of, with Prussia, 79, 81-2, 93-6
Derby, Lord, 52, 71, 191
Diamond Jubilee, 265-7
Dilke, Sir Charles, 163

E

Eastbourne, 179 ; Princess Alice Hospital at, 181
Eastern question, Princess Victoria on, 185-90 ; settling of, 199
Edinburgh, Duke of, *see* Alfred, Prince

Edward VII, King (Bertie, Prince of Wales), 68, 131, 260 ; birth of, 20-1 ; Albert's poor opinion of, 21, 28, 31, 65 ; education of, 21-2, 30-1, 51, 53 ; childhood of, 29-30 ; visits Paris, 34-5, 117 ; choice of wife for, 51, 56, 63-5 ; foreign tours of, 51, 57, 65, 73 ; in Ireland, 62 ; provision made for, 71, 83 ; at Alice's wedding, 75-6 ; engagement of, 78-9, 83 ; cruises in Mediterranean, 81 ; wedding of, 83 ; and Schleswig-Holstein question, 94, 98 ; indiscretions of, 97, 137, 161, 231-3 ; visits Germany, 98 ; meets William I, 120 ; enforced idleness of, 138-9, 256 ; on Louise's marriage, 151 ; scandal attached to name of, 160-3 ; reconciled to Vicky, 161-2 ; on Victoria's seclusion, 162-163 ; illness of, 164-5 ; at funeral of Frederick, 224 ; William's rudeness to, 232-4, 237 ; democratic way of life of, 250 ; in Russia, 253-4 ; and Henry of Battenberg, 256 ; and William's presence at Diamond Jubilee, 266 ; visits dying sister, 271 ; gives Osborne to the nation, 280-2
Egypt, 186-8
Elizabeth, Princess, of Hesse (Ella), later Grand Duchess Serge, 101, 103, 253 ; in England, 111 ; beauty of, 167
Ely, Lady, 154

INDEX

Ernest I, Duke of Coburg, 1, 9
Ernest II, Duke of Coburg, 1-2; visits England, 9; heir to, 25; at wedding of Alice, 75-6
Ernest, Duke of Cumberland, 19
Ernest Louis, Prince (later Grand Duke) of Hesse, 121; death of brother of, 170, 173; illness of, 179-80; marriage of, 248
Esher, Lord, 281
Eugénie, Empress, 34-5, 149

F

Fitzroy, Lord Charles, 128-9
France, on extension of British power in Egypt, 187, 258-9; friendship of, with Russia, 262; hostility to England in, 278
Franco-Prussian War, 136-41, 145-50; origins of, 134-6
Frederick, Duke, of Schleswig-Holstein-Sonderburg-Augustenberg, 94, 197
Frederick, Prince, of Prussia (Fritz), later Crown Prince and Emperor Frederick III, 81, 121, 161; betrothal of, 35-40; wedding of, 41-3; at Bertie's wedding, 84-5; estranged from his father, 90-3, 138; fights in Danish War, 95, 98; fights in Austrian War, 114-15; and bombardment of Paris, 140-141; liberal views of, 185; his opinion of William, 197, 202-3; deliberate obliterations of, 203, 212, 227, 231, 236; throat affection of, 209-15, 219; goes to England for treatment, 210-11; carries papers to England, 210, 274; is found to have cancer, 213-15; becomes Emperor, 216; death of, 220-1; and marriage of Princess Victoria, 222; publication of diary of, 228-30
Frederick, Princess, *see* Victoria, Princess
Frederick William, Prince, of Hesse, 147; illness of, 169; death of, 170-3
Friedrichskron, 220-1, 224-5, 236, 274
Frogmore, 125, 282

G

Gastein, Convention of, 107
Geffcken, Professor, 228-30
George IV, King of England, 2, 4, 7
George, King of Greece, 263, 265
George, Prince, of Wales, 237, 280
Germany, unification of, 145, 150, 182-4; unpopularity of, in England, 161; rancour of, against England, 268
Gladstone, W. E., 60, 70, 156, 188; and provision for Prince of Wales, 71, 83; and Victoria's seclusion, 157-60, 164; campaign of, against Turkey, 191

INDEX

Glassault Shiel, 126, 154
Granville, Lord, 70
Greco-Turkish War, 263-5
Greville, Charles, 5, 48

H

Hanover, defeated by Prussia, 112-13; Princess Victoria's unpopularity in, 118
Hanover, King of, 83, 98, 111
Hatzfeldt, Count, 218
Helena, Princess (Princess Christian), 26, 29, 83, 278; marriage of, 86, 106-11, 125, 127; charitable works of, 193-4; visits Berlin, 226; houses of, 282
Helena Victoria, Princess, 280
Henry, Prince, of Battenberg, marriage of, 206-7, 245; lacks occupation, 255-6; goes to Ashanti, 256-7; death of, 257
Henry, Prince, of Prussia, 195, 214; marriage of, 220; invested with Garter, 237
Hesse, defeated by Prussia, 111-13
Hesse, Grand Duke of, 105-6, 178
Hildyard, Miss, 49, 51, 103
Hohenlohe, Princess Feodore, 3-5, 75, 197
Homburg, 137-8
Howley, Archbishop, of Canterbury, 18

I

Ireland, Royal visits to, 62, 278

Irene, Princess, of Hesse, 112-113, 179; marriage of, 220
Ismail, Khedive, 117
Italy, 169-70; unification of, 182

J

Jenner, Sir William, 70, 158, 181
Journal of a Life in the Highlands, 126, 129-31, 176, 205

K

Kensington Palace, 6, 10
Kent, Duchess of, 2, 18; first marriage of, 3; and Sir John Conroy, 5; strictness of, 6, 12; injudicious arrogance of, 6-10, 12; William IV attacks, 11; and Victoria's accession, 14; death of, 60-2
Koniggrätz, battle of, 111

L

Lehzen, Baroness, 4-6, 10, 18
Leighton, Lord, 242
Leopold, King of the Belgians, 2, 28, 34; and Victoria's choice of husband, 9; Victoria's letters to, 9, 22-3, 26-7, 31, 35, 37, 47, 58, 61-2, 69-70, 85-6, 89, 98, 127; Victoria refuses to be guided by, 15-16, 73; on Victoria's first-born, 19; and Vicky's marriage, 37-8; visits England, 53, 69, 72; Victoria visits, 78; suggests husband for Helena, 106

INDEX

Leopold, Prince (Duke of Albany), 26, 125, 205
Leopold, Prince, of Hohenzollern Sigmaringen, 134–5
Lobanoff, Prince, 258–9
Loisinger, Fräulein, 223
Lorne, Marquis of, marries Princess Louise, 151–7; Governor General of Canada, 193
Louis, Prince, of Battenberg, 206
Louis, Prince (later Grand Duke) of Hesse, 105, 118; visits England, 53, 63, 83, 87–8; meets Princess Alice, 54; engagement of, 57–9; marriage of, 74–6; duties of, in Darmstadt, 86–7; visits Berlin, 103; on active service, 111–12, 146–9; illness of, 121, 179–80; becomes Grand Duke, 178–9
Louis, Princess, of Hesse, *see* Alice, Princess
Louise, Princess (Duchess of Argyll), 26, 29, 125, 191; marriage of, 150–7; personality of, 155–6; goes to Canada, 193; house of, at Osborne, 277, 282
Luxemburg, 117
Lyttelton, Sarah, Lady, 21, 27–8

M

Macdonald, Annie, 266
Mackenzie, Dr. Morell, treats Crown Prince, 209–11, 213–215, 219, 221; publishes account of Prince's case, 227

Macleod, Dr. Norman, 125–6
Marie, Empress of Russia, 104
Martin, Sir Theodore, 137, 270, 273; *Life of Prince Consort* of, 175–7
Maximilian, Emperor of Mexico, 117
May, Princess, of Hesse, 178; birth of, 174; death of, 179–80
Mechlenburg-Strelitz, Anna, Grand-Duchess of, 104
Melba, Dame, 246
Melbourne, Lord, 13; Victoria's dependence on, 15; and Victoria's marriage, 16–17
Mordaunt, Sir Charles, 160–1

N

Napoleon III, Emperor, 34–5, 117; defeat of, 138–9, 149
Neild, John Camden, bequest of, 33–4, 160
Nicholas II, Tsar of Russia, marriage of, 248–9, 253–4; visits England, 250–1, 259–262; accession of, 252; anti-English policy of, 258–9
Novikoff, Madame, 217

O

Osborne, 32, 276–8; Conroy's cottage at, 7; rebuilding of, 24, 63; visits to, 69, 76, 162; Alexandra at, 81–3; memorial to John Brown at, 204; tableaux at, 247; Edward's gift of, to nation, 280–2

INDEX

P

Palmerston, Lord, 37, 82, 96
Paris, Royal visit to, 34-5; International Exhibition in, 117; siege of, 140-1; Tsar's visit to, 262
Peel, Sir Robert, 15
Ponsonby, Sir Frederick, 271-5
Prim, General, 134-5
Prussia, Albert's conception of future of, 38-9, 145; and marriage of Victoria and Frederick, 41; hostility to Princess Victoria in, 79, 93, 97, 137-8, 185; seeks Schleswig and Holstein, 79, 81, 94-6, 107; reorganized by Bismarck, 80; abolition of freedom of press in, 90; Victoria's anger with, 107, 182; defeats Austria and her allies, 111-16, 118-19; at war with France, 136-41; hostility of, towards England, 137, 140, 185

R

Radolin-Radolinsky, Count, 201, 212
Raglan, Lord, 47
Regency Bills, 8, 11, 18
Reid, Sir James, 256
Reszke, Edouard and Jean de, 246
Roberts, Lord, 280
Rosebery, Lord, 254
Russia, war of, against Turkey, 186, 188-92; William represents his grandfather in, 201-2; Bismarck incites, to take Constantinople, 202; and Bulgaria, 208-9, 217; relations between England and, 249-50, 258-63

S

Salisbury, Lord, 217, 232, 264; and relations with Germany, 218, 234; and Tsar Nicholas, 261
Sandringham, 83, 163-5, 250, 280
Saxony, defeated by Prussia, 111-13
Schleswig-Holstein question, 79, 81-2, 93-6
Sigismund, Prince, of Prussia, 114, 117
Sophy, Crown Princess of Greece, 263-5
South African War, 268, 278
Spain, 134-5
Stanley, Dr. A. P., 73
Stockmar, Baron, 13, 21, 31, 47; on Princess Victoria's position, 48-9
Stockmar, Ernest, 45
Strauss, Frederick David, 123-124
Sudan, conquest of, 258-9

T

Tupper, Martin, 29
Turkey, revolt of Balkan provinces of, 185; Russian war with, 186, 188-92; Princess Victoria's method of dealing with, 199-200; conquers Greece, 263-5
Turkey, Sultan of, 117

INDEX

V

Victor Emmanuel, King of Italy, 182
Victoria, Princess (Vicky), later Crown Princess of Prussia, German Empress, 29, 34; birth of, 18-19; intelligence of, 20-1, 24-5, 28; education of, 21-2; engagement of, 35-40; her father's aspirations for, 39-40, 43; dowry of, 40; marriage of, 40-3, 267; her reception in Berlin, 43-4; her failure to "drop the Englishwoman," 44-50, 80; letters of, 44-5, 66, 91, 95-6, 134, 138-40, 183, 212-13, 223, 238-43, 269-75; birth of children to, 47, 54-5; visits England, 48, 63, 161-2, 234-6, 267; on Alexandra, 56; Memorandum of, 59; at Coronation of William I, 66-7; Liberal views of, 67-8, 91, 221; German hostility to, 79, 93, 97, 137, 140-1, 185, 210, 212-14; goes on cruise, 81; at Bertie's wedding, 84-5; and abolition of freedom of press, 90-3; and Schleswig-Holstein question, 94-6; Princess Alice visits, 103; on Prince Christian, 107; forbidden to come to England, 107-9; on war with Austria, 114-16; on Bismarck, 114-16, 184-5, 212; death of sons of, 114-115, 117, 196; unwise behaviour of, 117-18; unpopularity of, in Hanover, 118; on Franco-Prussian War, 136, 138-41; injudicious frankness of, 140, 143, 184-5; and education of William, 144-5, 194-5; reconciled to Prince of Wales, 161-2; on unification of Germany, 183; lack of logic of, 183-4; her "advice" to her mother on foreign policy, 185-90, 199-200, 263-4; rift between William and, 196-8, 202-3, 208, 214, 221, 223, 226-31, 236-8; scandalous stories told of, 210, 212-14, 220, 227, 233; cruel position of, on death of Frederick, 220-1, 223, 226-31, 236; and publication of Frederick's diaries, 229-30; loses her bitterness, 242-4; as an artist, 242; and Diamond Jubilee, 266-7; last illness of, 268-9, 271, 279; intends writing life of her husband, 269-75; death of, 274
Victoria, Princess, of Coburg, 248
Victoria, Princess, of Hesse, 101, 103; birth of, 85; visits England, 111, 121-2; education of, 119-20; illness of, 121, 179; marriage of, 206
Victoria, Princess, of Prussia, question of marriage of, 206-9, 216-19, 222
Victoria, Queen of England, early life of, 1, 3-12; relations of, with her mother, 5-6, 13, 14, 60-1; diary of, 6, 12, 32, 74, 84, 279-80;

293

INDEX

Victoria, Queen (*continued*)
choice of husband for, 8–10, 16–17, 37; meets Albert, 9, 17; ascends the throne, 12–13; indomitable will of, 14–15, 108; her need for a man's support, 15, 20, 127, 205; enjoys her Queenship, 16, 23; marriage of, 17; birth of children to, 18–20, 25–6; her dependence on Albert, 20, 26, 31–2; her fondness for quiet life, 22–3; relations of, with her children, 27, 283; incognito adventures of, 32, 64; legacy to, 33–4; visits Paris, 34–5; pro-German sympathies of, 38, 136–7, 159; seeks provision for her children, 40, 59–60, 71, 83, 110, 157–8; and Vicky's marriage, 41–3; retains her influence over Vicky after her marriage, 44–45, 48–50; visits Germany, 45, 55–6, 108, 217–19, 248–50; and Alice's marriage, 52–4, 57–60; her partiality for William II, 56, 194; gives herself up to grief, 61–2, 68–72, 74–6, 84, 88–9; visits Ireland, 62, 278; forms habit of seclusion, 70; at Princess Alice's wedding, 74–77; advises Alexandra, 81–2; intercedes for Crown Prince, 93; and Schleswig-Holstein question, 94, 96; unpopularity of seclusion of, 98–9, 110, 158–60, 163–5; her dependence on John Brown, 101–2, 127–33, 205; angry with Prussia, 107–8; meets William I, 109; her appetite for appreciation, 110; gifts of, to Alice, 119–20, 147; and her grandchildren, 121–122, 194, 247–8; publishes her *Journals*, 126, 129–31, 176, 205; her kindness to her attendants, 129–30, 266; her friendship with Augusta, 142–3, 154; on education of her grandchildren, 144–5, 149, 174; expresses dislike of foreign marriages, 151–4; asked to postpone visit to Balmoral, 158–9; ill with gout, 162–3; and illness of Prince of Wales, 164–5; on "rights of women," 168; and *Life of the Prince Consort*, 175–7; on Prussian "confiscations," 182–3; on Vicky's advice to "take Egypt," 187–8; and Russian advance on Constantinople, 190–2; reproves Duke of Argyll, 192–3; approves of William's bride, 197; on marriage of Beatrice, 207; and Battenberg marriage of Princess Victoria, 207–8, 217–19, 222; Jubilees of, 210–11, 265–7; visits Berlin, 217–19; letter of, to William II, 224–5; her anger against William, 232, 234; invites Vicky to England, 234–5; rejuvenation of, 245–248; Indian servants of, 246–7; and Russian marriage, 249–54; entertains Tsar, 259–62; appeals to William to intervene in Greco-Turkish War, 265;

INDEX

Victoria, Queen (*continued*). correspondence of, with Vicky, 269–70, 273; death of, 271, 280; increasing infirmities of, 279
Vienna, Prince of Wales and William II in, 232–3
Virchow, Professor, 209–10

W

Waldermar, Prince, of Prussia, 196
Wellington, Duke of, 5, 8, 11
"Willem," 87–8
William IV, King of England, 2; and Duchess of Kent, 7, 10–12; selects husband for Victoria, 8–9; assigns Victoria an income, 12
William I, German Emperor (King of Prussia), coronation of, 66; autocratic policy of, 67; estranged from his son, 90–3; refuses Crown Prince permission to visit England, 107–9; meets Victoria, 109; in Paris, 117; meets Prince of Wales, 120; and candidate for throne of Spain, 134–6; complains of England's lack of neutrality, 137; hampers Crown Princess's efforts, 137–8; re- presented by his grandson, 201; and William's employment at Foreign Office, 202–203; death of, 216
William II, German Emperor (Prince William), withered arm of, 47, 55, 143; Victoria's partiality for, 56, 194; at Bertie's wedding, 84; education of, 144, 195; rift between parents and, 196–8, 208, 214; arrogance of, 196, 215, 220; marriage of, 197–198; sent on missions by Bismarck, 201–3; opposes Battenberg marriage, 208, 217; accession of, 221–2; behaviour of, to his mother, 221, 224–8, 230; letter of, to Queen Victoria, 225–6; his rudeness to Prince of Wales, 232–4, 237, 255; visits England, 236–7, 251, 254–5; forces Bismarck to resign, 240–1; Imperial flamboyance of, 241–4; and Russian marriage, 251, 254; intervenes in Greco-Turkish War, 264–5; seeks invitation to Diamond Jubilee, 266; and his mother's letters, 271–2, 274
Windsor, 17, 23, 246–7; Ascot Week at, 52–4
Wolseley Lord, 246
Wrangel, Field-Marshal, 147

295

www.ingramcontent.com/pod-product-compliance
Lightning Source LLC
Chambersburg PA
CBHW032051220426
43664CB00008B/947